Pride and Joy

Alex Knight

First published in 2014 by Never Say I Know,
Church Farm, Aldbury, Herts. UK HP23 5RS

ISBN 978-0-9928-3980-2 (hardback)
ISBN 978-0-9559-5349-1 (paperback)

♦

Cover design by Frances Muir

Printed by Linney Group Ltd

A CIP catalogue record for this book is available
from the British Library

www.alex-knight.com

*This novel is intended to illustrate how the application of the Theory of
Constraints can help improve organisations. It of course does not constitute
professional advice or a promise of results in relation to the circumstances of,
or encountered by, any reader; and the author and publisher must disclaim
responsibility and exclude liability for any reliance placed upon it.*

1 2 3 4 5 6 7 8 9 10

Dedication

This book is dedicated to the memory of Dr Eliyahu M. Goldratt, the inventor of the Theory of Constraints. He passed away in 2011 and in my eyes was the greatest management thinker of our time. He was an educator, author, scientist, philosopher, mentor and a very special friend. *Pride and Joy* is a novel about the application of his unifying theory of management to something important to us all: the provision of high-quality, affordable healthcare.

I met Eli after following the well-trodden path of traditional education. He made me stop and think for myself and experience learning as fun again. Most of all, he taught me to never say '*I know*' and that anything worth having is worth sweating for.

Thanks

I want to thank my family, friends and colleagues who provided me with frequent support, encouragement and challenge. I am grateful to you all.

Writing this book has been a journey of constant discovery. It would not have been possible without the immense help, guidance and support of Stuart Wilkin, Helen Gibb, Tom Kemp and Bill West.

Most importantly, I want to thank all the caring and committed people I have worked with in many health systems around the world. It is your energy and endless commitment to your patients that has inspired me to write this book. I hope it helps bring you ever more pride and joy in what you do. We are indebted to you all.

Contents

Foreword

Healthcare is a fundamental necessity of all societies. Yet most countries struggle with increasing demand and costs. Medicine continues to advance at a rate faster than we can afford to pay for. The management of healthcare delivery systems has not kept pace; we manage by instinct and not evidence. Fire-fighting endless crises and poor patient safety have become the norm.

This story tells us that there is another way to manage. The other way requires an open mind, a willingness to collect data and continually improve. The gathering and analysis of data is done with a purpose: to achieve a breakthrough in performance in terms of quality of care, throughput and access, without additional cost. Impossible you might think. Far from impossible – it is possible and essential if we are to provide the healthcare our citizens deserve.

Delivering healthcare requires a complex system: many resources spread over time and space that interact to meet the needs of individual patients. We organise ourselves into professions, specialisms, teams, organisations, allocate them budgets and hold them to account accordingly. By sub-dividing we make working as a co-ordinated whole much harder. Yet in the midst of complexity there is simplicity.

I first worked with Alex Knight over fifteen years ago. We played the dice game, which features as a turning point in this story, as it did in my career. That game taught me that variation and dependent events are the norm in healthcare. To embrace variation rather than wish it away takes courage and leadership. A patient's journey requires numerous activities many of which have to be undertaken in sequence. Before blood results can be reviewed the doctor is dependent on the laboratory, which is dependent on the member of staff taking the blood, who is dependent on the equipment being in place.

The first time I played the dice game was with a group of surgeons. The story unfolded that surgical teams in fully staffed and equipped theatres were dependent on the availability of a porter with a wheelchair to bring the patient to theatre. Financial accountability in the sub-divided whole meant that the portering budget had been 'trimmed' and they had not maintained the wheelchair stock. The accountants were happy but now the most expensive resource stood idle while trying to find a porter who struggled to find a wheelchair. Leaders need courage to say that there should be porters with their feet up drinking coffee rather than surgical teams standing waiting for a patient. Throughput increased by over twenty per cent. We constantly collected data to find *'which resource causes most delay for most patients most often'*: evidence which helps identify the constraint of the system. Then you can act to improve the speed of flow for the patient journey.

Alex and his team have been on a journey, learning from Eli Goldratt about the Theory of Constraints then rigorously finding ways to apply the principles to improve healthcare. His wisdom and experience are distilled in this story. He is constantly generous with his time and knowledge – always seeking to develop others so that many flowers may flourish.

Dr Mike D Williams
Exeter
January 2014

Chapter One

Helter-skelter

Fighting fires again.

Just like every other day.

It's barely 7:00am on Friday as I walk into the hospital through the doors of the Accident and Emergency department, a habit I've never been able to break since I first started working in the health service. As usual the reception area is crowded so I walk towards the central treatment area where I see Mohinder, our emergency care clinical director. He's a good guy. I saw him working late last night so he must be filling another gap in the consultant staffing rota. He's talking to a patient who's lying on a trolley outside one of the cubicles. When he sees me he quietly raises his hands and signals with three fives and one finger that we have sixteen patients waiting for a bed. Mo knows this is all the information I need for now. I do my best to give him a supportive wave, but without a smile it probably looks more plaintive than supportive. I leave him to carry on treating, or more likely pacifying, the waiting patient, something no other medic I know can do so well. Mo is an excellent doctor who never, and I mean *never*, lets down the hospital or our patients. He has a calming way about him that simply reassures people.

It's not the best start to my day, but then sixteen patients waiting for a bed is about average considering our recent performance; it's been much higher on some days in the last few weeks. There will be the normal morning bulge in attendances but hopefully we'll have enough time to discharge some patients and free up some of the beds we need.

1

I carry on through to the assessment unit – often referred to as the AU. I don't recognise any of the staff but that's not so unusual when you have literally hundreds of front-line people working shifts. I approach a junior doctor to find out how things are going. I sneak a furtive look at his badge to discover he is Dr Ranjeev Malik, and then I look up to see he's doing the same. He knows no more about who I am than I know of him, and after an awkward and unnecessary exchange of pleasantries Dr Malik says:

"It's going to be a bad day. We already have patients waiting to come on to the unit this morning and the lady in cubicle three has been waiting for over five hours for a specialist doctor review. We are letting our patients down, and you are at risk of damaging your emergency target."

I thought it was *our* emergency target – not just mine! No matter, either way, I agree, we're letting our patients down. Dr Malik carries on:

"We are completely full. I have walked around all the beds in the unit and the place is full with sick patients. I am really not sure any will be going home today."

This unit is supposed to be a place for patients who require more detailed assessment before a decision is made to admit them to an appropriate ward or discharge them. Today, patients staying in the assessment unit are stopping those in A&E who need an assessment from being brought in.

I've heard enough to know that patient flow has started to slow down, and it's not difficult to extrapolate that there's a shortage of beds in the rest of the hospital. As Dr Malik is talking I see Jo, the director of nursing, walking towards me and I ask Dr Malik to reiterate the issue for her. Jo's response is as straightforward as always. She never hides the facts, good or bad, and her half-smile tells me they're unlikely to be good. And I'm right.

"I'll be honest with you, Linda, that's only one of our problems right now. I've just been into the admissions lounge to try to sort out beds for patients being operated on today and I think we're going to have to cancel a considerable number of them."

Many of these patients will have been waiting months for their operation, and it's an act of heresy in our hospital to cancel patients on their day of operation. When we've been at risk of this happening in the past I've personally taken over the management of the bed base and, if necessary, walked through every ward with Charlie, our medical director, to find patients we can safely discharge to create enough beds. Even when it works it takes all day and often results in less-than-harmonious relationships between clinical and managerial staff. Ten minutes ago I wasn't expecting today to be this kind of a day, and I know that if I take on this role now I can kiss goodbye to achieving anything else. Part of me wants to step into the breach, but I just can't lose the day and so I suggest Jo should call the hospital's bed manager and ask him to update her on the current situation. In my heart of hearts I know this is not going to be enough, but at least it will give me the chance to get to my office and check the planned number of operations today and see if there's been a rise in emergency admissions over the last few days.

It's just like every other day. I'm working on the latest short-term crisis. This isn't how I envisaged my career. My first ever management job over a decade ago was in the A&E department of a general hospital in middle England. It was a great place to learn the ropes, but it's so different here. One year ago almost to the day we had the formal opening of the new hospital – on that beautifully English day with the local press assembled in the sunshine in an unusually benevolent mood, and the mayor himself cutting the ribbon. It seemed like everything was set for us to flourish, but one short year later and we're not in such a bright place.

As I walk into our office suite I pass my boss's office. Bob doesn't look the happiest of bunnies either. In fact he has his head in his hands. I try to sneak past but then he looks up towards me. Damn these squeaky shoes. I should have taken them off and crept past, but that could have been even worse if he'd seen me! He looks preoccupied, in an eerily vacant kind of way. I walk on by but then have a sudden pang of conscience, stop and decide to retrace my steps. I pop my head around his door.

I don't expect him to be full of fun. Yesterday afternoon he visited our regional office, where he had the unenviable and distinctly unpleasant task of presenting our fourth recovery plan in six months. This particular plan had been hurriedly put together by our executive team at a rather acrimonious meeting the day before. With a predicted loss of around £15 million on revenues of £400 million per year, and a number of quality-of-care notices hanging around our necks, the whole planning session had deteriorated into a meeting where we were all defending our own patches. At the end of it I was actually ashamed of what we'd created. It read just like a string of excuses and horrible compromises to try to make the budget balance, only in a different order from the previous three plans and with the odd addition.

After two hours of discussions we'd left Bob with no real alternative other than to declare an across-the-board reduction in operating expenses of five per cent. Clearly this was insufficient to clear the current loss and give us enough breathing space to deal with the backlog of investment in staff training and equipment, but he had hoped it would pacify our masters for a few more months. I thought it was rather like trying to withstand a tsunami with an umbrella. Nevertheless, Bob and I had spent the rest of the afternoon creating a long list of cost-saving projects to achieve the reduction. We'd given it our best shot, but neither of us had left the session with any real confidence. We were using sticking-plaster when a more fundamentally radical treatment was required.

"Hi Bob. How's it going?" I ask.

"Well, that all depends on your point of view," he replies. "Come in and sit down, Linda."

I walk into the office and he offers me a coffee, which I decline. While a caffeine shot would be welcome, I don't want to commit to a lengthy discussion. Then, as I sit down, he takes an unnervingly deep breath and drops the bombshell on me.

"Linda, basically... I've been fired."

WHAT?!

I know our recovery plan wasn't exactly a work of genius... but fired?

"What happened?"

"Well," he begins, "the meeting was a disaster from start to finish. Region ripped our plans to shreds and told me there is no role for me in running this hospital." Blunt. "They've asked me to step down and work on some special projects. So that's me, Linda. Special Projects."

"How are you?"

"Been better. But hey – nobody's died."

I don't share Bob's confidence as my mind flits back to the conversations from earlier.

"Are you angry?"

"Not really."

Bob gives a sort of tired, resigned shrug. In a way it is probably a weight off his shoulders. His wife, Sheila, retired last year and has been asking him when they could go on holiday but, given the spiral of gloom the hospital has been hurtling down, Bob has been putting it off. So, I guess he could be off to Tenerife with Sheila before the end of the month.

"So who have they lined up?" I ask.

"Well, that's the next thing." He raises one eyebrow and fixes me with a look that gives me a slight shudder.

"The chairman will be here at nine and is going to ask you to be the interim CEO until they can find someone capable of turning this place around. You must keep that to yourself until you get the green light – don't let it get out, Linda. You can tell people that I've gone but nothing more."

I look down at my watch and then back up at Bob. He carries on:

"What do you say? I should have seen it coming but I never honestly thought this would happen so quickly. And I don't want any sympathy from you or anyone else. It is what it is, and quite frankly I'm relieved. This job has been a nightmare and for the first time in months I've been woken up from it. Now listen, I want to get out of here before anyone else turns up."

As I walk out of his office he calls me back to reassure me:

"Hey, listen. I'm fine."

Well, at least Bob's fine. I go to my office, drop my bag on the desk and wonder what the hell I'm about to let myself in for. Ten minutes later Bob's gone and I'm sitting at his desk which, it would appear, has become mine for a short while, and all I can hear is Bob saying: '*The chairman will be here at nine and is going to ask you to be the interim CEO until they can find someone else who is capable of turning this place around.*' Hardly a dream come true. I've always wanted to become a CEO at some stage and took the job here as chief operating officer because I knew the place was struggling and believed I could help turn it around. I thought this would be great experience before going for the top job. Right now it looks like this could quite possibly have been my worst career move to date.

As I get up to go back to my own office Cath, Bob's PA, walks in and says:

"Hi, Linda, have you seen Bob yet? I thought I saw him in the car park but it looked like he was leaving."

I sit Cath down and tell her the news about Bob's demise and explain that Bob will call her later. She's clearly upset. Cath is a wonderful PA, as loyal and devoted as any Miss Moneypenny and incredibly well organised. She's followed Bob around in his last three jobs and saved his skin on more than one occasion. She would have walked over white-hot coals for him. She gets up, takes a tissue out of the mansize box on the windowsill and returns to her chair. Cath had been in the meeting where we put together version four of the recovery plan and she'd seen for herself the mess we're in, not to mention the bickering and squabbling among the executive team. I make her a cup of tea and, mindful of Bob's warning, I tell her that I'll step in and deal with anything today until we know what's happening. After taking a sip of her tea and with a cheery, stoical, breezy note, she sits up straight and exclaims:

"OK, Linda, what do you want me to do for you?"

As it's Friday there's a meeting with the regional executive at 10:30am and Cath shows me Bob's papers at the side of his desk. I explain that the chairman is coming in at 9:00am and ask her to get a quick and confidential message to all the directors to meet in the boardroom at that time. I ask her to make sure they all understand this is a three-line whip.

As Cath starts texting the team Jo catches me in the corridor and starts to update me on the number of cancellations that have been decided on for today. That brings the bed crisis back into my consciousness with a clang, but I have to stop her and explain the news. Jo has worked at this hospital for over twenty years and has seen too many CEOs come and go. On the one hand she's always frustrated by the situation and the top-level handling, but on the other this latest news appears to be what she'd expected.

"The job is bloody impossible. Bob was a good guy, and it's not him who should be sacked. It's down to all of us."

Jo had also been one of the crisis team that put together the dreadful recovery plan which resulted in Bob being thrown to the lions. I can see she is as ashamed as I am to be mixed up in this. The hospital is a big part of Jo's life – she lives less than half a mile away and has been to hell and back in the last few years, fighting daily to keep her part of the ship afloat while watching CEOs step into and out of the revolving door. But, like Cath and Mo, she will be a godsend for me. If I'm going to have any prayer of keeping my head above water in the coming months I need people like her around me. Jo wants to know who is taking over.

"The chairman's coming at nine to talk to us," I offer.

"So are you taking the reins?" she probes.

I'm non-committal, which I am rather uneasy with. If I am going to try to resurrect the fortunes of this hospital, or at least stop it from crumbling, I need to engender a culture of trust among the senior team. And I feel slightly duplicitous keeping my hand close, and away from Jo. But she's no fool and I sense she has made an assumption.

"We cannot let this happen again, Linda. We need to stand up and turn this place around. I can see this hospital from my front window and I'm not prepared to see you be the next one to fail."

"I've been told to stay silent but I suspect you've worked it out, Jo. I think I'm standing in, but if so, it will be very temporary," I say. "Try to look surprised when the chairman speaks! In any case, I know his objective is to find someone who they believe can turn it around, and quickly."

She turns on her heel and says:

"See you at nine."

♦

The chairman arrives at 8:45am, when Cath is still rushing around trying to ensure everyone attends. She does it, as ever. We all sit around the boardroom table at 9:00am prompt, waiting for the chairman to speak. There seems to be a rather dismal and ominous mist settling a foot or so above the table while each of my colleagues wonders if the chairman has retained his lease of Damocles' sword. Mercifully it's all over in fifteen minutes. He explains the news – I am the temporary CEO and they are starting the search for a new CEO. He concludes by saying that everyone should give me their full support during this difficult interim period. Good of him. And then he fields the questions, of which there are precisely none! What is there to ask?

It is now 9:15am and the chairman is wandering around my office, dictating a note to all staff about Bob's departure and my temporary appointment. In an hour or so I'm supposed to stand in for Bob at the regional meeting. This is the meeting where all the local CEOs and finance directors meet to review the performance of each hospital in the region. Cath shows me the relevant documentation and I see we are red against ninety per cent of the measures. This is going to be fun.

I check with the chairman: should I stay here or should I go? I'm kind of hoping he says I should stay here and get on with the job but, of course, he makes it clear that I need to go and try to persuade the region that we can keep our show on the road. God loves a trier.

I pick up John, our finance director, from his office and he offers to drive. During the journey he briefs me again on the financial part of the recovery plan and says that in his view the proposed savings do not go far enough to ensure we hit breakeven this year. We're currently three months into the year with revenues down and operating expenses up, and we're actually predicting a £20 million loss rather than the £15 million we discussed earlier in the week. And breakeven by year end is the least that is expected of us. Who says finance directors are only capable of delivering bad news? Over the past few years John has taken on the demeanour of a young Ebenezer Scrooge, wielding a cattle prod at anyone who tries to loosen his purse strings. The perfect FD.

As we walk into the room it becomes quickly apparent that everyone knows each other well and I don't really know any of them; I've just met a few of them in passing. The boss calls us to attention and the meeting settles down. The regional performance director presents table after table and we are consistently appearing at the bottom of them all. I try not to catch anybody's eye so spend a lot of the time looking down at my file. After presenting the performance comparison charts he updates us all on the regional plans to unblock the emergency care pathway. Another CEO then presents a paper on their long-term strategy while my mind drifts in and out. My head's spinning a little; only three hours ago Bob was my boss and now

I'm listening to some guy drone on about how he's planning for his operation to become some kind of super hospital and take over the whole region, maybe even the world.

The regional boss catches me as John and I try to make a speedy exit and tells me that pretty soon some of his team will need some office space in our hospital to carry out an extensive review of our expenditure-reduction plans. Splendid – it just gets better and better.

On the way back I ask John why he thinks other hospitals can make a profit and we can't. I'm looking for a better understanding, but soon enough I'm thankful it's a short journey because after hearing the first fifteen reasons why it's impossible for us to make a profit I wish I'd never asked. In essence it appears almost all budgets are over-spent, we have the added expense of the new hospital building, and the prices we're able to charge don't take account of all the extra expense of treating patients these days.

As we walk into the hospital I'm determined to sit down with John and get him to help me understand the finances in more detail. But it is soon clear this is not going to happen right now as I hear Charlie, our medical director, shouting.

"Linda!"

He's closely followed by Mr Cooper, the clinical director for surgery, and Dr Staulous, the clinical director for medicine. They are all talking at once. Cooper is telling me he has patients waiting to go to theatre and no bed for them to return to because some of his surgical beds are occupied by emergency medical patients. And Staulous is explaining that the A&E department is like a war zone and some patients have been waiting there for a bed since the middle of the night. I ask them all to come back to Bob's office with us and we pick up Jo on the way. Even as I speak it catches in my throat and Staulous takes great pleasure in reminding me that according to this morning's note it's not Bob's office but mine now!

In Bob's office we're joined by Jo, and I start:

"OK, one at a time. Let's try to review the situation together and make a decision we can all agree on. Mr Cooper, you go first."

I pick Cooper because I think he may be the most difficult. He's an incredibly intelligent man, but years of being let down have left him with a cynical edge, and I suspect he thinks he's too much of a match for me. He doesn't disappoint.

"Well, it is quite simple really. I have patients, some of whom have been waiting many months and have already breached their planned care access target. They are down in theatre ready to go. I have surgeons ready to operate. But we dare not start the afternoon session because there are no beds to place them in afterwards. We went ahead yesterday and took a gamble that beds would free up but they didn't. As a result, many patients spent last night in the recovery room. Today it is just too dangerous to go ahead as two of the theatres are operating on complex cases and we cannot start until we know we have a bed for them. Bed management tried to cancel these operations earlier but I overrode them on clinical grounds."

Jo comes in:

"What about using the day case beds until the end of the day?"

She is looking for a compromise based on the hope that there will be no urgent need for these beds.

Mr Cooper briskly dispatches that idea.

"They are all full as well."

I turn to our clinical director for medicine.

"Dr Staulous, you next."

"I know the guys in surgery think it is our fault and in some ways I can understand that. Today we have over sixty medical patients lying in surgery beds but, unlike surgery, we cannot just cancel patients coming through the A&E door. It is possible, although risky, to increase the threshold of admission but we cannot say: *'Can you please have your accident tomorrow as we are full at the moment?'*"

Then he looks at Cooper and says:

"It's simple really. We need to open more beds."

Cooper agrees. But I know that while opening more beds solves the clinical issues it will make the finances worse as more beds need more staffing. I can sense John displaying the early signs of a seizure; we'll need a bed for him soon enough! So I push on, not responding to what is clearly a done deal in their eyes.

"Jo, how are the discharges going today?"

"Well, with all the pressure on finances we're opening and closing beds daily but at the moment we probably have close to nine hundred beds in total and currently we're estimating forty discharges today, although as you know that usually improves a lot as the day unfolds. I have done a quick trip around the wards and it looks like we have a lot of sick patients in beds at the moment. However much I understand the down side of this, I can't see any other option but to temporarily open Primrose Ward. I have no idea where we'll get the staff to cover it, but what else can we do?"

I turn to John, knowing full well that he's not about to agree.

"Well, both medicine and surgery are over budget on expenses, and agency nursing costs are over budget by nearly three hundred per cent. Also, revenue for surgery is down." Then he twists the FD's knife: "Linda will also remember in the plans submitted to the region only earlier this week we have committed to closing a number of wards, including Primrose, with an estimated annual saving of half a million pounds per ward."

I look around the table to see everyone looking back at me waiting for me to make a decision. Charlie seems to have no ideas to offer. I take a moment and walk over to the window. I see ambulance staff unloading a patient from an ambulance and two more queuing up behind. Then I notice a patient standing outside in her dressing gown, leaning on a drip-stand and smoking a cigarette. She's only a few feet away from our large red and white **NO SMOKING** sign. I take a deep breath and turn around.

I look at Cooper, in search of a tolerable compromise, being painfully aware that I'm not about to come up with a viable way forward any time soon.

"How many of these operations are really clinically urgent or have been cancelled before? Must they all be carried out today?"

He replies:

"Well, it really depends on what you mean by urgent. If you had been waiting in pain or for a cancer treatment I think you would say it is pretty urgent. Also, I think it is only fair to point out that these access targets you have required us to meet mean that if we do not operate on them today we will also be failing those."

I want to remind him that it's not me who set these targets and that we're all responsible for delivering them, but I take the less confrontational route and ask him, based on today's list, how many patients we could safely re-plan for the next few days. After some discussion and negotiation we agree a number, and both Staulous and Cooper agree to lead another ward round to try to free up

11

more beds. I ask Jo to take the lead on managing the bed availability throughout the day.

I know I haven't solved anything real but at least we have a way forward for the rest of the day. I'm sure that by tomorrow morning we'll be back where we started the day today, but that's the helter-skelter we're riding on at the moment.

As they all leave the office Cath pops her head around the door and says:

"You look like you could do with a coffee."

And this time I could.

The rest of the day is something of a blur. I answer phone calls and emails, drink coffee and have speedy catch-ups with countless members of staff. Some people wish me the best of luck and others jokingly ask how long I'll last. I don't think they mean it. But nobody is offering to solve the nightmare we're in, and why should they? Maybe nobody knows. Later in the day I get a three-line whip to attend a meeting with the regional bosses on Monday. They want to explain what they expect me to do in the short term. I'm not overly anxious to make such a swift return trip but it isn't my choice and I must keep an open mind; it may actually help us to get a quicker hold on the situation.

I agree to take John, Jo, Charlie and Mo with me and suggest to Mo that we have a quick catch-up first thing on Monday.

Chapter Two

Never... again

It's after 8.00pm when I pull into my drive. I bleep the Mini and it winks at me as I enter the house and trip over the mail. I pick it up and dump it on the breakfast bar, simultaneously kicking off my shoes and dropping my bag, before putting my shoes back on so I can retrieve my laptop from the car.

8:05pm and I try again, this time dumping the laptop on the breakfast bar, kicking off my shoes and turning to the fridge to be greeted by the welcome sight of an unfinished bottle of Sauvignon. I pour a glass, sit on a stool and push out a weary sigh. As I look across at this morning's coffee cup and cereal bowl, I muse that all I need now is a stage-trained cat wafting its tail in my face for me to become the classic stereotype of the single, professional woman of the twenty-first century. Too busy to have a relationship, too busy to wash up and helplessly hitched to the job. I should have more of a life though, shouldn't I? When was the last time I went out and not directly from work? When was the last time I came home, took a shower, got changed into clothes I like and went out?

But I love my job. No... I used to love my job. Almost seven years ago I'd just turned thirty and had the health service at my feet. Now I feel like I'm scrabbling around its feet. Days as bad as today don't come around often, although we're always fighting fires of one size or another. When does anyone get a chance to stand back and take the time to make a real strategy? Bob didn't. But ironically he'll have the time now that he doesn't need it. Maybe the special projects he's going to work on will shine a light for all us CEOs and acting CEOs. Hope springs eternal. I'm just about to descend into the '*what am I doing with my life?'* spiral when I'm rescued by the ring of the phone.

It's my friend, Dee.

"Hi, honey. Where the hell have you been?" This is her typical greeting.

"Oh hi, Dee, how are you?"

"Oh fine, just fine. As you haven't rung me for a while I've taken up a new hobby – basket weaving."

Dee has a pretty good line in sarcasm but this seems a little early in the conversation, so I probe.

"What have you been up to really?"

"This and that. Working hard as ever. Been to the gym a couple of times, there's a new instructor on the spinning class, have started to learn to speak Hungarian and, oh what was it, I'm sure there was something else? Oh yes... I've been getting a year older."

Damn it! As Dee is talking I flick my *South Park* calendar over to this month to confirm the dreadful realisation that I've forgotten her birthday.

"Oh, Dee, I'm so sorry."

"Yeah, yeah, you've been a busy girl. I know, what with your big job and your bonkers family to keep out of trouble. Anyway, what's the deal about being thirty-six? I can do it again next year!"

Dee's straight-up style is as reliable as her good heart. She can tease anyone with consummate ease but beneath it all she is fiercely loyal and a special friend. And, in fairness, my family is a pretty decent target for teasing. My mum has seemingly spent the decade and a half since I graduated and left home scouring the globe for a suitable partner for me, then scaring off any poor soul that I was cruel enough to introduce to her. My longest relationship was with a banker called Rob. We were together for three years, but with no plan to marry, Mum began to heap on the pressure. Anyway, Rob and I both paid more attention to work than we did to each other. We eventually split up amicably. Mum was obviously disappointed but gamely retook up her life's work in humiliating me and stalking hapless candidates. She only drew breath intermittently to irritate my retired dad who eventually ran out of resilience or will and succumbed to an irresistible offer to move to the south of France with his former PA.

So I only see Dad a couple of times a year now, which is a great shame. I idolised him as I grew up. He is such a reassuring man, so gentle and kind, and he worked hard to give us the best start in life. Mum was great too but it was always Dad who made me feel right.

When I say 'us' I mean me and my younger brother, Simon, for whom Dee reserves her most acerbic wit. Simon, much to everyone's amusement, married a beautiful, if slightly vacuous, headhunter called Simone. Even Mum could see the potential pitfalls of Simon marrying someone with only an extra letter in her name – '*Now I did like that Janet. She was a lovely girl... I wonder why Simon didn't settle for her.*'

Simone was hunting Simon's head when he worked as a marketing executive for a big pet supplies company. But Simple Simon (as Dee calls him) had his head turned, and Simone got more than she bargained for. They now have two lovely children, Lucy and Kirk. When they're all together they look exactly like those cloned, smug families of four that you see weekly on the front cover of the Money section of *The Times*, smiling nauseatingly as they wrestle with the dilemma of whether to invest in annuities or open an organic yoghurt factory in the Hebrides – '*We make all our decisions as a family as the kids' opinions are as valid as ours.*' Yoghurt factory it is then.

Dee delights in the comedy material they provide, ridiculing the choice of the name Kirk for a lad with the surname Seed: '*Kirkseed! It sounds like a suburb in Sheffield or something you'd varnish a door with. Or maybe something Simone would pour over a lightly tossed baby leaf and rocket ensemble.*' Years earlier it had taken me a while to pluck up the courage to let Dee know they'd only just removed Poppy from a prospective list of names for their daughter. When I did tell her she knocked over a table of drinks in the pub and lost any semblance of composure for a good five minutes. Then she didn't stop going on about it for three weeks.

"So, how are Simple Simon and the Barbie doll?" she asks.

I remind her that the Barbie doll is earning a six-figure annual fee. And Dee retorts:

"God knows how! Does she really dress herself? Anyway – how are you going to make it up to me?"

"Make what up?"

"Leaving me to watch the sixth series of *Friends* with a box of chocolates on my birthday!"

In truth, Dee had been laid low on her birthday by a nasty virus, but she isn't about to let me know.

"Well, how about tomorrow night? I'll take you to Carlucci's."

"You're on."

♦

Spending a relaxing evening in our favourite Italian restaurant was just what the doctor ordered. All day I'd felt guilty about forgetting Dee's birthday but equally I knew she wouldn't hold it against me. She might not let me forget for a while but she wouldn't hold it against me. And it's great to pass the time just eating and drinking and having a chat and a laugh.

As our coffees arrive Dee shows the usually expertly hidden caring side of her nature:

"So how are you really, Linda? You know I'll never forgive you for missing my birthday. But where have you been for the last few weeks?"

We'd already covered the current absence of bedfellows, family, and a myriad of other topics. But we hadn't talked about work. It was great to have a whole evening where work was off my mind, but I can't quite make it to midnight without a mere mention.

"I've just been really busy."

"Working?"

"No, running a Zumba class for retired accountants."

Spending a whole evening with Dee has had an effect. She smiles.

"Work's not great at the moment," I continue. "Fair to say, I'm not having a good time."

I then go on to tell her about everything that has kicked off at the hospital, about the perpetual fighting of fires, the politics and Bob's demise.

"So you're in the hot seat?" she asks.

"For a while. But I don't know if I can do it, Dee. Every single morning something goes wrong and not just little things, big things. It isn't like working in an office where if you make a mistake you lose some money or get sued – when we make a mistake people can die."

I catch myself as I can feel I'm darkening the mood, but Dee's my best friend and I haven't been able to speak to anyone properly about work. Mum doesn't understand and Simon's on Planet Simone and everyone at work is in the middle of it so they can't really offer anything new. I don't think Dee will mind.

"Tell me if I'm getting boring."

Dee opens her mouth and then shuts it again.

"We're lurching from one crisis to the next and I can't for the life of me work out why. Sure – things happen and we have to react, but every time we get one plate spinning others wobble. It's not as if we don't have the people. We have great people, highly skilled people. And it's not for the lack of measuring. We spend half our day collating data and completing returns. But somehow when we put it all together it doesn't seem to work."

"You know what you need?" says Dee.

"No, I don't."

"A holiday!"

Dee isn't trivialising my problems and it's not that she doesn't understand; for goodness sake, I've bent her ear over gallons of coffee for more years than I can remember. But she's a smart cookie. She knows when something can be solved and when it can't. And it certainly can't when the midnight hour approaches and the table witnesses the wreckage of both a red and a white. And, of course, she has a spare holiday ticket!

"You remember that Will guy I started seeing? Well, he said we should go on holiday together so I booked a week in Barbados for us. No sooner had the bill hit my credit card than the idiot got cold feet. What do you say?"

"Oh sorry, Dee – there's just no way. I can't, with work and everything being as it is."

"It's months away. Sure you can take some time off!"

"Oh, I don't know."

"You have to come. I'm not going on my own. Anyway, we can sort that out later. What are we doing now?"

"Going home, I guess."

"What? It's not even twelve!"

I know Dee wants to head off to her favourite club, the Circle Bar. We haven't been out dancing for months but I really don't have the energy. It's been a wonderful evening and I feel so much better, but we're both thirty-six, and at least I know when I've had enough fun and when it's time to go home to bed.

3:00am

The taxi draws away, Dee waving out of the wrong window as I bang my head on the front door trying to retrieve the key I've just dropped.

8:30am

The phone rings. It has a terrible shrieking trill and I fumble for my alarm clock until I eventually realise it's the phone, but not before noting the time. Oh God – what time did I get in? Must have been after two! I pick up the phone and gingerly put it to my ear.

"Hello. Oh, hi, Mum… what do you mean I sound tired? It's half past eight and it's Sunday."

Mum tells me that she's been invited to have lunch at Simon's. I'm wondering how this involves me when the situation suddenly becomes significantly worse. Apparently I too am invited, and Mum needs me to go because she sold the car when Dad left and Simon and Simone live over ten miles away.

"Can't you get a taxi?" I cling on to hope.

"I can get a taxi, Linda, but you have been invited and it would be rude not to go when you know Simone has prepared for six."

I suppose Mum is right. In any case I always like to see Simon. He's good fun, a loving dad and despite being a marketing executive, has plenty of interesting things to say. The kids are great too. They're at that wonderful age, eight and six, when they embrace every new experience with gullible excitement and believe everything I tell them. There have been times over the past few weeks when I've truly envied them and their blissfully uncomplicated lives.

Even Simone's alright when she is isn't straining to do a passable impersonation of a television domestic angel: '*Sunday lunch simply isn't Sunday lunch without a sticky toffee compote and a dollop of Moroccan vanilla ice cream…*' *POUT.*

So I accede to Mum's request and agree to pick her up at one. Back to bed.

◆

As I gaze out of my office window across the car park shrouded in mist I genuinely feel refreshed and relaxed. Spending time with family and friends has done me good, and as I pour a cup of coffee I vow not to leave it so long before meeting up again. It's 7:00am and the lady with the drip and cigarette is up for an early puff, accompanied by two other pallid figures. I muse that maybe it isn't an early morning mist after all, but a growing nicotine smog. Either way, it looks quite atmospheric.

A weekend away from work allowed me to gather myself and put things into context. Last Friday was a particularly hellish day, and while we muddled through to some sort of compromise I am under no illusion that anything will have materially changed. But I feel more up for it. The doubts I had when Bob left have been replaced by a determination to get hold of things. I need to understand the whole gamut of issues to be able to tackle them. But tackle them I will.

The end of last week passed in a whirl. And after an enjoyable family weekend the first thing I must do now is face the reality of another Monday when we're likely to run out of beds again. We're also due at regional office at 12:00 noon, when the bosses will tell me and the team what's expected of us in the short term. I don't see much point in preparing a detailed plan before we go. The last chance we had to display our planning prowess only speeded up Bob's demise! I'm confident that Mo, Charlie and Jo know their responsibilities and the challenges within their own departments, and that John knows the minute details of the figures, and I'm determined we show we've got our finger on the pulse. We're due to set off at 10:30am, which gives us a bit of breathing space if the traffic is bad. That gives me time now to continue working on a solution to the lack of beds, see what else has landed this morning and think about our visit to regional office.

At the meeting we'll need to say how we plan to get a grip on quality, meet the targets and balance the books. But my primary objective is to get out of there with no intervention teams descending

Mo looks up.

"Well, the AU was full and no doubt it will be the same this week."

Charlie looks weary.

"OK. With patients with diarrhoea needing to be treated in a side room and with the AU full, the patient was held in a cubicle in A&E. But as a GP referral he was a medical patient and not an A&E patient so no A&E doctors examined him. The nurses did the basic care but essentially he was waiting for a side room to become free on the AU. AU was waiting for a side room elsewhere in the hospital, which with the recent Norovirus outbreak are like hens' teeth. So, to cut a long story short, the gentleman waited six hours in A&E and the medics on the AU were in meltdown following the wrong medication dose incident, so no one went to A&E to assess the patient. He eventually arrived on the AU at the doctor handover time, then waited a further two hours to be assessed by the junior doctor on nights who appears to have prescribed an ineffective drug for the heart condition. The on-call consultant ward round on Saturday morning found the patient in a very serious condition and requested a visit from the outreach team but they were not available this weekend as we can only staff it every other weekend at the moment. ICU was full so the consultant got hold of Mo and insisted on an ICU admission. That was delayed due to the need to discharge someone first. The patient eventually got to ICU twenty-four hours after arriving at the hospital. Had he been seen and treated promptly he might well be on the road to recovery – now, sadly, he is fighting for his life."

I'm speechless. So many issues in one case. The lack of AU capacity, infection control, the lack of side rooms, medical doctors required to be in two places at once, A&E not staffed to care for GP-referred patients, the competence of junior staff working at night with minimal supervision, critical care without the necessary capacity, and the list goes on. Never mind the patient breaching the four-hour target in A&E!

I realise Mo is talking while I've been off in my own thoughts.

"Linda, you don't need me to tell you things have got to change around here. The surgeons are unhappy at always having to cancel patients. I've got exhausted consultant colleagues we really rely on to staff the acute medical rota. Gone are the days when the juniors did most of the work. This incident shows us the consultants have to be on top of every sick patient's details. The so-called general physician seems to be a thing of the past. Most now want to stick with their specialist work – the general medical work is just too onerous to be sustained into your sixties. I'm still young and want to make the system work, but look around you."

I know that medical patients today are passed from one consultant to another. The bed manager has more control over where the patients are looked after than any consultant. Mo explains that when consultants do the ward round the junior doctor who has taken the patient's history, done the investigations and started treatment can spend ages trying to find the patient or their notes. He says:

"Patients get moved from the AU without us knowing. We can be in the middle of a ward round and find the patient gone so we have to trek around the wards to find them. Often they are on a wrong ward, and that has got to be dangerous. I heard a colleague complain about one of his patients who was ready to be discharged but her social care package was not funded. This patient was moved wards five times by the bed managers while waiting for a nursing home, sometimes in the middle of the night, to create an empty bed for an A&E patient who would breach the four-hour target. It is outrageous that we treat patients in this way."

I feel sick in the pit of my stomach. My early morning bowl of porridge was not such a good idea. How have we got to this state? In one way it's quite easy to explain. As a good friend from my MBA days always said: '*Tell me how you'll measure me and I'll tell you how I'll behave.*' Now I see what he meant.

Managers in the service are measured by the things that are easy to measure and attract management attention – money and targets – yet that does not excuse or explain why many hospitals are drifting to it being acceptable to move patients in the middle of the night, leave doctors and nurses to cover gaping holes in care provision and only realise that safety is compromised when things go badly wrong for individual patients. In a sense I, along with many in the service, have come to compromise in the face of competing and irreconcilable priorities. How can this hospital save five to ten per cent of its budgets per annum for the next five years, meet all the clinical standards and waiting times, and focus on the needs of individual patients? Mo is still speaking:

"You know what? This weekend makes me more determined than ever to get the delivery of healthcare sorted in this hospital. The patients and staff deserve better. What we can do in the AU is limited as we are at the mercy of what happens elsewhere in the hospital and even outside. Patients arrive in waves from primary care and we can't get people home quickly as social services are too busy fighting their own fires. It is easy to blame others, and I do not want to do that, but we need a collective effort if we are to get this mess sorted."

Charlie is on the move. He has a clinic to go to. Before he goes I get the patient details ready to visit them later. Mo stays to provide me the details of the drug overdose patient and we brace ourselves for our meeting with the bereaved family.

The picture looks as grim as anything I could imagine and I find myself wondering whether my career is coming to a premature end. I think back to Bob and wonder what he'd do. He's probably had a blissfully long weekend after clearing his desk. But I do remember that whenever he saw me struggling with something or in a seemingly hopeless situation he'd often say: '*Focus on the things that can make a difference and stop worrying about things you can't do anything about.*'

So I take a look at the clock. It's now 8:35am. I ring John and ask him to call in to my office at 9:30am.

Chapter Three

Money

John's aware of the weekend's events but doesn't feel the need to offer conciliatory comment. And neither do I have the time to hear it. He sits down, financials in one hand and cup of coffee in the other. We get down to business.

"John, I need to understand why we're losing money and by how much. How much are we actually losing a month?"

John is not disposed to waffle or sugar-coat the truth.

"Approximately one million pounds a month at the moment. And that's getting progressively worse. We lost just over three million in the first three months of this financial year and my forecast is fifteen and possibly as much as twenty by year end."

I ask him how he got to that number and to keep his explanation simple.

"OK. Let me know if I'm going too fast or too slow. As you know, the profit, or in our case the loss, is simply the difference between how much money we bring in and how much we spend every month. If we bring in more than we spend then we make a profit. Of course, if we don't we make a loss.

"In its simplest form the money we bring in is directly related to the number of patients we treat. Each treatment has a price, or tariff, associated with it, so for each patient we add up all the treatments they receive and that tells us how much we can charge for their overall time in the hospital. Our revenue budget for this year is approximately £400 million."

"Where do we get their treatment information from?"

"Charlie tells us."

"Does he know the price of each treatment?"

"No, he doesn't. But in the patient notes is a record of the treatments a patient has had and we take those and professionally code them, and Finance work out the total amount to charge for that patient. It is just a case of going through each and every patient once they have been discharged and adding it up correctly."

I know it isn't always as straightforward as John presents it. Often these notes go back and forth many times, trying to clarify exactly what treatment the patient received and sometimes causing a serious delay between carrying out the treatment and invoicing. We can't actually be sure if we've missed anything out. It's frustrating, but we haven't come up with a better solution yet. Once we know the amount of money we can charge for each patient we add the figures up at the end of the month and invoice the various commissioning groups, and that makes up most of our revenue. There is also a small amount of revenue from private patients that we receive once we've invoiced their insurance companies.

As we're haemorrhaging money I wonder if the tariff we're using is simply too low, but John tells me it is agreed nationally before local adjustments are sanctioned.

I think back to my visit to regional office last week and listening to that sanctimonious CEO thrilling the bosses with his '*exciting plans for the future*'. I'm troubled by the thought that he can make money and Bob couldn't. I reword my thoughts for John's benefit.

"But how come we're losing money and others are making money even though they charge the same tariff?"

John spells it out for me:

"We have to work out the expenses associated with carrying out any given treatment. In essence these fall into two categories. Firstly we have the totally variable costs which vary directly in relation to the number of patients we treat. So if we carry out a thousand hip replacements we use a thousand joints. Drug costs are variable as well.

"Then we have the costs that do not vary directly with volumes, the costs of running the hospital, including the building, staff, doctors, nurses, managers and even the finance team."

Anticipating my next question, John takes a blank piece of paper from his file and starts to draw a pie chart as he explains how our costs are broken down.

"The totally variable costs amount to about twenty per cent of our annual revenue, and that equates to a budget of £80 million. Of that figure, drug costs are around £73 million. Our annual operating expenses are likely to work out at £335 million which, when you add the £80 million a year of totally variable costs, will make an annual total of £415 million."

So there we have our £15 million loss in a year. John continues.

"By far the biggest annual operating expense is staff costs – around £270 million, or eighty per cent of the £335 million. Management costs only make up £12 million of this, and almost everything else is doctors, nurses and other clinical staff. The annual cost of the building and service charges, is about £35 million and various other costs make up the rest."

With the aid of John's pie chart the numbers are pretty simple to understand in isolation, but I still don't understand why we're struggling and others aren't. I ask John if he has similar data from elsewhere. Reluctantly he pulls a sheet from his file showing the figures for a hospital about fifty miles away and in a comparable area. The headline figures show them with annual revenue of £450 million, costs of £430 million and a profit of £20 million last year. Drug costs as a percentage of total is similar to ours and our management costs are slightly lower, but that won't be the case for too long as we've many unfilled posts. Attracting good staff to a poorly performing hospital is never easy.

Our running costs are slightly higher than theirs due to our new buildings and infrastructure, but this is only a small percentage of the difference. That had been my number one speculation of the cause of our loss, but clearly I was wrong. I look down the sheet for the crucial figure and immediately the main difference becomes acutely clear. Our percentage of front-line staff costs relative to total revenue is higher. Surely it can't be that our nurses and doctors aren't working hard enough. I just don't buy that.

John, not predisposed to making me feel any better, goes on to explain that the situation is actually worse than it might seem as we have also been increasing our spend on temporary agency staff over the last few months. As he talks I think to myself that I'd be dangerously wide of the mark to assume the answer is to reduce clinical staff. I know only too well that the dossier of complaints we have is about to outgrow Cath's biggest cabinet. In a moment of gloom I reflect that it's the only thing increasing faster than our losses. But I can do something about the pile of paperwork quicker than I can the losses.

I have a quick look at the latest batch of complaints in my tray. Most of them are about waiting and queuing and quality of care. The disaster that unfolded over the weekend is a much starker reminder than any foreboding pile of paper. Then John summarises.

"So, our revenue is determined by volumes and standard prices and our costs are a combination of variable and more fixed operating expenses. On the face of it our staff costs are higher than others, and that's the big difference. That's why we make a loss and they make a profit."

But I still can't buy that.

"That doesn't make sense. It doesn't match up with what's actually happening out there on the ground. Everyone is overstretched. Look, John, I'm not convinced our staff numbers is the issue."

What I do know is that before 10:30am we'll have to set off for regional office, so I thank John and he heads off. It's 10:20am now so I close my office door and sit down for a final chance to gather my thoughts. At the meeting we need to be crystal clear about some positive actions we're going to take, even if we're still not sure of the cause. We can't afford to go back to the long list of wishful savings. But then having some clear actions to resolve financial issues is no good if they damage patient care. We can't have any more avoidable clinical disasters. But we do need a win of some kind, and quickly.

◆

I head out to the car park with Mo, Charlie and Jo. Cath has already sent my hastily drafted notification of the clinical disaster to regional office and I guess that will be item one on the agenda. In line with policy, the governance team has already reported the incidents up the line. We agree to go together in Jo's Mazda and meet John there.

The traffic is awful and I'm glad we left plenty of time for the journey. This gives us the chance to either talk through our strategy for the meeting, try to unravel the horrific clinical incidents of the weekend or just stay quiet with our own thoughts. We all opt for the latter, for the first ten minutes at least. Then Charlie leans into view and speaks.

"I saw you were in deep discussion with Chuckles. What did he have to say?"

Charlie gets on OK with John, on the whole, but he can be pretty disparaging when he wants and has developed a weary cynicism over the past couple of years, which he combines with a sometimes annoying and slightly odd illusion that he's a joker. I think the cynicism and joking is Charlie's defence mechanism. He's always been a committed professional but has become battle-worn and exasperated by the unremitting advance of bureaucracy in the service over recent years. I indulge him:

"Chuckles has presented me with the less than cheery news that we're currently losing £1 million every month and, wait for it, that's increasing."

"Management costs?" Charlie ventures predictably.

"Nope."

"Building?"

"Nope."

"What then?"

"What do you think?"

Charlie shrugs. So I tell him.

"It's you, Charlie. You and all our doctors and nurses. Our staff costs are out of sync."

"It's the doctors and nurses who keep the place running," he retorts. I've pricked his veneer of jocularity, which always fails to conceal the fact that he still truly cares about his work.

"How much are we bringing in?" he asks.

"Hopefully, £400 million this year," I reply. I go on to explain how the patients' treatment costs are calculated from the clinical coding and tariffs he submits and he returns to his role as jester.

"Ah, now I have more sympathy for the ladies in the coding department. With my writing it is a wonder we ever get any money for the patients I treat."

Jo interjects.

"There are men as well as women working down there, you know. Maybe you should go and see what they actually do."

She winks across at me as Charlie replies:

"You know, I may just do that. Could be fun."

Jo brings us back on track.

"Just explain the figures to me again, Linda, and keep the pace glacial so I can keep up."

Jo is self-deprecating and always tough on herself when it comes to numbers, and yet I know she is probably the most reliable source of real data in the whole hospital. There have been countless times when we've been trying to work things out like the number of outpatient appointments, where patients don't turn up, or the number of patients discharged in the mornings, and time and time again her intuitive thought turns out to be much more reliable and speedier than any orchestrated data search. Charlie is impatient.

"So how come we are really making such a loss? Are we not getting the money in or are we spending too much? This is exactly the conversation I have with my wife when she wants to book the next holiday. Last year we went to Mauritius. It cost me a fortune."

Jo rolls her eyes and I tut. Mo is too polite to do either but knows as well as we do that Charlie can be such a pain when he really puts his mind to it. I remind myself that I didn't take two weeks of my holiday allowance last year and quietly fume. But then I don't like going on my own and I'm not entirely sure that if I went with Dee I'd return home unscathed.

Jo is more concerned by how she can understand the position well enough to be able to explain it to a thousand staff. And after I have recounted John's gloomy summary she checks her understanding.

"So, just to be clear, for every £100 we get, £20 of it is spent on drugs and consumables, and most of the rest is on staff and most of that is doctors and nurses."

Charlie doesn't believe it.

"Not a chance. Who comes up with these numbers?"

He's desperate to find an answer, and an answer he's comfortable with. But we're in danger of searching for random answers without actually getting to grips with anything that will make a difference and give us hope. We may even fail to find it. But with the brains and experience we have in the car, combined with John's contribution, we should be able to solve this. Anyone can come up with a collection of random answers without actually validating anything. We need to form a consensus, but equally I know it's my job to ensure that everyone is heard and their thoughts are taken into account. And much as he'd like to, Charlie knows we can't just blame the people who come up with the numbers. He says:

"You know, in the good old days we got back what we spent, but I'm not sure those days will ever return. If a patient stayed a day longer we got paid an extra day, but no more."

He's actually as committed to the cause as he always was. And the really sad thing is that the cynicism we often see now is probably the final stage of an individual who was originally keen to change the world, has done his best, run into obstacles and been frustrated. He became a sceptic and over time ended up as a cynic. But I keep reminding myself that at least that shows he cares. If he were just passive that would be a nightmare. As my mind wanders I'm almost relieved when he has another dig.

"Are you absolutely sure it's not the colossal tier upon tier of management that we now employ? In the past we never had that huge, cumbersome expense."

"I'm sure," I smile. "Anyhow, you're always going on about the importance of evidence-based medicine so can we please wait and see the evidence about our costs before you come to any half-baked conclusion?"

Meanwhile, Jo has latched on to the issue around agency staff hire.

"If we're massively overspending on expensive temporary staff to fill unfilled posts, surely we should push and find more permanent nurses wherever we can. Why don't we really focus on finding good, qualified nurses as fast as possible?"

This isn't the first time Jo has talked about hiring more permanent staff, but previously Bob had refused to lift a recruitment freeze which was initially announced as temporary but seems to have gone on for years. Jo's earnest thought prompts Charlie to take a helpful stance.

"You know, when I think about it, I'm sure some of our work isn't getting across to the coders accurately. I'll use my next doctors' meeting to go through it and make sure everyone realises how important it is. We really need to get on top of this."

It seems like we're making some progress so I call John on his mobile to let him know what we've discussed. He's on board with

Jo's thoughts on permanent staff but counsels me not to present invoicing as a panacea to our problems on the basis that it's a rather thin solution, not to mention an admission of inefficiency.

As we pull into the car park at regional office I feel we are reasonably well prepared considering the circumstances. I have briefed the team as well as I can and we're all clear about the rules of engagement. We'll just tell it as it is. John will give a clear update of the financial position, including the inevitability of further losses, and at the very least we'll be able to demonstrate that we can read the pulse.

We walk across the car park and Mo, who has been silent throughout the journey, catches me and says:

"You know, the way you've analysed the position makes it easier to understand, but why haven't we looked at it in such detail before? Management is new to me but it isn't brain surgery, is it? The numbers are pretty simple to understand, just like any small business. At least now I can show everyone in the A&E department that we cannot solve our problems by adding more and more staff. We're going to have to change the way we do things."

I feel better than I did when we set off. We're all on board and have grasped the gravity of our predicament. Now we want to do something about it. But what we don't have is a consensus of the underlying cause of our loss or a solution of any kind. We have cleared up some misguided understandings and the facts are a little clearer, but we don't know why our operating expenses are high and yet many staff feel overstretched. I think I understand the size of the problem but I'm still unsure about the way forward. And human nature has pushed us towards different, unconnected actions: Mo will communicate to his team that more staff is not the answer and Charlie will tighten up the coding and invoicing. But that's not the end of it by a long stretch.

Our analysis is incomplete but at least we've gone through it together, albeit on the hoof. John meets us in the foyer, looking as organised and dispassionate as ever. It's the kind of emotionless attitude we need, though I didn't miss it during the drive over when I think we had a better, more open, discussion without the clinical dissection of the cold, hard facts. Impending doom in minute, slow-motion detail can be disheartening at best. As we shuffle around waiting to be called up it strikes me that the last time I felt quite like this was at school, as I stood outside the Headmaster's office with non-regulation earrings in my blazer pocket. Even the lady on reception seems to have a sniffy air about her. I guess she didn't expect to see me again. I touch my left earlobe and drift momentarily before the stark outline of Kieran Bamford, the regional director, and his trusty sidekick, Ashcroft, loom into view.

"Linda, we're in the board room."

And good morning to you too.

We follow the two regional office mandarins to the board room where I'd suffered my first humiliation as acting CEO the previous Friday. The five of us sit in a line, across the table from our inquisitors. Ashcroft notices that we don't have a slick PowerPoint presentation and makes a point of closing the screen before sitting down and pouring a glass of water, not carbonated, naturally. Charlie helps himself to a glass that is carbonated and mutters an expletive as it fizzes out of the bottle and on to his file.

Kieran briefly looks upward and then speaks.

"As you haven't prepared a presentation shall we get straight on? I'm sure I don't need to spell out the financial difficulties your hospital is facing and so I'd appreciate you taking me through the changes you feel are necessary to bring the finances back into some semblance of order."

Charlie begins to speak as he continues to wipe his section of the table with what I can only think is part of his summary. This is not how I was expecting things to progress. I rather thought John would set the agenda by going through the detail of the numbers first, but I only manage to get out an '*erm*' before Charlie ignores me and continues. We're really on the back foot but I just have to trust him now.

As he talks through his understanding of the finances he actually does a good job, and I thank God we all prepared this together. Actually Charlie reels off the figures with such ease that I suspect the wily old dog has seen them before and has been playing with me on the way over. He's obviously gone through them in some detail and even manages to keep a straight face when he explains that our management costs are lower than those of some other similar hospitals.

Ashcroft looks perturbed, but Kieran offers a shred of encouragement.

"I have to say it's quite refreshing to see a doctor who is not only interested in the finances but actually seems to understand them too. Is he right, John?"

John nods and Charlie nonchalantly wipes the last drops of fizzy water from the table in front of him with considerable panache, before Kieran turns to Jo to quiz her about staffing costs. She is beginning to explain the actions we discussed to reduce the overtime and agency nursing costs when Ashcroft interrupts.

"Am I right in saying that per head your nursing staff are the least productive in the region?"

"I'm not sure about that," says Jo.

"I am," says Ashcroft.

I look at Jo in fear of her leaping across the table and grabbing Ashcroft by the throat. Thankfully she keeps her cool and simply becomes more focused. She's normally less confident in high-pressure situations like this but she's determined to give it her best shot and certainly doesn't let us down.

Seemingly satisfied with Jo's account, Kieran turns his attention to John and the temperature rises noticeably as he goes through the figures line by line.

"How can you let agency costs run out of control for so long without doing a single thing about it?"

There isn't an answer. Looking at the figures in the cold light of day is a very different scenario than trying to impact on them when everyone in the hospital is fighting fires. When John is let off the hook Mo is the next to speak. Kieran asks him about A&E, and Mo outlines an ongoing clinical risk of low doctor numbers and shows the extent of the currently unfilled posts. Kieran is unimpressed.

We have been trying for months, but with our reputation it's difficult to attract any new staff, let alone good doctors, but Mo, discretion allied to his ability to read a situation, simply agrees. He then takes them through the detail of the weekend's clinical incidents and Ashcroft takes notes throughout, before Kieran surprises us all by saying:

"Not really what you wanted in your first week, Linda, but I'm not going to hold that one against you... yet. You're following the procedure. Just give me an update next Monday."

They've obviously taken it seriously, but it's clear that Kieran simply doesn't want this to alter the direction of the meeting. He wants absolute clarity and focus on the matter in hand. He turns to me and says:

"Linda, as the temporary CEO everything that happens in your hospital lands on your head, not just the latest run of disasters. You have to be absolutely clear about what is expected while you are there. And that is to control this completely unacceptable rise in operating expenses. We need to see a properly detailed plan to explain how you will bring this hospital to breakeven, as an absolute minimum, within the next three months."

Three months! What do they expect, a miracle? He continues:

"We're working hard to find an experienced replacement for Bob, and we will keep you informed of our progress. In the meantime, we will be sending in a team to validate John's analysis and specifically to see which clinical treatments cost more than in other hospitals. To get your hospital back on an even keel you must establish which treatments you are not cost-effective at delivering and move them elsewhere."

I can once again feel the dark clouds of failure gathering over our heads as Kieran summarises that the new CEO, when found, will be given the opportunity to review the team and decide if there's a case for wholesale change. To make matters worse, he tells us he wants a thorough ongoing audit of our performance measures – all one hundred and forty of them! He wants me to report on some every day, some weekly and some monthly. Maybe we'll have to report when we go to the toilet too.

♦

As we walk back to our cars I feel I have to congratulate Charlie.

"Well, you came out of that OK. And the way you handled the fizzy bottle was imperious."

"Actually," he smirks, "I quite enjoyed it. I think they wanted to give us more of a hiding than they did."

Jo says: "They didn't do all that badly. Three months to raise the Titanic, and as for '*the new CEO will be able to review his team*', well, thanks a heap."

"Well, he or she is not here yet," says Charlie. "We are still here to fight another day, aren't we? And let's face it, those guys in regional office are scared of us front-line doctors. All we have done is bought some time to try to sort out this mess."

This was a side to Charlie he hadn't allowed to surface for too long. I thanked him for putting his head above the parapet. It's obvious to me that behind all the jocularity and sniping he's a critical part of this hospital.

John looks less happy, I presume because of the region's decision to send in a team to review his financial reports, but when I ask him, it's clear his mind has been working throughout.

"The gap between our revenue and our operating expenses is causing the loss, right? Well, if we take away even one penny of our revenue the gap will get bigger and our losses will get bigger," he says.

Charlie jumps in.

"But surely our costs will go down."

"Our totally variable costs will go down because we will be treating fewer patients," says John. "But unless we start firing more and more people our operating expenses will remain unchanged. The amount we will have to save to break even will grow. For every one pound drop in revenue we will have to save an additional 80p. And remember, our main operating expenses are our staff."

Jo brings the figures to life.

"It's an impossible ask for our staff. We have serious operational performance issues and major clinical issues which are going to require us all to change the way we do things. So let's go ahead and make the best possible improvements. And as the only way to save money seems to be by cutting staff then, hey, go for it and improve yourself out of a job. What sort of motivator is that?"

Jo doesn't mean to, but she deflates the atmosphere like a pricked balloon. I feel the need to rally.

"Hey, come on. We had a good, well OK meeting. We've managed to gain some time. At least we weren't thrown out."

In all fairness it could have been a lot worse. Not our predicament, but our treatment by regional office. We've survived, for the time being anyway, but my future career prospects continue to look pretty grim. I don't have much time to turn this mess around. And there's been no hint that they might let me have a go at the CEO's job as anything other than a caretaker. At this very moment that certainly looks like a poisoned chalice in any case.

Jo and Charlie both take calls on their phones and as John drives away I have the chance to speak to Mo. He's been quiet all morning so I ask him what he's thinking.

"You know, Linda, I felt devastated this morning after what had gone on over the weekend. And that was terrible... truly terrible. But it was just a symptom of a far greater ailment. I wish more of our doctors could have seen what we have been talking about here. It is no fun. But it is serious. We all work in our silos but there is a much bigger picture, of which we are all just a tiny part. It seems to me that if we can get the big picture in focus then we give ourselves a better chance to make our work more manageable. We will get better at what we all do. We will all feel better."

"Are you really interested in all this management stuff?" I ask.

"Well, I have to be now, don't I?"

"In that case I have an invitation you might just like."

Chapter Four

Stevie

A couple of weeks ago I received an invitation to an evening event at the business school where I completed my MBA some ten years previously. The event is part of a series of presentations and this one is entitled '*Challenges and Opportunities in the Global Pharmaceutical Industry*'. It's the kind of thing I'd usually file in the bin but I noticed it's being hosted by Stevie Vokes, an old friend. He's the only colleague from back then who I've kept in touch with, and although I haven't seen him for at least two years I view him as a good friend.

When we first met, though, we didn't hit it off. Me proudly holding on to my northern heritage and roots, confronted by a leading candidate for that year's Upper Class Twit Awards. Gosh. He was posh. And opinionated. To be fair, I remember being fairly relieved when he opened his mouth on the first morning. A friend of my brother's once told me that if you can't spot the class idiot by lunchtime on Monday it's almost certainly you. So when he announced himself to be the '*achingly bored heir to the third largest privately owned business in the South East's Growth 100*', I knew I was safe.

But as the year passed it turned out I was wrong. Stevie wasn't actually the class idiot – far from it in fact. There were other candidates queuing for that accolade, and once Stevie had overcome his initial craving for attention he turned out to be a pretty insightful student and loyal friend. He could still be an embarrassment to be with from time to time, but equally he could be the most charming man I've ever met. We spent a lot of time together, helping each other in our studies and socialising enthusiastically. And after graduation we carried on meeting, although less frequently as the years passed.

So it was nice to get this invite and, as it was Stevie, I was happy to go. It could even offer us something that might help us in our current predicament at the hospital. Hopefully I'd learn something new. While the health service isn't your typical business, I know a bit about the pharmaceutical industry and sometimes you find that business problems transcend sectors.

I set off with Mo, an open mind and looking forward to seeing Stevie again. Mo's keenness to come along confirmed to me his interest in the business side of the health service. His eyes had been opened at our meeting at the regional office and, because of the bright man he is, he'd quickly identified that any operation of our size can only thrive if the top people understand what's going on. Brilliant people are not always the most collaborative; ask any academic. So a brilliant person who's also a team player is like gold dust.

As we drive over, everything that's going wrong at the hospital is floating around in my head. Mo can see I'm deep in thought and politely asks if I want to chat.

"Sorry, Mo, I was miles away."

"I haven't thanked you for this invitation, Linda. I appreciate you asking me along."

"You might not be thanking me by nine o'clock," I reply, with some sincerity.

I explain the dynamics of the collection of people he's about to meet. The successful, the ambitious, the ruthless and the over-achieving will all be there, bound by their egocentric views of life and their love of bigger and faster cars than they need. It's a sort of college reunion, but what Mo will witness this evening happens at every MBA alumni event. It's a rite of passage. This is Stevie's opportunity to stand up and tell his course chums of yesteryear just how well he's doing.

"How well is he doing?" asks Mo.

"I don't actually know," I admit. "Over the last few years he's been travelling all over the place, which is why we haven't met up. Now he's running his own company. All I know is that he was determined to do anything other than join his dad's business."

We make our way up the long gravel drive and the business school comes into view. It's a beautiful old building, home to twelve lecture theatres, countless studies and a high-tech business centre. It's surrounded by beautifully manicured lawns and topiary, and is mirrored in a tree-lined lake in the early evening sunshine. It's a far cry from the grey car park at the hospital, with its carpet of cigarette ends. I park my Mini between a Porsche and a Range Rover. It always amazes me how Land Rover manage to sell so many of those things almost two hundred miles away from the nearest hill.

As we walk towards the main entrance we see a small sign in the grass pointing towards a marquee on the neighbouring lawn, where we're greeted by an elegantly presented reception.

"I didn't realise we were coming to a wedding," Mo quips, as a waiter offers us a canapé.

"Well, as I know Stevie, this is exactly his style. Classy, attention to detail and an excellent host."

There are about twenty or so people milling around and I don't immediately recognise anyone. But then it was over ten years ago and not all of the delegates will be classmates. I help myself to another canapé and then stuff it in my mouth as I see a gangly, tweed-clad gentleman walking towards me with outstretched hand. I transfer my glass of orange juice to my left hand and hold out my right.

"Good evening!" beams the man, before turning to greet a slightly bemused Mo.

I manage a muffled '*hullo*' as I crunch my cream cheese and leek toast, which was bigger than I expected.

"Thank you so much for coming this evening. Who are you with?" smiles the man.

"I'm an old friend of Stevie's, we were on the MBA together," I explain.

"Stevie?" The man looks puzzled. "Is he in business or horticulture?"

"Business I suppose. He's the organiser and speaker here."

The man now looks at a complete loss and Mo looks the other way.

"He's speaking on the challenges facing the pharmaceutical sector," I explain, trying to help the poor man, who replies:

"But this is the planners, organisers and sponsors reception for this year's Chelsea Flower Show."

Mo is still looking at the car park.

"The MBA talk is inside," says the man. At which point we quietly offer our farewells and good luck wishes, put our glasses on the table and slide away. In my defence, the business school would never have tried to make ends meet by hiring out the space to external organisations in days gone by. It's a sign of the times I suppose.

Minutes later we're in the Lemon Suite, part of the business centre, which Mo points out was very well signposted. I scan the room to see if I know anyone as Mo waves his finger gently up and down his face.

"Linda," he whispers.

"What?"

"I think you have a blob of cheese on your cheek."

I wipe it off.

I look around and see a number of familiar faces, one of which belongs to the pretty Clare, who comes over to tell me she's just back from holiday in Barbados with someone called James. They're now engaged and in the throes of planning their wedding in the Far East. Yoghurt factory in the Hebrides within ten years, I suspect.

It certainly looks like most people in the room have done well, judging by the tailored apparel and remarkably slender phones wafting around. There's nothing wrong with people doing well for themselves. Well, most people that is.

"Oh no!" I whisper to Mo. "It's that odious man, Robert Cynch."

To my horror he spots me looking at him and makes a beeline towards us.

"Lynn!" he bellows.

"It's Linda," I say as I reluctantly offer my hand.

"Of course it is. How the hell are you?"

Why is it that people like Cynch can't just say '*How are you?*' Why do they have to say '*How the hell are you?*' or '*How the devil are you?'* as if to hint that they subliminally hope you're enduring some fiery discomfort? Or am I being neurotic? I tell you though… I'm thoroughly irritated within eight seconds of meeting him. I stretch every sinew of my will and manage to be polite.

"What are you up to now, Robert?"

"What am I not up to!" he drones. "Tax partner at BFBFK, three non-execs and on the regional board of UK Sport. Look out for me in next year's Honours List!"

What a muppet.

"How about you, Lynn?" he feigns interest.

"Health Service COO, well acting CEO," I reply.

"Fan-bloody-tastic! Mind you, I don't envy you trying to sort that mess out. It's beyond repair, isn't it? Well good luck, Lynn," he says as he spots someone more interesting.

"It's Linda."

Mo smiles at me.

"Nice man, with, I suspect, an impressively inflated opinion of himself." Mo's rarely so cutting and is being supportive.

"You know, I hated him all the way through our course and now I remember precisely why."

We're then approached by another well-dressed man. Smart suit, clean shirt and nice tie. Wow, so different from the man I so often saw in jeans and a T-shirt, but I don't need a reason to be pleased to see this guy.

"Stevie!"

We hug and smile, and hug again. Then I introduce Mo, and Stevie thanks us both for supporting him. He has to go and prepare and we agree to catch up after the event. Mo and I get a glass of water and move into the hall where the talks are taking place. I'm really looking forward to this as I know Stevie has taken some of the stuff we learned on the MBA programme, one theory in particular, and is applying it to real life.

We take our seats in the middle of the third row and by 7:30pm the room is full, seating about a hundred guests. As the main speaker, Stevie is on last and, after listening to the first two, I eagerly wait to see what he's prepared.

♦

Stevie begins.

"The pharmaceutical industry. If we look back over recent decades we can see that almost all companies in the industry have made substantial profits that would be the envy of many other industries."

He shows a slide of the profit and sales for a number of key players, and for many years it has just gone up and up.

"A closer look will show you that actually the growth in profits has continued but it has slowed down. The growth rates are not as large as in years gone by."

He zooms in on the more recent years and sure enough you can see profits have slowed down.

"So, the question I want to explore tonight is this: is it possible for this industry to not only return to previous profit levels but to actually exceed them?

"Is this of interest to you all?"

He's greeted by a positive murmur, rows of nodding heads indicating a range of enthusiasm and Cynch exclaiming:

"We would not be here if we weren't, old boy!"

So with this sanction he continues:

"The first thing we need to understand is why growth in profits has slowed down.

"As you are probably aware, this is an industry where the opportunity to make money only comes after massive investment in extensive research and development. Therefore, when you finally have one of the few drugs that actually makes it through to production and on to the market you have to try to sell as much of it as you can as quickly as you can. Why? Because there is only a limited time period to get a return on your investment before either your competitors launch a better-performing drug or the generic producers come in and a price war starts. Companies need to ensure availability for anyone who wants to buy. A common tactic is to employ a large sales force to ensure not a single opportunity is missed."

This helps to explain why those sales reps are so pushy at their 'conferences' they arrange for our doctors. There is a question from the floor.

"Yes, but why has profitability suffered?"

"Well, some would say that the cost associated with R&D has just gone up and up. But actually, the other important factor is that the period of patent protection is constantly under pressure and with the competitors' new drugs also coming to the market the window of opportunity that the company has to exploit the drug is itself reducing. As a result it is no longer just a gamble of whether or not the drug makes it to the market, and now there is a bigger and bigger game of roulette in persuading customers to change to their newer drugs as opposed to the competitors'. You can predict many pharmaceuticals are constantly having to resize their global sales forces."

And this is precisely what I don't need right now. If the pharmaceutical companies try to push more of the latest drugs on me, how am I supposed to buy the next blockbuster as well? We don't have an endless pot of cash; far from it. Stevie illustrates his point nicely with a number of examples of supply chains which have over a year's worth of drugs in them to try to ensure a sale is never lost, and yet they still end up with short supplies.

Stevie goes on to explain that after the initial investment in R&D, the increasing competition and the shortening time period before the generic suppliers move in, there is a need for the pharma company to maximise the sales of the new drug because it's an all-important and increasingly limited and competitive period. This is the main opportunity to gain a return on their investment. But he explains that this is not as simple as it might seem as even with sophisticated forecasting techniques the true likelihood of the take-up of the new drug and the actual sales in any one region is not known until the launch has happened. There's always the need to ensure no potential sale is ever lost, but there's also a risk of flooding the globe with excess stock that will never sell. He takes his time to point out that a competitive edge can be gained by any company that can deliver much better availability with substantially reduced stock across the system, while experiencing unpredictable demand.

He continues to explain that during this limited period of exploitation the supply chain can become over-populated with too much stock of some drugs in one location around the world, and too little of others elsewhere. Producing too much of what was not actually needed uses the capacity required to replace shortages of other products elsewhere. This misuse of capacity in the chain of production and supply inflates the time it takes to replenish stock where it's needed most. This often causes further short supplies across the range and geographies, and puts even greater pressure on the limited capacity. In the worst instance, a negative loop starts.

I try to relate this to the hospital. It certainly seems many patients queue at many stages of their journey, and these queues may be inflating the time it takes us to treat patients, but I can't yet see how this is masking our capacity.

Stevie then looks back at the examples in a different way. He replaces the existing mentality with an approach that focuses on making only what is required to guarantee availability. He explains how with this approach he has seen lead times reduced by fifty per cent and a surprisingly large amount of excess capacity exposed.

Wow, that's one hell of a claim! I certainly don't believe that by eliminating delay in a patient's treatment we can reduce their overall length of stay by fifty per cent; after all, for many patients, much of their length of stay is associated with their time to recover. But I can see that if we could eliminate some of the queues it would help, as I know for sure these queues extend the length of stay of some patients.

Back to the pharmaceutical industry. Stevie is explaining how this approach can be implemented across the regional distribution centres and the whole global supply chain. Everyone else is listening intently but I'm away with the fairies. My eyes have been opened to the possibility that delay not only increases journey times but also wastes precious capacity. In the pharma industry it seems Stevie achieved the improvements by only producing what was required to guarantee availability. I can't see the equivalent in our world.

Mo leans over and whispers:

"You know, Linda, this is exactly what I see happening every day. In the mad rush, someone calls me to say: '*You must review this patient in the assessment unit now*', and yet a few days later I see the same patient still there. What was the rush all about? Meanwhile another patient who I could have discharged was delayed, which stopped me treating the next patient in the queue. We are constantly responding to whoever shouts the loudest."

♦

As I listen to Stevie's talk, two things strike me. Firstly, I'm pleased that he seems to have matured into a serious and considered guy. There's no sign of the attention-grabbing angst of a decade ago and he certainly hasn't turned into one of those self-important 'achievers' that are populating parts of the room.

Secondly, there's a confidence in his words and simplicity in the explanation. Much of what he says is striking a chord with me and the step-by-step approach he takes is in stark contrast to our habitual lurching from one crisis to the next. It's clear to me that our strategy is anything but clear. If only I could defog just one tiny part to begin with...

And listening to Stevie has made me impatient too. I need to get to the core of the hospital's conundrum as quickly as possible. I'm desperate to speak to him. All I need is a shred of encouragement and one simple steer to get me started. The depressing start to my tenure as acting CEO has knocked most of the stuffing out of me but I think there's something worth looking at here. And I don't have a better plan up my sleeve.

While my mind has been wandering, Stevie has been summarising and opening the floor for questions. He points to a gentleman to our left, who announces himself.

"Gerry MacDonald, Hipcock and Dirge national loss adjusters. Mr Vokes, I'm interested in what you have to say but you need a track record of results if you are going to gain credence. Commenting on industries is fine, but as you surely appreciate, ultimate proof can only come through many examples. How many successful examples of your work do you have?"

Stevie smiles.

"I have four and I will keep going with this validation unless I disprove the approach. Many opportunities are lost while we wait for one hundred per cent assurance, but then as we wait for that security we cannot really say we deserve the entrepreneur's spoils."

"I suppose it's a case of '*do what you've always done and you'll*

46

always get what you've always got," says a chap in front of us.

"Unless you do what you've always done a little differently," answers Stevie. And with this his gaze turns towards the back of the room and the next question.

"Bob Cynch, BFBFK!"

Oh God. Wait for this. Mo leans across and whispers:

"Why is he shouting?"

Robert gives his most insightful opinion for the benefit and spiritual enrichment of all present.

"Stevie, what I need to know is which company you are going to work in next so I can make a killing on the stock market."

Stevie laughs this off before desperately looking for another question. I have one of those moments when your energy seems to surge. So I speak up.

"You have a new approach from my viewpoint, but how could you apply it in the health service?"

"I have no intuition in this environment but I do suspect it is possible," he replies.

I continue:

"You see, it's incredibly complicated. In all other industries you get orders but we get patients. We don't know what's wrong with them. They just turn up and can have any one, or more than one, of tens of thousands of categories of illness or injury and this happens twenty-four hours a day, seven days a week."

I'm on a roll now. I don't hear any impatient noises emanating from the room so I continue.

"Nothing's predictable. Some recover in five days, some in ten, some unfortunately never. When you make mistakes in manufacturing you get scrap. In the health service you get worse. The flow is uncontrollable and if the tide is against you, patients could end up on the wrong ward and that can be very bad for the patient. Everybody tries their best, but a nurse or junior doctor outside their area of expertise is under unfair pressure. And that's before you even consider variation in efficiency and aptitude. It can be a nightmare."

"So how have you decided to manage that?" he asks.

"We chase fire after fire and make sure the extinguisher is always to hand. That's the only way we know how to do it."

"How do you work out which fire represents the biggest danger and which to put out first?"

I shake my head.

"With great difficulty. We have people doing improvement projects all over the hospital but we don't really know which one is having an effect."

There's a brief pause before a chap at the back of the room speaks up.

"We have that problem too. I know she's talking about a hospital but in our businesses we seem to relish the number of improvement projects we can come up with. I'm sure some of them do more harm than good."

Stevie nods in agreement and then turns back to me.

"So you try to manage the flow of patients through the hospital by improving a number of things at once and hoping that something catches. Meanwhile patients continue to wait for treatment."

The audience has become more attentive and Clare raises her hand:

"When my future mother-in-law had pneumonia she went into an emergency unit and was then transferred to three different wards over the following week."

There seems to be a growing realisation in the room that I'm talking about a bigger and more tangled operation than most businesses when Cynch lowers the tone with a clunk.

"It's simple inefficiency and profligacy. We hear all these bloody doctors moaning about their hours while they stagger home with their wheelbarrows full of cash. An eighty-hour week is nothing special when you have to make your own money rather than just gleefully accepting someone else's."

"Well, I have a doctor sitting next to me." I reply. Mo smiles at Cynch. "And it may be worth remembering that, as he buckles under the weight of his wheelbarrow, he has a Doctorate while all most of us have is a Masters."

Stevie brings us back.

"It must be difficult to decide which area to put efforts into improving. Surely the question we must be answering is: of all the things we could improve, which should we attend to first?"

"To be perfectly honest I have no idea if what we do ever makes an improvement," I reply in a moment of candour.

Stevie says:

"Your operation may appear considerably more complex than most businesses so, if the theory I've applied in the pharmaceutical industry is valid, I expect it is possible to make a big improvement. I wouldn't rule out the possibility of increasing throughput and reducing length of stay by up to thirty per cent. What difference would that make?"

"Throughput?" I ask. "What do you mean by throughput? And do you really mean thirty per cent reduction in length of stay?"

I'd give anything for that right now. Stevie explains that the more complex the system appears, the more likely it is that people have resorted to local optimisation. Local optimisation degrades the performance of the system as a whole, and as a result the more the local optimisation, the more improvement we should expect. Another question to Stevie:

"What about applying these focusing principles in a project management environment?"

Before he can answer, the Master of Ceremonies explains that we must now stop as we have run out of time. He thanks us for our attendance and Stevie for his contribution and suggests maybe Stevie could come back another time to address the issues of projects.

As the attendees drift away I wait for the chance to speak to Stevie. He's shaking hands with a couple as I wander over.

"Great talk."

"Thanks."

I know Stevie well enough to be sure that when he said thirty per cent he wasn't showboating. He may have been an arrogant so-and-so back in the day, but he never showed off about anything he couldn't back up. And I have also detected a new maturity in his manner. He has the same confidence but a much more balanced approach. So, to send out a howitzer like thirty per cent in front of a reasonably aware collection of business acumen I know there must be something to it. And I'm desperate to find out.

"What on earth did you mean by that figure of thirty per cent? What do you know that I don't?"

"Would that solve your problems? If we could reduce, by thirty per cent, the time it takes to carry out all the tasks to support the patient's recovery, would it mean more patients would go home in a more timely manner?"

"Damn right it would. If I could speed up patient flow by five per cent I'd be a hero. I'd be able to transform the hospital."

"Linda, if we reduce all the tasks by thirty per cent we have to see if it will have an impact on length of stay. This will only happen if these tasks are currently causing the elongated stay. This is why we have to check it out. If it is not the cause then we have to find out what is. I'll come and explain it if you like."

"I'd love you to come more than anything in the world right now, Stevie, but I don't have any money."

"No matter. I'll try to help. But I have some conditions."

I'm not sure what to expect.

"I need two things: time and access. I want to meet with your senior team and I want you all to give me the dedicated time I need. I expect it to take two days. No mobile phones, emails or interruptions. I'll also bring two of my colleagues with me and you'll give us access to the small amount of information I request."

I look across at Mo and he gently nods.

"You're on."

Chapter Five

Crocodiles

It's 5:45am as I pull out of my drive and head off for work. I don't know whether I've convinced myself things could be worse or if the current spell of good weather confirms I have Seasonal Affective Disorder, but I feel distinctly perky. On reflection it may have something to do with the two coffees I glugged before leaving the house.

Half an hour later and I'm sitting at my desk looking at the piles of paper which Cath has helpfully sorted into internal reports and external returns, patient complaints and items that can wait. I wander across to the window to see if cigarette-and-drip lady is having an early puff, but she's not there. I hope she's OK.

I think back to last night's presentation and my chat with Stevie. It was brilliant to be able to catch up with him and his talk has given me a real boost, almost a renewed sense of hope. The explanation was so clear. But what happens next? The way Stevie explained his case study bore very little resemblance to how we manage things at the hospital. Could it really help us? And ultimately, I may have a choice to make. Am I expected to follow the well-trodden path or the path less travelled? Not a question I'm inclined to ask the chaps at region, but it's something I have to work out myself.

I email Stevie, asking him to call me when it's convenient. One minute later the phone rings.

"Morning, Stevie."

"Hello, Linda. You're up early. Couldn't you sleep?"

I could ask the same question but instead I tell Stevie I've been thinking about his presentation and want to know when he can come and speak to us.

"I can come next Monday for two days. We'll need to get started early. Is eight OK?"

I say it is and he tells me the way it will work. He'll begin with an analysis and spend two uninterrupted days working with his and my team. From our side he asks that we're joined by our finance director, the medical director, nursing director, Mo, and someone from the information side who can provide rapid answers. That's the A-Team plus one. How can I possibly say no? I've asked for his help so I need to make sure he gets everything he needs. The following week I've cleared the diaries and the team is assembled.

♦

John, Charlie, Jo and Mo are already in our biggest meeting room when I arrive with Stevie and his two colleagues. John has brought Sam from the data team with him. I smile at Sam, remembering how I'd embarrassed myself the first time we met. It was a couple of years ago and I was in the data office with John when Sam wandered up and asked me if I wanted a coffee. As he asked I was sure he gave me a big wink. So I smiled, said '*Yes*' and winked back. It was only when he returned with the coffee that I realised he has an involuntary facial twitch. I wondered why John had given me such a funny look.

I've already told John, Charlie and Jo about Stevie and why I've asked him to come to the hospital, and I introduce Sam. When I spoke to the others the previous week I sensed a mixture of curiosity and concern. Jo wanted to be sure I knew what I was doing, hoping the meeting would help but advising me to keep it in-house for the time being. John had looked faintly quizzical, presumably trying to work out how an outsider could undermine his work, and Charlie, a little surprisingly, was all for it.

Stevie breaks the ice.

"So, we have two days to find a new way forward for this hospital. Best get on with it then."

Stevie has brought Tim and Tam with him. Tim is dressed in jeans and a casual shirt. I guess he might be in his thirties but I could be wrong. He explains that he's known Stevie since they were young and they've worked together on various projects for many years. Tim's role is in turning Stevie's ideas into working solutions. He says this with a little tease in his voice and smiles at Tam. Stevie then explains that Tim has a PhD in natural science and I notice John's eyebrows rising a little.

Tam looks rather younger and is very attractive, a point which hasn't escaped Charlie's notice. She explains that she did a degree in teaching five years ago but, after qualifying, became totally disillusioned with the education system. She met Stevie at a conference and became part of his team.

After we make our introductions, Stevie begins.

"OK, let's get started. Linda has explained to me that as a hospital there are three areas you are all concerned about: a growing concern about the quality of care you provide, your operational performance against targets, and then there's the constant nagging of your weak financial performance."

When Stevie explains that I've told him about the recent tragedy at the hospital, Charlie and Jo look a little uncomfortable. But Stevie carries on.

"Your more general conclusion is that a similar tragedy could be repeated, and your operational and financial performance could also continue to deteriorate. Moreover, your real concern is that your efforts to try to improve all of these are not producing results quickly enough and you spend your time fighting too many fires without effect.

"My starting assumption is that although they may appear disparate effects, there must be a common cause to these issues and our first task is to identify the common cause and understand why it appears to be so difficult to resolve."

Stevie goes on to explain that firstly we need to check if the three issues, which he calls undesirable effects, really do exist. And if so, we need to understand the severity of each. Then he uses an analogy of a crocodile at the door to describe the issues within the hospital. He explains that he uses the crocodile as it has some particularly nasty traits. It creeps up on you unexpectedly, has razor sharp teeth and once it gets a bite of you it's virtually impossible to escape from. This persona is sufficient to generate enough fear in humans to get them to act. I picture a ten-foot crocodile inflicting an underwater death roll on some hapless victim as Stevie explains that he uses this analogy to give an indication of the risks of not changing successfully. It helps us understand just how severe the situation really is. And it also makes me wonder what has stopped us from running away from it with a little more energy.

Stevie has gained our attention and everyone present wants to hear what he has to say next. He turns to his colleague.

"Tim. When were you last in a hospital?"

Tim explains it was as a child when he and Stevie were playing with the lawn mower in his parent's garden. Ah, those halcyon days when children and adults could have harmless fun without the drudgeries of health and safety madness. Anyway, while chasing each other around he managed to push the lawnmower over Stevie's foot and apparently it was a rather bloody mess. He recounts that after a hurried trip to casualty, Stevie was patched up and fully mended. I guess the purpose of this anecdote is to illustrate how little they know about the modern-day running of a hospital.

Point made, Stevie says:

"Let's attempt to understand the size of these three undesirable effects by examining the flow of emergency patients through the hospital and seeing if we can understand where they are most severe. Just like Tim and me many years ago, some of the patients arrive through the A&E, some walk in and others arrive by ambulance. Is it as simple as that?"

He looks around the table to find an answer. Jo obliges.

"The other stream of emergency patients is those who have been referred by their GPs. This is either when they have seen a patient at their surgery and the presenting problem requires more investigation than they can do there. Or maybe they've done a home visit and called an ambulance because they believe the patient is very ill and may need admitting."

Stevie asks Jo how many patients arrive a day and for an approximate ratio of how many are in each category. Jo seems to be enjoying the opportunity to contribute early in the meeting and says that she can give a pretty accurate answer. She's been working in this hospital for many years and this is one of the key pieces of data she keeps her eye on every day.

"The total number of attendances is about six hundred a day and the most we've had in any one day has been over seven hundred. The split between the categories is about two thirds walk-ins with GP referrals, ambulance admissions and a few others making up the rest."

Sam nods his confirmation, I think. Stevie continues.

"Presumably not everyone ends up being admitted. Some will go home requiring no further time in the hospital."

Jo says that eighty per cent either go straight home or are referred back to their GP, and the rest are admitted. She tells Stevie of the service target to either treat and discharge the patient or admit them into a bed within four hours of them arriving. The current target is ninety-five per cent.

"Are you meeting this target?" asks Stevie.

I feel the need to speak up.

"This is one of our biggest problems. It's one of the prime measures against which this hospital is measured and we've found it increasingly difficult to meet. To be honest, we haven't consistently met this target for the last four months and our performance is still deteriorating."

In fact, during the last week we even missed the ninety per cent mark and the whole issue was one of the main reasons Bob lost his job. Currently we're one of the worst-performing hospitals in the region, brutally evidenced by the weekly league tables that hit my desk. Charlie's indignant:

"It's a bloody ridiculous measure. It's as far away from quality of care as you can possibly get. It's purely political and at worst can be counterproductive."

"What happens if you continue to miss the target?" asks Stevie. "Who pays the price in the end?"

Charlie looks puzzled and so I interject.

"Actually, Stevie, it's normally the CEO who goes first and then, dependent on the financial picture, the FD follows."

John snaps his pencil. So I explain that it's not uncommon for the rest of the managerial team to be removed. Only the doctor and nurse side of the leadership tend to stay. I tell Stevie that before Bob, who lasted three years, the hospital had a string of CEOs in indecently rapid succession.

"So why are the doctors and nurses safe?" asks Stevie.

"Under their contracts they often just retake up their clinical roles. We're lucky here that we've had some continuity with Charlie and Jo. Many other struggling hospitals just keep spinning the revolving doors."

Stevie summarises by asking if it's fair to say that although some of the group may not like the way it's being measured, providing timely care is an important aspect of quality of care and that in this instance the crocodile has real teeth. Fail to meet the target and the consequences can be terminal for some. And so we have validated that the undesirable effect does exist and is so severe that we're missing a key target at this first stage. Then he asks what happens to the patients who are admitted. Jo answers:

"With a very clear pathway, such as a suspected stroke or suspected heart attack, they'll go straight to our stroke or cardiac unit. Most others are supposed to go to the assessment unit, where more detailed investigations occur over the next twenty-four to forty-eight hours. Then a final decision to admit or discharge is made. If they need admitting they are then supposed to go to the ward dedicated to their required care."

Tim says:

"But what actually happens?"

Stevie interrupts:

"Tim. Do you already have a hypothesis to your own question? Why don't you answer it yourself?"

This is interesting. Stevie clearly thinks Tim has jumped in too early. Charlie clears his throat and smiles at Mo, while John tries to stick his pencil back together. Sam winks at Tam, who mercifully doesn't wink back. After a few seconds Jo graciously speaks again.

"You're right, Tim. This is what is supposed to happen but it's not always what does happen. Sometimes the assessment unit is full and so the patient either stays in A&E for a few more hours until a bed becomes available. Or while they're waiting for a bed in the assessment unit a bed might become available on a different ward and the patient is moved straight there. It may not be the correct ward but it's better than being stuck on a trolley in A&E."

A&E is a place for patients to be seen, treated and discharged if appropriate or passed on to the next stage for further diagnosis or treatment. It's not a place for patients to stay. Also, when a patient is moved to the assessment unit, sometimes while they're waiting for their investigations to be completed a bed becomes available on the correct ward but is given to another patient whose correct ward is full.

As we discuss this, Charlie adds a note of cheer.

"Of course, sometimes it works really well. As the assessment is completed a bed is available and the patient goes straight to the correct ward. But when I think about it, the last time that happened our achievement was eclipsed by Neil Armstrong hopping on to the moon. Unlucky really."

For Jo this isn't a joke. Four times a day there is a bed meeting with all the operational staff and matrons to try to resolve these issues. There have been days when the operational team take on the role of porters, pushing patients in beds around the hospital to save the latest risk of a four-hour breach. She says:

"When this gets really bad we have patients backing up in both the assessment unit and A&E. Sometimes we can even have ambulances waiting to offload patients into A&E. But if there's a long delay we have to send the ambulances to one of the other hospitals. And that's when we've completely failed."

I recall one day last week when we were very close to diverting to another hospital and I saw Jo outside trying to pacify the ambulance crews. She knew that while they were waiting to offload patients they were compromising their own service levels. The whole service is measured and every part and member feels the pressure. On that occasion a reporter from the local paper was taking pictures. Jo, in the midst of trying to manage an unmanageable situation, took umbrage with our local journalist and told him it was wrong of him to take pictures of patients, but I suspect that was just a tiny trickle down a hardened duck's back.

When I see situations like that I long for the day when the press has nothing to report but a good news story about this hospital. I dream of them saying how well the hospital is run – very briefly of course – and then I wake up.

Throughout Jo's explanation I've noticed Tam taking notes and I can see there are lots of boxes and arrows on her page. And then Stevie draws our attention.

"So, the undesirable effect we have spoken about does not stop at A&E. The provision of high-quality and timely care in the right location can be an issue for emergency patients throughout their passage of care."

Charlie shrugs. And noticing this, Stevie asks for his opinion. So Charlie explains that Jo's headache worsens because the admissions she described only account for less than half of the total admissions. Other patients start their journey with a referral from their GP to see one of our specialist consultants through an outpatient clinic. Just like in the emergency stream, the diagnosis reveals that some patients need no further treatment and others can be treated without an admission. But there's a smaller proportion who will require admission into the hospital for their treatment. This can either be for an operation or other clinical treatments. We call this the planned stream of care as we're able to give the patient an actual date when they'll be admitted. Of course, many patients are waiting too long for their admission date. Charlie elaborates:

"Let me tell you about one of our elderly ladies who required a gall bladder treatment. She had been waiting several weeks for her operation and had deteriorated greatly, noticeably losing weight by the time the operation was planned. They had to cancel her on the day of the operation because of a lack of beds. The following week they did it again. And again a week later! She was really distressed and was told to come back later in the day to A&E. This is a route sometimes used when a case has been cancelled a few times. They tell the patient to go to A&E when they know they are running the emergency list and then sneak the patient in through the emergency door."

I look at Charlie in the hope he isn't going to confess or spill all his guts but he isn't bothered. He goes on to tell another story where a patient was cancelled, but it hadn't been recorded as a cancellation. It then took another four months for the patient to come back to the top of the list. When they called to arrange the operation the patient's son explained that his father had passed away.

We all look around the table at each other. And the silence lasts a good while. Charlie's stories have brought home the chaos that a lack of beds can cause. The undesirable effects, as Stevie calls them, in high-quality and timely care are also evident for planned care patients. Stevie appreciates the sensitivity in the room right now, and it's clear to us all that poor quality and timeliness of care is a common theme across both the emergency and planned care streams. He begins to push his questions in a different direction.

"So, once a patient does get on to a ward, what are the steps in their journey?"

Charlie explains that every patient is different. We might see a twenty-five-year-old man who looks very fit but there are complications and he takes much longer than expected to recover. And with our frailer patients it's often very difficult to predict how long it will take for them to go home or into further care. Stevie seems to be working out a hypothesis to check and is keen to understand more about the variation in the recovery time. Jo explains that the time it takes for a patient to recover is not the only consideration. Many times there are issues in getting patients discharged. Even those patients that go home are not always straightforward. She says:

"We had one lady who was admitted through A&E and was brought in by her daughter. She had a mild form of diverticulitis and after four days of treatment was ready to be discharged home. But when we started to arrange the discharge we discovered the daughter had gone on holiday after dropping her mother off at A&E and had taken the keys to her mother's flat with her. When we tried to contact the daughter she announced that she wasn't coming home for another two and a half weeks and that her mother would have to stay in hospital until she returned!"

I look at Stevie, who listens motionless, and then at Tim and Tam whose eyes have widened. Jo explains the clinical risk to the mother in a prolonged stay as well as the impact on other patients waiting for both emergency and planned treatment. The average daily operating expense per patient also means it would probably cost less to keep her in a four-star hotel. With this case, the hospital arranged for the locks to be replaced but by that time the mother had spent five more days than she had to in the hospital. The poor lady was desperate to go home, mainly because she was missing her cat.

This type of example where family is the cause of the extended stay isn't a one-off. The hospital can sometimes be used as a boarding house to meet family needs. But Stevie wants to know if the process of discharge in this case could have started earlier. Why did they only find out about the keys once the mother had recovered? I think he's trying to clarify whether in this case the family is the major cause of disruption and extended stay, or indeed if clinical recovery is the major cause of variation, or a mixture of both.

Jo describes another case which caused disproportionate hassle, when they tried to get a patient from out of town discharged back to their original home. She describes the nightmare of administration and paperwork and the number of different stakeholders involved.

Stevie pushes again. He wants to understand if there is a disruption during the journey which results in a length of stay going beyond that which is clinically required. In truth, it's quite normal for disruptions or just simply late decisions to result in elongated stays.

"This is a crucial point," he says. "Even fifteen minutes into a car journey of two hours, if you have gone nowhere you don't need to wait until the two hours are up to predict you are going to be late. You can compare the expected arrival time with the latest estimate of remaining duration of the journey to see if you are likely to be late. I am keen to confirm if the variation in total length of stay has an element of varying recovery time and an element of delay and if these interact with each other."

Stevie asks for Tim, Tam and Sam to investigate the length of stay by treatment type and the variation in length of stay, and to create a graph by treatment type. Sam knows this will be an involved and time-consuming task and agrees with Tim and Tam that they'll work this evening for as long as it takes. I can't fault the commitment of the whole team in striving for a better understanding, and that gives me real hope.

♦

An hour later we break for lunch but without doubt we have confirmed that poor-quality and untimely care is an undesirable effect that is occurring across both the emergency and planned care stream. It's also clear that our attempts to resolve this are taking a lot of time from our front-line clinical staff.

This is a very rare day. It's a day when I feel, rightly or wrongly, that my brain is in the process of slowly being defogged. I offer to buy Stevie a sandwich at the hospital's most hygiene-conscious coffee bar. As we walk through a busy waiting area my phone rings.

"Well, if it isn't the Scarlet Pimpernel!"

"Hi, Dee. What's happening?"

"I've had an exhausting morning looking after the new intern in the office."

Dee is head of marketing at the town's university, and rarely has an exhausting morning. It's not that she doesn't have a demanding job, quite the contrary. But she has the happy knack of being able to take everything in her stride. She certainly gives that impression and I often wish that I could be a bit more like her, in that way anyway.

"What's so exhausting about looking after an intern?" I ask, reasonably.

"You know. You can't get on with anything, particularly if they have a brain the size of a pea and the dynamism of a spoon."

"Surely it can't be that bad. Isn't the intern about to enter his final year?"

"Of course he is. He's one of ours… and he's as thick as a plank!"

Dee, the true professional, describes the university interns as *'intelligent, committed and work-ready, sure to energise your business'*, in all her knowledge-exchange publications. Never *'as thick as a plank'*.

"Can't you just give him a prospectus to proof?" I suggest, helpfully.

"Well, I could… if he wasn't so good-looking."

"Ah. I see. Anyway, what are you doing now?"

"I'm coming to buy you lunch."

I'm just about to explain that I'm already booked when she hangs up. I smile at Stevie and put my phone back in my pocket. Then, my heart sinks, not in a terrible way, more of a kind of *'oh no'* way as I spy a grinning Dee striding towards us.

"You're here," I observe.

"You don't miss a thing these days," she replies, then offers her hand to Stevie: "Hello, I'm Dee."

"This is Stevie," I say. "I'm really sorry, Dee, but we're in the middle of a pretty intensive meeting today and we've just popped out for a sandwich."

"Oh, that's OK. I only have half an hour anyway. I can't be too long. I don't want my intern to get his tie stuck in the laminator again. Where are we going?"

I look at Stevie.

"It's fine," he says.

Dee winks:

"Oh that's good, sweetheart. But I wasn't really asking you."

Stevie smiles and we wander into the coffee bar together. I have the confused emotion of being happy to see Dee, as always, but my glee is tinged by a sizeable slice of dread of what she's going to do or say. If the worst she does is hit on Stevie then I'd probably take that right now.

We order three coffees and three paninis (safe enough) and sit down. Dee looks at Stevie:

"So what do you do?"

"I'm a friend of Linda's."

"Bloody hell! Is that a job now? I know there are some pretty nebulous positions in the public sector but that takes the cake. Executive head of friendship for sad health service boss... I bet it pays OK though."

"Stevie owns his own business," I say, trying to introduce some semblance of maturity.

Dee raises her eyebrows and I steel myself, waiting for the next announcement.

"Now that sounds a little more worthwhile."

My heart sinks further. Over the next ten minutes Dee proceeds to give Stevie the benefit of her opinion on all that is wrong with the health service, the bit that is right, why paninis are a con, how the Beckham brand was further enhanced by a move to Paris, and how exposure to reality television is a reliable barometer of intellect.

She then advises us to prepare well for our afternoon, plops her upturned, half-eaten panini in her coffee cup, kisses us both on the cheek and strides off, clamping her phone to her ear.

"You have very interesting friends," says Stevie.

I smile sheepishly.

◆

We all reconvene in the meeting room, and after summarising the morning's discussion Stevie turns to John and says:

"Can we move on to the finances? John, can you summarise the financial position for us all?"

John replies:

"Yes, our performance is deteriorating every month. We could lose as much as £20 million this year."

"And what has happened to revenues over the last few years?"

"They were rising by a few per cent per annum, although this is slowing down."

"This is an unusual situation and I want to ensure we are all very clear about the situation. Many companies would love to have a year on year rise in revenues but in your case this has been associated with increasing losses. In this period of revenue growth it is clear your total cost of treating patients has risen faster than the growth in revenues. I have taken the liberty and asked Tam to prepare this on a slide for us to investigate further."

Tam plugs her laptop in to the projector to show a table of our revenues over the last five years, the increasing losses and what she has annotated '*total medical costs*'.

"The table confirms that the total cost of delivering clinical services is rising faster than the associated growth in revenues. Yes?"

There are cautious, but unanimous, nods around the table, as Tam shows a second slide – this time a graph showing one line of revenues increasing annually and a second line of medical costs growing more quickly. This demonstrates succinctly the growing gap. The graph actually goes back further than five years and shows how we used to make money, but even in those days the costs were rising faster than the revenues. The crocodile has been there for us all to see during the last ten years. It has slowly sneaked up, and now its ugly face is staring right at us.

I search in my own mind for an explanation. John is more concerned by the source of the data, and Tam explains.

"All this information for any hospital is publicly available. I just got it from your financial accounts over the last ten years. I've had to represent some of the data in this format as I've subtracted some

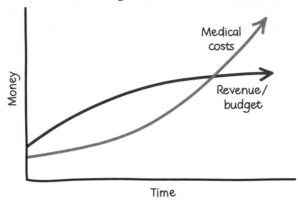

**A graph showing that medical costs
are rising faster than revenues**

of the special items relating to one-off incidents. But on the whole I think it's a fair representation."

Charlie certainly looks impressed. And John acknowledges that the data looks accurate to him. I've had a bit of a *'Eureka!'* moment; hopefully the first of many. I also feel a bit of a fool. It's so obvious when presented like this. A simple summary of our financial history shows that the problem's been systemic for many years but we'd not really noticed the growing importance of it. The crocodile has been watching us for the best part of a decade. For sure, once costs exceeded revenues a few years ago it was impossible for us to ignore as it was the beginning of our loss-making run. We have been fooling ourselves for a while that it was tough times, but actually the problem has been slowly magnifying year on year. As I glance around the table I see that everyone else is experiencing a similar insight. It is now obvious to me that it is only a matter of time before more and more hospitals will feel this financial pressure mounting.

Stevie funnels down in an attempt to understand this phenomenon in a bit more detail, asking:

"Have revenues gone up because the price you can charge has gone up or are you treating more patients?"

After some discussion we all agree it is a combination, but in some areas of the hospital we also know the actual number of patients treated within a year has gone down. Stevie seems a little unconvinced with our response and asks Sam to put it on his list to check. While he did this politely it struck me that Stevie was treating Sam as if he worked for him rather than the hospital. I half expected Sam to say it was going to take a while. In the data office they have a queue of requests for information, and normally the response is '*it'll have to take its turn*'. But it's clear that Sam is as interested in the outcome as the rest of us:

"I can have the answer by morning."

John offers to clarify what has happened to prices and volumes, so we can be clear about the increase in revenues. I'm pleased that John seems to be on board. Stevie continues:

"What makes this even more interesting is Linda tells me that in most instances your totally variable costs as a percentage of revenue are relatively low."

John reminds us all that the totally variable costs are those that vary one-to-one with the number of patients treated.

Stevie continues.

"Normally in such a situation an increase in volume results in an increase in profit, not loss. This is worth us trying to understand why."

♦

Stevie seems happy that he has clarified the headline financial situation and says he just needs another couple of hours to further cement his understanding. The statistics that Sam, Tam and Tim are to present tomorrow should provide more clarity. But in the meantime he asks for more examples of operational performance issues and concerns over quality of care. Jo tells of an out-of-region amputee with mental health issues who has been in the hospital for over six months. They've just discovered that some days he gets dressed and goes out for the day before returning to his bed for a sleep. And Mo tells us about the tragic recent case of the lady who was dying and wanted to go home. It took fourteen days to sort this out and she died the morning the ambulance crew turned up to take her home.

Over the remainder of the afternoon Stevie asks us to go over these cases and the ones discussed in the morning again and again, to fill in all the details of what's happening at the hospital. He also gets us to review a cross-section of the recent complaint letters. While he does this, Tim is slowly constructing a diagram summarising the patient flow through the hospital. Stevie goes through each case again, highlighting the impact on flow through the hospital and damage to quality of care, the finances and the operational performance. He also highlights just how often we're using extra staff, paid at a premium, to cope. And then at 5:30pm exactly he puts down his pencil and smiles across at me.

"Thanks for your time and honesty today, everyone. I believe that when we have Sam's figures in the morning we will have everything we need to have a full picture of the current reality."

"How the hell can you say that?" asks Charlie.

"All I am going to say tonight is that it is now clear the undesirable effects are playing out across the whole system, they are growing in severity and they are clearly connected."

After everyone has left I go to my office with Stevie and we sit down. I want to know more about the process he was using today in gathering the information, and with all the craft of a senior Whitehall mandarin he responds with a question.

"Linda, is it fair to say that all we have done today is clarify the size and position of two key undesirable effects, namely the operational performance and the finances, as well as highlighting many examples of problems with quality of care?"

"Yes, I guess so."

"OK. But even though we have done a good job in clarifying this, I suspect many of your people are already painfully aware of these issues. We know there must be a common cause. We just need to articulate it in a manner that explains why it has been so difficult to solve and then we just need to create a solution. Tomorrow we need to work out how the hospital is full of good people who understand the size of the crocodile and the sharpness of its teeth, but have failed to implement a sufficient response. What is holding them back? Is it a lack of understanding of the size of the pot of gold that awaits them or is it something else holding them back? Is it the fear of the journey of change or are they unwilling to let go of the current ways regardless of how sharp the crocodile's teeth are?"

I'm not exactly sure what he means but I think I can see some of what he's getting at. We've never really taken any risks at our hospital; from a management perspective, that is. We've gambled with operational standards from time to time. But as far as strategy is concerned it seems Stevie is suggesting that we believe the risks and obstacles to changing are more dangerous than continuing to live next to the crocodile. We could end up as casualties ourselves either way. Stevie suggests there may be some other force driving us to stay where we are. Maybe we fear that if we change we'll have to leave something behind that we truly treasure. We need to discover the cause of the inertia to properly understand the problem. Stevie stands up.

"Let's call it a day, Linda. But remember, we are going to have to find a way that simultaneously improves the quality of care, the operational efficiency and the financial performance. Trying to solve them independently is a monumental waste of time and effort. We have to address the common cause of all three."

Chapter Six

Ever-flourishing

I can't wait until tomorrow. I want to find out how we create a solution to the problem we've been discussing today. So I talk Stevie into joining me for dinner at Les Deux Epis, a lovely restaurant near the hotel where he's staying, while Tim, Tam and Sam set about crunching the numbers. On the way to the restaurant Stevie tells me his hotel has put him in a smoking room, which he really hates. I'm embarrassed. It was me who booked the rooms so I make a mental note to call the hotel to sort it.

Having ordered our wine, Stevie leans towards me and says:

"Linda, I assume we are out to dinner because you are keen to understand how we can create a solution for your hospital, not just because you want to hear a solution."

"I'm just grateful you're here to help, Stevie. I don't expect to be spoon-fed," I reply.

"OK, so as our very first step I want to start by checking if you agree with my conclusions from today's analysis."

Stevie has always been a good reader of people and he knows me well.

"If I have read you correctly you will not be happy with just turning the hospital around. You want the hospital to become a flourishing hospital and that is not going to be easy, otherwise your predecessors would have already done it. It also seems you are not the only hospital engaged in this kind of endeavour. The newspapers are riddled with similar stories. But nevertheless, in your situation this is going to require not only an improvement in both the quality and timeliness of care, but a rapid improvement. It has to be rapid and sustainable because we have uncovered today the growing daily risk of a catastrophic failure in care."

I listen carefully as he pours us both a glass of water and he continues:

"Linda, many times today we have heard the cry for more resources to address this requirement; and most particularly, front-line clinical resources. However, it has not taken much for us to notice that whenever this is raised, your finance director is quick to raise the equally important need for, once again, a rapid improvement in financial performance. John is evidently experienced enough to know the temptation to meet this requirement through belt-tightening is overly simplistic and likely to be insufficient. He has regularly pointed out that you are already in a situation where medical costs are greater than revenues, and are still rising faster than revenues."

It is at this moment I start to realise what it feels like to be stuck on the horns of a dilemma. Stevie carries on.

"What we have learned today is the real risk to quality of care from the slow and insidious reduction in front-line staff. We see this in the complaint letters: so many of them are about the basic provision of care. What's more, this type of slow degradation, experienced by many a hospital in far better health than yours, also has its impact on staff. Over time I predict they get more and more worn down and it is not long before even the most dedicated staff become cynical about what is happening. Over time, cynicism turns to apathy and apathy will sometimes result in catastrophic failures. You can apportion blame for the final failure in care but this is denying the underlying cause of the situation."

This makes me think that even our own Charlie shows the early symptoms of what Stevie's talking about but his cynicism, rather than turning to apathy, almost seems to act as a foil for his burning passion for the hospital to get it right, and his frustration when we fail. It's almost like a safety mechanism, but how much longer will it last?

We talk about the risk of a negative loop taking hold where excessive pressure causes a string of mistakes; failures become normalised and higher mortality levels occur. Clearly I'm responsible for solving it but it's now more obvious why it's proven to be so difficult to solve. Adding front-line staff to meet the needs for a rapid improvement in quality and timeliness of care is in direct conflict with reducing front-line staff to resolve our financial situation. Now I understand this really is the dilemma we face, it's easier for me to talk through the full ramifications. It's becoming clear to me that it's not simply a matter of me making a choice.

◆

Stevie's steak tartare and my confit arrive, along with the sommelier armed with the Côte de Beaune which, on Stevie's gesture, he offers for me to taste. I act out the ritual swishing, sniffing and sipping. Then I manage the perfect facial expression of deep thought, followed by recognition, followed by munificent approval that leaves the sommelier desperately stifling the urge to applaud wildly.

As I poke a small mound of wilted spinach, Stevie continues.

"So you're keen to understand how we can go about solving such a dilemma, yes? Well, the inevitable temptation is either to relax the financial requirements or the requirements for safe and timely care for all, or seek a tolerable compromise where you continuously add a little staff here and trim a little there. I can understand how it is very difficult for any of you to predict how such actions made in one part will create consequences elsewhere: cut back on the physiotherapy budget and hope this does not result in longer patient-recovery periods and the need for more nurses elsewhere. There is a huge risk of this approach making things worse. An even more cavalier approach is to cut front-line staff everywhere and see who squeals the loudest, but unfortunately in this environment patient safety will be put at further risk. As part of creating a new direction, what you and I need to do tomorrow is ensure everyone understands that the requirements to rapidly improve the quality and timeliness of care and the finances are real, and any relaxation of either of them will mean you can never become a flourishing hospital."

"Stevie, I get it," I say, "but if we're not going to compromise, what are we going to do?"

"We are going to seek a solution, any solution that simultaneously meets all the following requirements:

- *rapidly delivers a flourishing hospital*
- *rapidly improves the quality and timeliness of care*

- *rapidly improves the financial performance*
- *without exhausting staff or taking imprudent risks.*

"Why don't you think about that overnight and we can return to it with everyone else tomorrow."

As the coffee arrives I realise Stevie has only had the chance to eat half of his meal. I ask for the bill while he discreetly reaches over and helps himself to a chocolate. What I don't notice, and what Stevie certainly doesn't notice, is that his jacket sleeve, having hung briefly over a candle flame, has started to melt, which he only realises when he smells burning, at which point he leaps to his feet and wafts his arm around. Then I notice his napkin too is smouldering and I instinctively throw the contents of my glass over it, spattering the white satin table cloth, not to mention Stevie's trousers, with red wine. Not content with that, my sweeping action upturns Stevie's brandy balloon, the remaining contents of which give the growing flames renewed vigour.

By now we are holding the excited attention of the whole restaurant as Stevie plunges his hand into the ice bucket on our neighbouring table, apologising earnestly as I burst out laughing.

"Bloody hell, Stevie! I thought I was clumsy but that was spectacular."

"Thanks. It was nothing," he mumbles as he rolls up the remains of his soggy, charred napkin.

"You know, I thought the story of Tim running over your foot with the lawnmower was made up to set the scene, but I can almost believe it now."

Stevie admits it's a true story as I pay the bill and leave a bigger-than-intended tip. I'm still giggling as we leave the restaurant and agree to go back to his hotel bar for a more relaxed nightcap and to catch up on old times. We settle down in a quiet corner and are about to reminisce when Stevie spots Tim, Tam and Sam wandering in.

"Hey, look who's here. We should go and join them," he says.

"How's it going?" I ask them and Tam is about to speak when Stevie suggests we leave the work-talk until the morning. We deserve a breather. Tam says:

"Good plan. What happened to your jacket, Stevie?"

I snort a giggle and Tim looks at me quizzically. Meanwhile,

Tam seems to have taken a shine to Sam, having spent the best part of four hours with him and Tim in the data room. She's regaling him with tales of skiing in the Rockies and diving off the Great Barrier Reef as Tim rolls his eyes.

I go to the bathroom to freshen up and as I squirt Mulberry gloop on my hands I hear a toilet flush followed by a familiar voice.

"What are you doing here?"

"Dee! Are you stalking me?"

"I could ask the very same question," she replies. "I have a water-tight explanation why I'm here on a Monday night. Our Vice Chancellor is schmoozing with a Russian aluminium magnate, looking for inward investment as ever, and I'm here to add a touch of class. The Russian chap has just pulled a pile of money out of southern Europe and the VC can smell moving cash half a continent away. At last the VC has gone, and Mr Socanovich and entourage are off to beddie-byes, so I was off home. Anyway, I left you a message at teatime. Have you got time for a chat?"

I know it's pointless resisting, so we walk back to the bar for me to introduce her to the others.

"Hello again, sweetheart," she beams at Stevie. "You two are spending a lot of time together. Not that there's anything wrong with that of course."

Tim and Tam look at each other before Dee turns her attention to them.

"Linda isn't going to introduce me. I'm Dee. And you are?"

"I'm Tim."

"And I'm Tam."

Dee looks at me with furrowed eyebrows and turns back to Tim.

"You're Tam."

"No, Tim."

"I'm Tam," says Tam. And then Dee turns to Sam:

"So you must be Tom."

"No, I'm Sam," he smiles.

"You're kidding me. Tim, Tam and Sam! You'll be telling me Tinky-Winky and Po are just about to appear!"

As I glance around the room I'm secretly praying that Sam's face doesn't twitch and looking for the nearest hole to jump into if it does. My prayers are answered and Sam, who says he's tired, decides to leave.

A receptionist comes across and says that they've managed to change Stevie's room and upgrade him before asking:

"Do you need one key or two, sir?" At which point Dee turns to Tim and Tam and smirks.

"Come on, kids. Let's leave the grown-ups to it. What are we having?"

"I'll have a Scotch," says Tim.

"Peroni for me, please," says Tam.

Dee leans over the bar with all the panache of a twenty-first-century western gunslinger and calls:

"Excuse me, barman. One bourbon and coke, one Scotch and one beer."

♦

Within the hour Dee has seemingly exhausted Tim and Tam, and Stevie has retired to bed. So I'm left in the comfy seats nursing a coffee with my friend.

"Sorry I screwed up your date tonight," she says.

"Come off it, Dee. You know it wasn't a date."

Much as I love Dee and her omnipresent joie de vivre, she and it can sometimes get on my nerves. She easily takes the rise out of anyone and anything that has the misfortune to drop into her view, and while I know she bears no malice I sometimes wish she could be more deferential, not much, just a tiny bit. And not to me – we're mates. But every time she meets any new acquaintance of mine she charges in like a young Miss Marple on speed.

And I can't afford to live in that world any more, fun as it may be. If I have the slightest pretence of being a CEO in the health service I can't have a public persona that even Bridget Jones would frown upon. I desperately need Dee to keep me sane, but at the same time I can't appear frivolous or silly when I'm out and about. So I tackle the issue, saying:

"You have to stop turning up and laughing at the people I'm working with Dee, it's just not grown up."

"Not even if they're funny?"

"You think everyone's funny, even when they're not."

"OK." She looks unusually perturbed, then looks at her phone and says:

"Listen… I have a busy day tomorrow and I have a couple of messages to answer so I'd better be off. I'll see you soon when you have a bit more time."

I wonder what calls she has to make while she kisses me and leaves. I thank the reception staff for sorting Stevie's room and then take a taxi home, listening to my own messages on the way.

◆

The following morning I wake at 5:00am and I see that I have a new missed call on my phone. Someone's up early. I listen to the message.

'*1:23am… Hi, Linda… it's me. Listen I've just spoken to my mum and… Carl's overdosed. He's in intensive care at your hospital, Linda. My mum's in pieces, and frankly… I don't know what to do. Ring me when you can.*'

Oh no. That must have been the call that Dee was making last night – to her mother. Her only brother Carl is in intensive care. I pick up my phone, but as it's still just past 5:00am I think better of calling her. So I send a text and decide to go in early to see him.

◆

At 8:00am we all gather in the meeting room. Stevie is pacing up and down, saying nothing. It all feels a tad embarrassing and we're not sure when or whether he's going to start the day, or whether he'll just keep pacing. Finally he turns around and starts by going through with everyone our discussion over dinner. What I find interesting is that it's almost a word-for-word repeat, but this time he presents the dilemma through a diagram.

Stevie starts.

"So are we all in agreement on the objective to be an ever-flourishing hospital?"

Amid unanimous nodding Charlie speaks up.

"Yes, if ever-flourishing includes our ambition to excel in research and teaching."

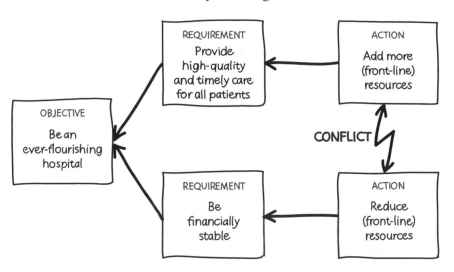

Charlie too gets universal agreement, as does the first requirement to provide high-quality and timely care for all patients. It is clear to us all that this is not the case now. Stevie continues:

"But let's remember, in a simple world where there are no financial pressures, higher-quality and timely care could be achieved with more front-line resources. But in the current environment the hospital needs to reduce front-line staff to address its worsening financial position, and this is the core of the dilemma we face."

Stevie perseveres in reviewing the diagram until everyone is in agreement. He then turns to me.

"Why don't you go through the criteria we discussed last night, against which any solution should be judged, and then say whether you are prepared to relax any of them."

I'm not sure whether I like being put on the spot, but after a long pause I have my answer.

"Unequivocally no; I believe we can find a better way forward with Stevie's guidance. No compromises. We must find a solution that meets all of our requirements simultaneously. Yesterday evening Stevie and I discussed four crucial requirements."

I pause a second before laying down the rules of engagement.

"We can only say our strategy has truly succeeded if it meets these four criteria: one, it rapidly delivers a flourishing hospital; two, it rapidly improves the quality and timeliness of care; three, as well as the financial performance; and four, without exhausting our people or taking imprudent risks. Yes?"

I look around the room to see what looks like universal agreement. So Stevie takes a large glug of coffee and continues.

"Let us look again at the dilemma you face. We have already established that adding front-line staff is in direct conflict with reducing front-line staff, and a compromise will get us nowhere. So let us look elsewhere."

He points to the arrow connecting the requirement for higher-quality and timely care with the need to add more staff.

"Do we believe there is a way of rapidly improving the quality and timeliness of care without adding front-line staff? You could say everyone needs to work harder, but we have already seen the pressure your staff are under." Stevie pauses before continuing. "There may be a breakthrough here but it is not the direction I wish to explore first. This only leaves us with the choice to explore why we believe reducing front-line staff is necessary to improve financial performance."

Charlie interrupts:

"We all agreed yesterday that medical costs are already greater than revenues, which is why we're losing money, and John has pointed out in no uncertain terms that medical costs – especially staff costs – are growing faster than revenues. Isn't it obvious? I can't believe I'm saying it but that is why the only apparent route is to cut staff."

Stevie continues:

"This is the mindset I want us to review this morning. I want to talk about an idea that directly challenges this. The idea is based on approaches I have applied to other industries but it is a relatively new idea. Firstly, it has never been applied to this environment, and secondly, and let us be absolutely clear, it is an idea that definitely needs scrutiny. So before we think through how to implement it, I want you to help me rigorously scrutinise the idea itself. All my experience has also taught me that rigorous scrutiny requires a process. It is often difficult to share ideas with others and yet in most instances, if the idea is a good one and is to be turned into a full solution, it requires significant upgrade and engagement from those who will be implementing it."

John jokingly adds:

"Stevie, just tell me how much it's going to cost and I'll tell you if it's a good idea."

Mo is quick to move us on.

"Stevie, a lot depends on the complexity of the idea. I agree we need a new idea but relaying a new way forward to our staff fills me with utter dread. Last night I tried explaining what we talked about to my wife and she thought I'd lost the plot."

Stevie reminds Mo that our understanding of the dilemma the hospital faces came from our shared inquiry and analysis, and simply telling someone the conclusion of an analysis will often fail to gain their agreement. He continues.

"If you think it's difficult to get your wife to agree, imagine how difficult it will be for us to get people who are directly responsible to agree. One of the important lessons from yesterday is clearly the need to engage everyone in carrying out the analysis, as it is this that leads to a shared understanding.

"Let us start by clarifying the objective of being an ever-flourishing hospital. Rather than simply trying to treat ninety-five per cent of patients within the access target, or having no 'never events', you want to be recognised for the very best care. Or rather than lifting pressure off staff who are disgruntled and feeling overstretched, you enable them to be truly proud to come to work in this hospital and enjoy everything they do. Or rather than aiming to break even, you create enough profit to invest in all the staff training, equipment and research that the hospital needs to grow and flourish. Are these the desired effects you all want?"

Mo speaks up:

"Everyone here will agree with you on these outcomes. But we need to be convinced that they are truly achievable."

"He's right," says Charlie. "If I had a pound for every half-baked, grandiose scheme seeping out from the region over the past few years I wouldn't be here now. We can smell horse manure from a mile away."

Charlie is actually overplaying that particular ability. At the outset of some previous ideas we thought they were good, only to find when we started implementing them that there were some unexpected outcomes. We lost credibility and the cynics had a field day.

Stevie seems buoyed by the challenge.

"Exactly. We have to be confident that the idea will cause these desired outcomes or we will flounder. But remember, we are not dealing with mathematical cause and effect. We are dealing with practical cause and effect. I believe the idea I am about to show you is valid in the environment we discussed yesterday. So let's check it."

Everybody nods. Then Stevie places his finger to his lips and, after a few seconds, says:

"One more thing before we start to look at the proposed direction of solution. We also need to explore the negative ramifications of success. Anyone with an idea naturally focuses on minimising negatives but can often become so engrossed in the positives they forget to see the wider implications of success. Remember yesterday when Jo pointed out that if we were not careful we would be asking people to turn their successes into cost savings and that the only cost saving was to reduce front-line staff. That's what I'm talking about. Let's not ask turkeys to vote for Christmas.

"Let's refill the coffee before we carry on."

◆

Stevie paces up and down again for a few moments, then says:

"It is obvious from our discussions yesterday that your hospital has a finite number of clinicians and managers who must meet not only the needs of every patient but also the need to improve the performance of the hospital on many fronts simultaneously. Clearly, you are all working very hard and I suspect, like in many other hospitals, management and clinical attention is itself a bottleneck, where the demands on your time are exceeding your capacity. As a result, it is vital that any new solution helps you focus your efforts. It should guide you to stop working on the things that are not actually improving the performance of the hospital as a whole and focus your attention on those few areas that will make a big difference quickly. As a starting point we must ensure that both the everyday management and the improvement processes are patient-centred and improve both the quality and timeliness of care for *all* patients."

Charlie looks particularly enthused by Stevie's assertion and Mo says:

"I agree, Stevie, but you are clearly suggesting we need a process that improves the quality and timeliness of care of all patients simultaneously. But every patient is different and it's only through diagnosis that we start to understand the real needs and problems of each individual patient."

This prompts Stevie to make his first specific proposal:

"My advice is that each patient has a purely clinically derived planned discharge date (PDD) set by a doctor-led multi-disciplinary team (MDT) within twenty-four hours of arrival, and the team updates this every day as the patient's clinical needs unfold. This will ensure we have the first building block for a robust and trustworthy patient-centred priority system that everyone can follow."

"As we are clearly performing well below the national average, why don't we just focus on this for the time being?" asks John. "I'm assuming it will be a nightmare to get all the doctors to agree to your proposal."

"The core of this approach is to set the PDD on individual, clinical grounds alone," says Stevie, "rather than exhorting everyone to try to achieve better than the average with every patient. This will also ensure that all our efforts are focused on improving the quality and timeliness of care for each and every patient."

Charlie interrupts:

"I'm pretty sure the one thing all our clinical staff will agree on is a clinically based discharge date rather than the mumbo jumbo we work to at the moment."

Stevie explains the problems that can arise when people working in silos are unable to see beyond their own remit. If they cannot see the bigger picture then they inevitably fall into the trap of local optimisation, in other words, looking after their own priorities at the likely expense of others. This local prioritisation then results in a disjointed organisation where there is little or no synchronisation across departments.

"When you have mis-synchronisation you inevitably end up with conflicting priorities, and this is what leads to bad multitasking by some departments."

Rather than being a badge of honour, ineffective multitasking is the leading trait of a busy fool and does not improve the quality and timeliness of care for any patient. He continues:

"The next building block is designed to ensure a rapid and

sustained improvement in financial performance. My proposal here is that we implement an approach that will help us identify and eliminate which task carried out by which resource is most often causing the most disruption or delay to the most patients.

"This will help us in two ways. Firstly, it will help us identify the major disruptions to patient flow across the whole hospital and focus our improvement efforts, but secondly and much more importantly, in this environment it will help us identify the multitude of local measures that try to optimise each part of the system rather than improving patient flow through the whole system. It is these measures that must also be abolished and replaced with a few simpler system-wide measures. You will flounder if these local measures are not abolished and improving patient flow is not the primary objective."

"Amen to that," says Charlie. "In other words, measure me in an idiotic manner and don't be surprised if I behave like an idiot! Why do you believe we have ended up with such a ridiculous number of measures and more arriving each day?"

Stevie responds:

"Well, we are driven to develop measures that focus on the finer resolution only when we don't know what to do, and that leads to ever increasing detail which paradoxically diverts management attention to the parts rather than the whole. By abolishing these local efficiency measures you will be surprised just how often you will stop doing the things you shouldn't have been doing, or shouldn't have done yet. You will then be able to focus all of this time on the few disruptions to patient flow across the whole system. This will accelerate your improvement efforts, release capacity and free up clinical and management attention."

The idea of the combination of one robust and trustworthy priority list for everyone to follow, and a process to identify and address the dominating cause of disruption to the most patients, is attractive to me. Particularly if it heralds the end of the bitching and moaning that goes on while we pursue a multitude of improvement initiatives, and helps us reduce the myriad of local efficiency measures.

I also remember a conversation I had with Jo a couple of weeks ago when she described a situation in the scanning department. Staff there have dedicated each session to a specific patient type to minimise their own downtime, with the outcome that some patients are staying longer than they need to. I have another of my '*Eureka!*' moments and smile to myself. Charlie looks at me quizzically.

Stevie then explains that the PDD should not be changed because of a non-clinical delay.

"That'll just put us under more pressure," says Charlie.

"Yes and no," says Stevie. "Most parts of the hospital will be able to cope with these updates to priorities; it is only the few key resources that will struggle and this will help us identify them earlier. We can then focus our efforts to resolve these few underlying causes that are really damaging our performance, once we know what they are. Charlie, if we update the PDD for every non-clinical delay that happens we are building in acceptance to these delays and will never be able to identify the dominant cause."

Stevie goes on to say that we must also understand the implications of delays and develop an approach that will ensure the patient flow through the various departments is maintained. Not all disruptions or delays will actually affect the PDD, and reacting to every disruption or delay would soon wear people down, so we need a way of identifying when an outstanding task is putting the PDD at risk. He proposes we use a green, amber, red coding system to protect or 'buffer' each PDD. As the remaining durations of outstanding tasks become known we can easily see the risk any outstanding tasks put on the PDD and prioritise accordingly. Stevie goes to the flip chart and draws what this would look like for one patient. If a specific task is constantly putting many patients' PDDs at risk then we will be able to see this, as it will most often not be finished until the red zone, close to the planned discharge date.

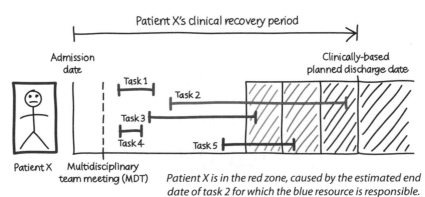

Patient X is in the red zone, caused by the estimated end date of task 2 for which the blue resource is responsible.

He then draws a number of patients in parallel and shows what this looks like across many patients.

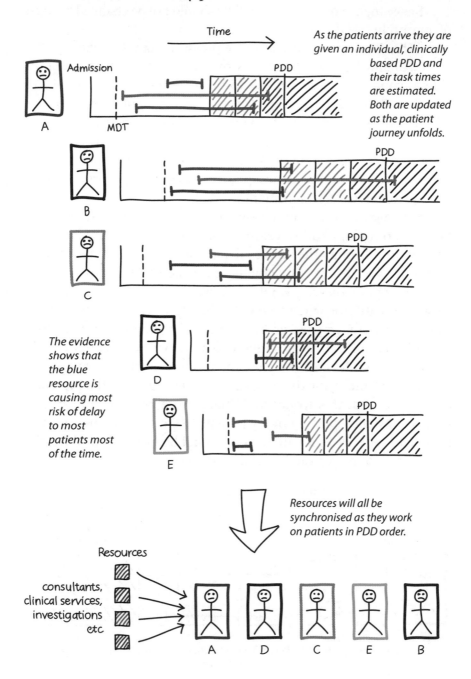

As the patients arrive they are given an individual, clinically based PDD and their task times are estimated. Both are updated as the patient journey unfolds.

The evidence shows that the blue resource is causing most risk of delay to most patients most of the time.

Resources will all be synchronised as they work on patients in PDD order.

With such a simple measure we have successfully identified where to focus our improvement efforts.

I look around the table and see that everyone is listening intently to what Stevie has suggested, and Charlie is keen to test the idea.

"The time to complete all the supporting tasks varies a lot. On one day I can get a scan within a few hours; on other days the patient may have to wait days. And sometimes it can be an outside service or even the family that lets us down. How will we find out if one of these tasks is going to take longer than we originally expected?"

Stevie replies:

"When we were driving in to the hospital this morning it soon became obvious that we had insufficient time to get here and have a coffee before the meeting started, which I would have liked. As I pointed out yesterday, I did not have to wait until the end of the journey before I realised that wasn't going to happen. It is the longest outstanding remaining duration that gives us this information. So what we need to know from the critical resources is how many more hours or days they need to complete the tasks on those patients who are approaching their PDD. Everyone needs to know which patient to work on next for the whole process to succeed. Everyone, and I mean everyone, must follow the one list."

Charlie adds that on rare occasions there may be an immediate life-threatening need for a patient, but he gets the point that we need a list that everyone can follow.

♦

From where I sit, we seem to be adding some practical steps to the clarity of analysis we developed yesterday. And now it's John's turn to check our progress.

"Stevie, you said we should also judge the proposed approach by its financial stability. How much resource do you think is being wasted by the lack of synchronisation and bad multitasking?"

If we could get the key resources to follow the same list and update it, the impact could be immediate. And if one resource continues to follow their local priorities it would become quickly apparent. I'm on the right lines. Stevie says:

"If everyone follows the same list many more patients will reach their PDD and much less resource will be wasted. The work that Tam, Tim and Sam have done overnight strongly suggests that the time currently wasted must be at least thirty per cent, and time is money. Think what you could do with that in terms of training staff in best clinical practice and how that would also eventually result in a reduction in the length of stay."

John perks up and says:

"And with that free capacity should I assume that rather than shutting down wards you're going to tell us we should be using this to reduce the backlog and earn more revenues?"

"Exactly!" says Stevie. "And with this combination of improved quality and timeliness of care, through focusing our improvement efforts on the few disruptions causing the most delay, and using the freed-up capacity to treat more patients within the same resources, we will be in a situation where revenues are now growing faster than medical costs. This will give you the breathing space you need before I ask you to consider a more ambitious plan."

Jo has listened intently so far and I can tell she is desperate to believe we really are taking the first positive steps to a breakthrough.

"But what happens if a delay happens right at the end of the process? The patient will miss their PDD."

Stevie says we must be pragmatic.

"You are right, Jo, patients will still be delayed but in much smaller numbers. We just need everyone to understand the cultural shift needed. If you are the cause of delay and you can solve it then this is your top priority. Just get on with it. If you are genuinely unable to resolve it then you must escalate as early as possible."

Previously, escalations were random and often seen as bitching or moaning, but under this system they are both important and urgent and offer a huge insight into where efforts should be focused. I want to nail this down. I suggest that each relevant doctor should lead a review of all patients' progress against their PDD every day and to highlight new and outstanding tasks and escalate if required. I want this to become the heartbeat of the whole hospital. Charlie objects.

"Do you really understand what you are asking for? Some days the doctors have outpatient clinics or theatre sessions first thing in the morning or they may not even be on site."

"How long would it take?" asks Stevie.

"I guess if the clinical staff got everything ready it'd take half an hour or so," replies Charlie.

"Why don't you do it first to test it?" I suggest helpfully, and thankfully Charlie smiles. I understand that his initial reservation may still be valid but at least if he gives it a try we'll have evidence of the size of improvement that's possible.

Mo, who has been silent throughout, returns to the issue of gaining agreement.

"If we are going to have any chance of changing the way we work we clearly need everyone on board," says Mo. "We need the hearts and minds of everyone in the place. If anyone looks after their own unit or continues to use their local measures and accepts compromises, it won't work."

"You're right," says Stevie. "But I do have a way of helping there. It involves getting everyone in a big room and showing them that in reality we only need a relatively small number of global measures to ensure you stay on track and focus your improvement effort. In effect, it involves getting round a table and treating people like adults. But that's for another day."

♦

All the way home my mind is buzzing, tossing around the discussion we've had over the past couple of days and the seemingly simple approach that Stevie thinks will answer all our prayers and lead us to a blissful life. I wonder how many initiatives we've tried in my time as COO at the hospital and how this could be different. The biggest thing in Stevie's favour is that I don't think he's said anything that isn't logical. So why shouldn't it work? But then again, if it's so straightforward why haven't we done it before?

I think back to what he said about the human tendency to measure more and more things when we don't know what else to do. I can hear Cynch and his types saying '*if you don't measure it, it won't get done*'. But then Stevie says the measurements that make us do things often damage our overall effectiveness. I guess Charlie had it right. The plethora of local measures has left us with an organisation bursting at the seams with talented people who can no longer use their talent. And on that cheery note I drop my laptop in the hallway and head for the kitchen, or more accurately, the fridge.

As I survey the contents and muse what Simone would do with a courgette, half a melon and a can of baked beans, I remember Dee's frantic message from early morning. I feel bad that she probably had something on her mind last night when she had her calls to make and maybe didn't think I had time to talk to her, but I was a bit fed up at the way she'd spent most of the day gatecrashing what, to me, was a series of important conversations. She should have known. But then if she was worrying about her mother's call-back request then I should have been more forgiving, and certainly more aware. Before you speak it's always good to remember that you never know what the recipient of your comments is currently dealing with. That's not always easy but I feel like I've screwed up as a friend.

Carl is the apple of his sister's and parents' eyes. He was such a promising student, a brilliant musician and an incredibly gregarious character. Eight years ago he got a First in Medicine at Durham University and then naturally took two years off to travel the world. When he came back he surprised everyone, and disappointed his mum and dad, by joining the army. He loved it at first but the tours he went on not only sent his mum frantic with worry but also took their toll on him. We were all so proud of him when he came home, but he seemed to have lost some of his spirit.

Last year he left the army and said he wanted to give himself time to work out what to do next. He stayed at home with his parents and seemed to be pretty much together, helping around the house and gardening for their elderly friends. He also started writing for a magazine and was considering a career in journalism. He certainly has a talent with words. He wrote the lyrics and some of the music for his band's first CD. He plays the lead guitar in a heavy metal band called Scarecrow. I went to see him play in Hammersmith with Dee last Christmas. He was good, but after the concert I couldn't hear for a day.

Soon after, Dee confided in me that she was worried about him. He seemed OK on the face of it but he was prone to extended quiet periods, which everyone put down to army stress and hoped it would pass. He'd had three girlfriends in the year, none for more than a month, which seemed odd for such a good-looking and talented lad. And although Carl had always been partial to a beer and a spliff, he was drinking and smoking more weed by the day. All the band members had some drug habit or other, the bass guitarist's being heroin. But Carl assured Dee he was just smoking pot. It relaxed him and she couldn't begrudge him that.

The promising student I remember from eight years ago seems such a long way from the frail person I saw in the intensive care unit this morning.

I look at my phone and see that Dee hasn't replied to my text from this morning, so I give her a call. Her phone goes to divert and I leave a message. Then I return to the fridge and suddenly I'm not hungry. I've kind of gone past it. I hope and pray that Carl gets better soon and that Dee isn't too fed up with me.

Chapter Seven

Be Linda

Wednesday morning presents the first opportunity for me to begin to put into practice some of the things we talked about with Stevie. I look at the ordered piles of paperwork on my desk, three days' worth now, and think to myself this plan had better work. I walk over to my window and am partly relieved to see that cigarette-and-drip lady is there again this morning. Maybe she had a lie-in on Monday. I'm just about to call intensive care when there's a knock on the door and Jo pops her head around.

"Hi, Linda, listen I'm sorry to drop this on you but we've had a diarrhoea and vomiting outbreak on three wards this morning, so we've had to close them to admissions. Can you come to today's bed meeting?"

"Sure I can," I say, seeing this as an early opportunity to introduce some of Stevie's ideas.

Although I've been to many of these meetings, there's always a sense of foreboding when I walk into the room and this time is no different. The room itself has little natural light but has five large screens on the walls. It's the hospital's war room. The hub of daily decision-making. The first screen shows a minute-by-minute picture of the emergency arrivals in the hospital. We can see exactly where all the ambulances in the region are and also how many are heading to the hospital at any one time. We know their expected arrival times and the early diagnosis of the arriving patient. The second screen shows the number of people currently in A&E and how long they've been there. It's an early warning system of patients breaching the four-hour target. A quick glance tells me we have fifteen in breach and many more about to breach. That does nothing to lift my sense of apprehension. Normally I would accept that this is going to be a very bad day.

The third screen shows the ward's empty beds and the expected number of discharges today. And this is the screen that frustrates the hell out of me the most. It always looks like there are precious few discharges due and yet I know that by the end of today, somehow a miraculous increase in the number of discharges will magically materialise. So what's the point of the screen, for pity's sake? The fourth screen shows us the hospital's estimated resource levels and highlights areas where we don't have a full complement of staff, as well as areas where we have more than we predicted we would need. This method of staff resource-planning always feels more like an art than a science. To add to the frustration, we often meet the urgent need for staff in one area by taking on temporary staff at higher cost, while in other areas we know we have staff looking for something to do. Even though we have put great effort into cross-training staff, all too often we end up with a costly mismatch.

The final screen signals the overall status of the hospital in the form of a block chart. At the bottom of the screen it denotes that all is calm in the hospital, higher up there will be a series of escalations and towards the top there's a major incident which requires us to shut the hospital to new emergencies and divert patients to other hospitals. In all the time I've been here we've never got away from the top half of the screen, and today we're at the second highest level of a serious internal incident. If we don't resolve the current bed availability issues we'll have to call a divert to other hospitals, which is not only a major disruption to the whole region but also results in a mountain of paperwork to report the reasons. The dichotomy, of course, is that when we have no new patients arriving at A&E it also affects our future revenues, not to mention adding further damage to our already tattered reputation and alerting the local newspaper hacks. The pensive mood is palpable as we sit down to join the inner group gathered to survey the wreckage of the night. With three wards closed following the outbreak of D&V and a growing backlog in A&E, the vital signs are a tad grim. We all inwardly brace ourselves, knowing that we're bound to end up right in the dilemma of trying to ensure safe and high-quality care for the patients on the wards, as well as those waiting for a bed – not just the emergency patients but also those with an operation planned for today.

As Jo opens the meeting I resolve to get some of the ideas we discussed with Stevie put into practice, but I need to bide my time. She reviews every patient waiting for a bed, asking how we can solve it, and it quickly becomes clear that the problems we described to Stevie are playing out in front of my eyes. It's a nightmare to find a bed for almost every patient. We end up with male patients in female bays and many patients being placed on the wrong wards. I can already hear Staulous and Cooper shouting for more beds, ringing in my ears. Jo asks the doctors to do another review of all the patients in the hospital and I can see some of them starting to get annoyed. One says:

"If I spend the afternoon doing another set of ward rounds I will have to cancel this afternoon's outpatient clinic. Are you going to tell the patients?"

Another offers the thinly veiled threat that he'll have to cancel a theatre session to find the time for another round. He says that finding his patients on the wards is like searching for the big five on a safari. He doesn't even start with his own ward as it's full of other patients!

This is the moment to grab. I say that the problem is a lack of clarity about who's going to be discharged. And that opens the floodgates.

"I think you'll find that all the patients are still sick and none will be discharged today. Look at the screen," says one doctor.

The statistical chance of this is small, but my problem is that the only way we can find patients to discharge is to review them all across the whole hospital and this could take the rest of the day. Doctors are never happy discharging another doctor's patients so such an exercise will involve many doctors for many hours and with relatively little success for each of them. They would see it as a monumental waste of time. A second doctor pipes up.

"It's not as easy as you may think working out in advance when we can expect a patient to be discharged."

"This is exactly why we need to review it every day and I have a system to propose. We need to set a planned discharge date for every patient and then track the progress..." I begin, but am shot down by the second doctor.

"It will be more work for us and we don't have the time." Then a third says:

"Even if we know the discharge date nobody will follow it. The physios are often the problem."

"The whole flaming social care system is the problem," says a fourth.

Two of the doctors have already stood up to leave and Mo can see the frustration on my face. He starts to chat with a couple of his colleagues but I see them shrug. When the room is empty enough I vent my spleen.

"Unbelievable! Two days pulling the whole hospital apart, dismantling it piece by piece, coming up with a credible plan, and then watching a room full of people just bloody well throwing it out! I could cry."

Mo, who has hung around, curls up the right corner of his mouth and sighs. And then Jo looks at me with the kindly, stern air of an auntie who has just heard me swear for the first time. I'm imagining her shaking her head in disappointment. At least I hope so. She says:

"You know, Linda, that's exactly the point."

"What is?" I snap, before correcting myself. "Sorry, Jo, what is?"

"With Stevie we spent a long time talking about and analysing the situation. We really gathered the evidence to validate the problem clearly. What you did just now was charge in at the first opportunity to state what you believed to be the cause, and then went straight to a solution, which would sound completely ludicrous to everyone. And they told you so. Linda, look in the mirror. Our time with Stevie helped us to change our understanding but as far as the doctors are concerned it doesn't look like you've changed the way you're behaving. Same old, same old."

"But we didn't have enough time," I say.

"That's exactly what they said."

Then Mo suggests that we hold one-to-one meetings with the doctors to try to gain their agreement again. That seems like a plan, and having calmed down I call Dr Staulous to set up a meeting with him and Mo.

During lunch I visit Dee's brother Carl. Thank God he is recovering well. He's pleased to see me and probably a little relieved that I'm alone, rather than being with his big sister, who I suspect will give him a pretty hard time. As I chat with him, for a moment I experience acute empathy with the thousands of visiting friends and family who sit at the bedside of their loved ones in hospitals countrywide. Some in hope, some with relief and some with despair. The reality hits home, and hard. We simply have to succeed in turning this hospital around.

♦

As we sit in Staulous' office I find myself impressed by the orderly layout, tidiness, and brightness of the room. There's a picture of Staulous and Cooper sitting in a restaurant in the mountains in ski gear, with their mates and just one lady in a white ski outfit. Underneath the strapline reads **Drinks with the Countess**. I wonder what that's all about. Then the man himself arrives.

"Afternoon, all," he beams.

"You're in a good mood," I say.

"Well, I must say you looked a little unhappy this morning, Linda," comes the reply.

"I was just trying to help us all and I came up against the same old objections."

"Well, maybe they are valid then."

"Maybe so, but you know as well as anyone the state this hospital is in. And it doesn't have to be that way for the rest of our lives."

My earnest plea seems to strike a chord with Staulous and his tone is considerably softer than that of his colleagues in the bed meeting.

"There is always going to be game-playing, Linda, but we are all under pressure. Take our track record in emergency medicine… it is awful, and people take it personally. Nobody makes mistakes on purpose. We are not proud of our care standards and operationally we know we are all over the place."

Mo adds the third dimension, explaining that we're also losing over one million pounds a month. Staulous looks perplexed then repeats my mantra that surely it doesn't have to be this way. We're an operational mess, our care is poor and we're losing money. Yet we have good people throughout the hospital. It just doesn't stack up. We are all struggling with this conundrum when Staulous says:

"So, Linda, you are the boss, why is it like this?"

"I don't know," I admit. "But that's what we need to find out if we're going to change for the better. One thing I can say is that I'm coming to the conclusion that the problems we're facing are not isolated. There may be a common cause for our ills and my job is to find it."

"Linda, am I right to assume that you are here because you want my help?"

"I actually need more than your help. I need you to take a lead on this. I need this to be led by someone all the doctors respect."

The silence is excruciating but I hold my nerve, keep my mouth shut and wait for his response.

He tentatively starts.

"So you say you think there is a common cause but you are not sure what it is. Is that correct?"

"Absolutely."

The silence prevails for a little longer and then he continues.

"You must have a hunch. You seemed to be saying in the meeting earlier that the core of the issue is a problem with patient flow."

I explain that we've spent two days on this topic and concluded that when patient flow slows down and the demand on A&E continues, we see a deterioration in quality of care, a need for more resources to cope, and patients' lengths of stay increase. Staulous nods.

"This makes sense to me. Managing and improving patient flow seems to be the overriding objective of managing the operation of this hospital. Did you talk about how to do it in your two-day management pow-wow?"

I resist the tease, instead explaining that we concluded on the need to translate the objective of improving patient flow into a practical mechanism that everyone would understand. This will also help us pinpoint where we need to improve the most.

He comes back with the obvious challenge.

"But why aren't people doing this anyway? And what convinces you it needs a doctor to lead this?"

I decide to take each question in turn.

"Your first question is the key one. I think we have many great people trying their best and yet the performance of the hospital is not good enough. We need to systematically establish the answer to this first question. This is what I tried to explain in the meeting. Clearly I made a hash of it and just raised the barriers, and as a result I never got to explain the approach we've been working on."

"OK, Linda, I am all ears. You can try it out on me."

I go on to explain that the core of the approach we've been thinking about is based around setting a clinically based planned discharge date for each individual patient and then uncovering what resource, policy or behaviour is most often causing the most delay across the most patients. If it's to truly be a clinically based planned discharge date for each patient, I explain that what I was trying to say in the bed meeting is that it should be set and constantly monitored by a cross-discipline, clinical team, and the best person to lead such an initiative is the doctor caring for the patient.

"Put like that it makes more sense."

After another pause where Staulous gets up and walks around his office and where Mo puts a finger to his lips as a hint for me to wait, Staulous says:

"OK, I will give it a go on three wards and let's see what happens. Linda, you do realise that if we find a common cause then there will be no excuses, we will have to deal with it. Otherwise this will just fuel the current perception that nothing ever changes around here."

My mood, indeed the mood of all three of us, is in stark contrast to the negative outcome of the bed meeting. Within forty-five minutes we've agreed how to implement the approach as an experiment for eight weeks. Staulous will lead it and insists he'll start the very next day. He instructs his PA to put together a data collection pack and promises to communicate the plan to the other doctors. I want to kiss him.

Mo calls Charlie and Jo and we meet back in my office where we explain that Staulous is on board. At last we have some excitement.

"That's fantastic," says Jo. Charlie winks at me and says:

"Stevie better be flipping right or you'll be the village idiot."

"Thanks a heap, my esteemed colleague!"

This is a big moment. We realise it is just an agreement to an experiment, but we sense we are gaining traction.

◆

Staulous, being an insider, easily gains agreement from all the relevant doctors to follow an experiment. He later admits they did tease him, saying he'd gone native when he started talking about the finances. But the plan was agreed that on three selected wards we'd create a list every evening of those patients who are clinically fit to go home the next day. We'll then record how many of these actually do go home the next day and keep the data for a month to see if we can identify which resource is most often causing the most delay across the most patients. The next step is to produce a priority list of patients for everyone to follow to see if the number of discharges per day increases.

Following Staulous' update I'm almost walking on air. It seems an age since I let my guard slip after this morning's debacle and I really feel excited. It's a feeling that I haven't had for a long time (at work anyway) and I show the first sign of creeping insanity by smiling to myself in my office. Cath pops her head round the door.

"It's lovely to see you smiling, Linda." Then she hesitates as if she doesn't want to spoil my fun.

"I'll put a coffee on. You have a visitor at three."

"Who's that?"

"Mr Ashcroft. He's been here to see his finance team and walking around talking to people."

Something inside me dies. I'm convinced Ashcroft can turn milk sour by looking at it. What on earth does he want? It's typical of him to show up when I've just had a really good hour.

It's 3:00pm on the dot and he arrives. Cath has put the coffee and our best biscuits on my desk. I move the milk away as Ashcroft sits down, then I see Charlie breeze past my window with a cheery smile and I let out an involuntary tiny whimper, before composing myself sufficiently to ask:

"So what brings you here?"

"I need a progress report on your cost reduction. What have you done since we met?"

I quickly decide that the best strategy is to tell Ashcroft what we have really been doing this week. I don't actually have anything

95

else to tell him and the success I've had today with Staulous gives me confidence. I take a deep breath.

"I'm looking at our whole operation rather than the finances in isolation." Ashcroft's glower tells me he's expecting weapons-grade waffle but I continue unabated:

"Finance is just one area of concern here. There's likely to be a common cause to other ills as well as just the numbers. We also have operational inefficiencies and care issues, so we need to isolate the common cause. We have implemented a controlled experiment across three of our biggest wards to analyse the causes of discharge delays. And that's the starting point to check our hypothesis."

Ashcroft looks at me for a moment, narrows his eyes and then raises his left eyebrow before saying:

"Linda, I hope you don't mind my asking… but are you feeling OK? I haven't the faintest idea what you're talking about."

Before I can re-order my thoughts to try to explain myself a little more clearly, Ashcroft has risen to his feet and walked out of my office with a cursory:

"Just get it sorted."

I have to say I'm not particularly bothered. I'm happy in my own mind that we're doing the right things, and in any case Ashcroft leaving early is always a bonus. I'm spending the hour I've saved going through the ever-growing, outstanding pile of paperwork teetering on the corner of my desk when Cath arrives. She has kindly looked into Dee's brother's case and brings the welcome update that he is continuing to improve, so the day has taken an upturn again. Then she says:

"And I have Mr Bamford on the line. Can I put him through?"

"Yes."

I puff out my cheeks then pick up the phone.

"Kieran, how are you?"

"I'm fine thanks, Linda. And you?"

"I'm good."

"Are you sure you're OK? Thing is, I've had Ashcroft on saying that you refused to talk to him about your financial proposals. He says you gave him a load of gobbledegook."

I stop short of trying to explain our strategy to Kieran on the phone, instead saying:

"I'm looking at a bigger picture."

"Linda, I don't really care which picture you're looking at, provided you have the time to stop your hospital haemorrhaging money. Do you understand me? Don't start grasping at straws or setting off on some half-cocked idea. You can't afford to be diverted."

"I know what I'm doing, Kieran."

"Well, Ashcroft doesn't think so and I'm inclined to trust his judgement from time to time. He has a lot of experience in the health service and is by no means an idiot. Don't let me down, Linda. You are a caretaker CEO and I already know you are capable of doing a good job at COO. But I don't want to have a problem placing you back in a COO role. Do you understand? Please don't give me that problem."

Aaargh! That was a bloody disaster. I've made myself look like an idiot in front of the top man at region – with Ashcroft's help. He thinks I've lost my mind. The wind has all but disappeared from my sails, and Charlie walks in to see my head on the desk. When I tell him of my meeting with Ashcroft and subsequent call from Kieran he suggests I speak to Stevie. He's already determined that, as we've decided to walk down the less travelled route, we should hold our nerve and stay on course. He doesn't want me to wobble, but my confidence has taken a hefty knock.

"Stevie was here only yesterday. What will he think if I call him now to ask for more help?"

"Do you care? We want to get sorted, don't we? Speak to him."

I agree to think about it and Charlie leaves. About twenty minutes later I receive a call from Stevie.

"What are you doing tonight?" he asks.

"Going home."

"Well, I'll call round with a bottle of wine and a pizza then."

"Where are you?"

It transpires that Stevie has stayed over for another day to meet a client based nearby. It also transpires that Charlie and Jo have contacted Stevie to tell him I need a lift. They're good friends.

♦

It's 7:30pm when I arrive home and I flick on the television to the news channel. I can do this safely in the knowledge that however spectacular the hospital's failings are, we're never likely to hit the national news. At least I hope we don't.

As I half watch images of a crime scene somewhere in Manchester I feel numb. Exhausted. It's not so much the hours I've been working, more the mental and emotional pressure. It's been a rollercoaster of a day. There was the usual fighting fires and fending off head office, but added to that I've experienced the excitement of sniffing a route to a breakthrough, the excruciating frustration of failing to implement my ideas at the first attempt, the delight at Staulous' response and then the pure dread of realising that, having spoken to Kieran, I may well be having a Martini in the last-chance saloon.

I could have kicked myself when the doctors walked out of the bed meeting. If I had real leadership ability then that wouldn't have happened. Sometimes you just need to get stuff done. You need to take charge and lead from the front, and be tough on those who are not following your lead. But that's not my style, and in any case, I'd defy anyone to take a firm stance with that bunch at 8:00am on a Wednesday. This type of situation can be tough in any senior management role, but when you're dealing with professionals and their associated intellects and egos it can be daunting. Sometimes you need to keep people on board by not pushing forward too fast. But in our position at the hospital we don't have long. Thank goodness I have Jo, Charlie and Mo on my side. I can see how lonely Bob must have been with hundreds of subordinates, plenty of bosses and stakeholders, and not one peer.

The doorbell chimes.

"Pizza delivery!" It's Stevie. "Were you talking to yourself?"

"Were you looking through my window?"

"No… I just heard some murmuring."

"It was the telly."

Stevie puts the pizza and wine on the coffee table and I go to get some glasses and a kitchen roll while asking:

"Why do I want this job, Stevie?"

"I didn't know you did."

"I don't know either, to be honest. I've had a hell of a day again. One minute you think you're getting somewhere, then you realise you're wading through treacle. Nobody wants to change. Well, the guys you met are all on board, but only one other soul in the whole place is."

"I'm not sure of that," says Stevie. "Let me show you something."

He takes a piece of paper from my file and divides it into quarters, drawing, in turn, a pot of gold, a pair of crutches, a mermaid and a crocodile. He says that I already know what the crocodile is, and we have already talked about the pot of gold waiting for us if and when we succeed. But the mermaid and crutches? Stevie explains that these two illustrate why people resist change. If you're on a beach and can see the pot of gold at the top of a cliff and can hear the crocodile snapping ever closer you may be persuaded to sit tight by two thoughts. The first is of the mermaid, particularly if you are infatuated and are unwilling to give her up to head off for the gold. After all, mermaids can only survive close to the sea. The second is one of fear – what were to happen if you lose your footing and fall in pursuit of the gold? That fear is represented by the crutches. I give Stevie a quizzical look.

"Blimey. When did you write this analogy? The last time anyone talked to me about a mermaid was 1982. And isn't it a little sexist?"

"OK, well if you're struggling with it, whenever I mention the mermaid you just think of David Hasselhoff."

"That doesn't help."

Mermaids apart, it does sort of make sense, but what does the pot of gold represent for me? It isn't simply cash. Is it sustaining health care for all? Maybe that's what I believe in. What is it about becoming a CEO that is a pot of gold? After my conversation with Kieran this afternoon maybe I should be looking for a career change. For the hospital the pot of gold must include something like a truly happy workforce. I certainly have no doubt what the crocodile is. It has big teeth, looks unnervingly like Ashcroft and right now it's my ass it's going to try to bite first (horrific image). But then what about the mermaid? I guess in relation to this job I certainly had more peers to talk to before I took it on and more time to talk to them. Don't get me wrong, I'm desperately keen to make this work, but if I can't, I wouldn't be disappointed to go back to somewhere that makes me happier. And while I aim for the pot of gold – in this case a flourishing hospital – I can't give too much thought to the crutches. If I crash and burn trying, then so be it.

"So do you want this job?" Stevie asks. And I still can't answer.

Do I really want it and could I even do it? Before I'd taken Mo to Stevie's talk at the MBA reunion, I'd probably have been happy to simply do my best and avoid rocking the boat. But there's a big part of me that would love to make this the best hospital in the country. The ideas we've developed with Stevie are common sense, but who says we'll even be allowed to implement them. They're so far from the normal route that the likes of Ashcroft would love to see us fail. And what makes Stevie, and now us, think we're right? And why on earth do I think I have the right to play with people's lives with such a grand experiment?

"Are you eating the pizza or analysing it?" asks Stevie.

"I'm sorry. There's so much bouncing around my head. I'm analysing everything."

"But if I know you as well as I think I do, you have already decided what you want to do."

But I haven't. I've already had a taste of the ridicule I can expect if this goes wrong. I've only dipped my toe in the water of a fresh approach and the regional boss is getting ready to certify me. How can I gain the courage to break into a new way of working? I have to have real confidence in the decisions we make.

"Your confidence will grow," says Stevie, "just as soon as your confidence in your project grows."

"But I don't actually know what it is I'm trying to be confident in. Is it my own ability, is it the people I rely on to save my skin, or is it your damn theory, Stevie?"

Uncharacteristically, Stevie loses his cool.

"For Christ's sake, Linda, just be you, stop messing around and go for it. You can spend your whole career lying to yourself and kowtowing to the likes of Ashcroft – or you can be yourself. Just toughen up. It's up to you."

"Life's not like that," I retort. "It's easy for you to say '*go for it*' but it's not your ass on the line. The people I'm dealing with are not idiots. They often behave like that but they're certainly not. And they're just waiting for me to fail..."

Stevie interrupts.

"On every single occasion when we had a row at university, did you ever express the slightest concern for what anyone else thought, let alone protecting yourself? You've changed, Linda."

He said that with a recognisable devilment that took me back more than a decade. But credit to my old nemesis, I can feel the blood churning inside as I start to feel alive again. The future of my role and the task of creating the best hospital in the land unfolds before me in my mind. I'm having an adrenalin rush and I can actually visualise what a happy hospital will look like. I look at Stevie and say:

"You're right. I'm not going to give up that easily. Are you here to help me?"

As he picks an olive off his pizza, Stevie looks at me and says: "Of course I am. But it doesn't really matter what I do.

"You just have to…

Be Linda."

Chapter Eight

Murphy

So I just have to be Linda. What exactly does that mean? What does it mean to *be* Linda? Surely I should know that better than anyone else, even Stevie. I have always tried to be nothing other than true to myself. Sure, I've learned the dark art of operating politically if I need to, but I'm not by nature a political animal. Clearly Stevie thinks I need to wise up to my new responsibility and seize the moment. He's always on the end of a phone, which is a godsend, but I really feel like I should be able to work this out for myself. I just need a little guidance now and then and Stevie is always ready to help. I need to summon all the tenacity I can, and find the initiative to make it happen.

I have a marvellous group of people around me in the hospital, an eclectic group of people, and each one of them talented and committed to the cause. And when I need to get away from it all, I couldn't have a better friend than Dee. Stevie's already spotted that, and has also worked out there's a lot more to her than the ballsy joker she likes to portray; she's so sharp she's a danger to herself and better with me than against me.

And it's all very well Stevie telling me to be Linda, but he could do worse than heeding his own advice. He told me last week that he's writing a book on modern-day scheduling techniques but he isn't getting very far, much to the annoyance of his publishers. Apparently he hasn't written anything for the last three weeks. He needs to just be Stevie and get on with the things that will make a difference for him.

But then I experience a pang of guilt. Stevie has already committed a lot of his own time to helping me at the hospital, and when he called me the day after his visit I felt more than a little guilty asking for his time again. I know he's busy, but selfishly I want to pick his brains and investigate every thought in his head (to know what he thinks) about our predicament at the hospital.

I don't feel guilty for long though when, a few weeks later, he invites me on a weekend trip to the Netherlands. And not a sightseeing trip at that. He says that if I want to pick his brains, he'd have time over Friday and the weekend and I would also have the opportunity to see some of his work in other environments – firstly at the university on Friday and then at a pharmaceutical seminar on Saturday. I don't have anything planned for the weekend, and if I'm going to be working I might as well be working on something that's important.

◆

The cold is harsh and biting as I stand on the pavement outside my house, bag in hand, at 4:00am on Friday. Stevie texted me five minutes ago while I nibbled the corner of a particularly unappetising slice of wholemeal toast. I don't know why I tried; it's a ridiculous time to be up, let alone to be eating. He said he was here, so I'm now dutifully standing out in the cold, dodging to avoid a stray carrier bag that floats past on the chilly breeze. Grim. Then the headlights of Stevie's car light up the corner of my street as he appears. As he comes to a stop, his boot opens so I throw my bag in before sitting in the passenger seat.

"I thought you said you were here."

"I am."

I grunt ungraciously, but not entirely inappropriately for the time of day.

"So why are we setting off in the middle of the night? I thought your lecture was late this afternoon?"

"Ah, well," Stevie smiles. "We have the indisputable pleasure of flying with WW Airlines this morning, an experience everyone should enjoy before they die."

WW Airlines is not their real name, it's Stevie's nickname for them but he won't tell me why. He has a choice, of course; he could drive another hour and a half to a different airport with a different airline, but this one is only fifteen minutes away.

"Not to say they should experience it immediately before they die!" he adds.

Although this is Stevie's humour, it is quite cutting even for him, so I muse that he too is grumpy at this time of day. And as we approach the airport I realise that today is likely to be one of those bad days Stevie is hinting at. The airport only has a single road into it and when volumes of traffic are higher, around school holidays and public holidays, apparently it struggles to cope.

Stevie says:

"I've done this so many times before that I now know everyone will be late into the airport, everyone will be late through security and customs, and most of the planes will leave late as well."

In the car in front, a couple, who it seems have not travelled from here before, have panicked and decided to abandon the queue, dump their car in medium-stay and struggle out of it with their luggage to make a run for it.

"There is still about half a mile to the airport," says Stevie. "I should call them back really."

"Why don't you?"

There is no reply as Stevie shrugs and we sit in stationary silence. Finally, as we creep the next hundred yards, we overtake the couple. A moment later they have moved ahead of us again but by now the guy has turned bright red and is struggling under the weight of his two gigantic suitcases… and the last stretch is uphill. I feel sorry for them now, especially as the road opens up in the last fifty yards and half the cars peel away to drop off passengers and the other half head to the short-stay car park.

This trip is going to be two days long and Stevie tells me, as we indulge in the luxury of the short-stay car park, the cost of parking will be greater than the cost of the flight. But with this amount of traffic outside, it will almost certainly be mayhem inside. And it's not long before we're queuing through security and passport control. The sign on the wall reads:

Due to increased security requirements it may take longer for you to pass through security. We apologise for any inconvenience this may cause.

I wonder if the cause of the increased time is the security requirement or actually the lack of capacity at peak times. It's not always easy to forecast short-term demand but this is the holiday season, for goodness sake. I nudge Stevie.

"Why don't they get more people on?"

"I suspect," he replies, "it is policy to keep the capacity the same to control costs and just let the customers wait. I've never understood this because the more time people spend queuing, the less time they spend in the shopping centre between customs and departures; it's a classic case of stupid local optimisation."

As we stand around in limbo I decide to use the time productively.

"Did you have a look at my email last night? I sent it with the figures for the past six weeks."

"Yes, I did."

"And?"

"They're good."

I thought they were better than good. We were delighted.

"Come on, Stevie, I know it's early but you could show some enthusiasm."

"Whoopee."

Now I'm getting irritated.

"Don't you think we're progressing more quickly than we'd hoped, Stevie? I do. We're much closer to achieving the access target in A&E and we've achieved this through reducing length of stay rather than throwing in more capacity. What's not to be impressed by? One of our senior matrons in A&E thought it had been a low-volume week until I showed her it had actually been a week that was higher than the average attendance. How can you beat that?"

Stevie can see that I'm a little perplexed.

"Yes, this is all good news, Linda."

"But?"

He pauses a moment as we make a tiny move forward.

"Do you understand why your progress has been so great, because I sure as hell don't! At this moment I can't work out how and why the actions taken have achieved the size of the results in the timescales."

"Does that matter?" I ask.

Stevie is disappointed in me.

"Of course it matters, Linda. Unless we predict the size and pace of the results before we take the actions, we will never know whether it was actually our actions that caused the improvement, or how effectively we took the actions. I was confident the idea of using planned discharge dates (PDDs) and a list to follow would work, but I was still unable to predict the exact size of the benefit and the pace. After I looked at your email this kept me awake for most of the night."

No wonder he's so grumpy. But he's making sense. When results from an action are better than expected it demonstrates just as clearly as when they're worse than expected that we do not really understand the causality between the actions and the effect we have been trying to create – the results. I suddenly feel slightly less chipper and return to my out-of-bed-too-early mood, so little is said for the next ten minutes.

After queuing for twenty minutes to get through customs and security we've just enough time to grab a coffee, which turns out to be a great coffee served by someone with a great smile. Thank you. We are both briefly uplifted but our joy is short-lived as we and our three hundred fellow passengers are herded into a windowless sheep pen. I recognise the couple from the car chase; the red-faced man is still flagging and his wife is looking distinctly cross.

While we collectively suffer this human rights indignity I start to think about the hospital again and ask Stevie for his thoughts. He explains that for his part he's trying to work out why so much progress was made. After all, our hospital is just a particular type of service industry. Our thoughts are interrupted by splendid news:

'Ladies and gentlemen, we are very pleased to announce the imminent departure of flight WW1374 to Schiphol. This is an allocated seat flight and your seat number is on your ticket. This is a new service we are offering and after extensive research, ninety per cent of our valued customers agreed that an allocated seat would enhance service. Everyone with ticket numbers one to thirty can now board the plane through the front entrance, and all remaining passengers through the rear entrance.'

Stevie is unimpressed.

"Well, would you believe it? A new innovation, allocated seats on a plane! Nine out of ten cats prefer it and yet for the last fifteen years, the airline has been happily promoting the benefits of their choice of seat service. Of course that isn't to say that I wasn't the one out of ten who actually preferred it as it was; the challenge of predicting the gate and getting there in time to get a good seat relieved the tedium."

We make our way through the gate and within a gloriously short five minutes we're in our allocated seats. As I take a cursory look at the laminated (some time ago by its dog-eared appearance) safety sheet, Stevie taps me on the arm with his pencil.

"This is actually quite interesting."

"What is?"

"Any system, whether it be a hospital, a manufacturing plant or an airport, has a process of dependent events. And, as we've experienced this morning, we have moved from car park to passport control, to security and then the plane. But each step experienced statistical fluctuations. Sometimes they are natural variations and sometimes they are a result of an unexpected event."

He goes on to say that predicting our journey time to the airport and through customs to the gate is one thing; but how do we do this when, instead of just one person passing through three or four steps, we try to predict the time it takes for many different customer orders of many different descriptions to pass through many different resources (some of which are shared)? That is the task that manufacturing plants face. With this added complexity, how can we then build a schedule that gives us sufficient confidence that we can make a real commitment to each and every customer when their order will be ready? How can we be so confident that even when we have a surge in demand we know we can cope and will not let our customers down? In essence, how do we build a robust schedule which can meet a series of differing customer demands with timely delivery?

This is indeed a conundrum. And one into which Stevie has done quite some investigation. He explains to me one well-used approach that he has seen.

"Many organisations have, for the best of reasons, started with the customer. When does the customer need his order fulfilling? That is the starting point and should be complemented by your own service levels. Hopefully the two should meet. If you know when your customer needs the delivery, you work back from that and schedule how long you think it will take to make the order, with some sort of contingency factor to take account of variation and unexpected events."

"So, if the customer's order is required in six weeks we simply work out when to start the order to ensure the delivery date is met," I offer.

"Which is exactly what we have done today," he replies. "You set your alarm at a time that you thought would ensure your arriving at the airport on time."

"Assuming you had done the same."

"Yes. And then we had to make a judgement about how much time to leave between the gate closing and getting up, allowing for things to go wrong."

In industry, you can calculate the times of each step in the process and factor in the variation in these times and any known queues. The fastest Stevie has ever done his journey to the airport is ten minutes. Walking from the car park to security takes a further five, and from security to the gate probably less than three minutes. But leaving home with only eighteen minutes to go before the gate closes is a tad reckless and almost bound to result in you missing the flight. In reality we tripled that time to take into account the variations.

Stevie can relate this process and strategy to his work in industry. In a factory most products are a complex assembly of many different components, where each component in itself can undertake many different steps in its production. It's not unusual in more complex industries for there to be thousands of components requiring hundreds of different steps each to produce; just imagine how many components it takes to build a plane. Establishing how long it's going to take for all the components to be ready for final assembly is quite a task. He then explains to me that firstly we need to know the bill of materials, which is a breakdown of exactly which components are required for the particular product the customer has requested, and the sequences of the tasks required to create each component and sub-assembly and final assembly.

"You can try to do this for yourself," he says. "A plane needs a fuselage, at least two wings, a tail fin, at least two engines, an undercarriage, and then things like toilets and seats. The total number of components is huge."

This process also requires us to know the touch time: the time it takes to physically create each component. Then we need to know the number, location and size of queues already in the system and what other customer orders are standing in front of the various resources. Unless we plan to jump the queue we're going to have to wait our turn. Stevie continues.

"The experience in manufacturing has often been that when a schedule was finally calculated, quite often certain components needed to start their journeys in the past!"

This happens because when the original due date was committed to, scant account was taken of whether or not there was sufficient capacity to meet the date. The schedule was then adjusted until it appeared to produce a workable system.

"From today's journey it's pretty easy to see that the summation of the queuing time is much higher than the summation of the touch times," he says. And he goes on to explain that in some industries this calculation became so complex that the schedulers decided it would be easier to base the time to release the products into the system on the average time it had taken to produce such a product in the past. Exactly as we had done with our journey to the airport this morning.

"But how do we judge the amount of safety time to include in our estimates?" I ask.

Stevie smiles.

"Tell me how paranoid you are about missing the plane and then I'll tell you when to set your alarm clock."

It wasn't long before scholars realised that this predetermined production lead time varied considerably as the work in the system varied. How long does it take us to get through security? It depends how long the queue is. Actually, passing through the gate probably took us one and a half minutes and yet the total time was more like twenty minutes. It is not the capacity of the system alone that determines the lead time, but the amount of work in progress. Double the work in progress, double the lead time at least. Double the number of people queuing in one day and you double the time it takes to get through security. It's not that capacity is less than demand, or the queue would go on forever. It is just that the capacity struggles to cope with the variation in demand in a timely manner. Stevie's thoughts are interrupted again:

'Good morning ladies and gentlemen, this is your captain speaking. Please listen to the following safety announcement given by our crew; and however frequently you fly I would ask that you give it your utmost attention. Thank you and enjoy the flight.'

This is the only useful and necessary announcement on the flight, but it is, as always, lost in the mélange of marketing blurb oozing constantly from the public address system. Although he is a frequent flyer Stevie agrees with it.

"I do wish people would shut up and listen to the crew," he whispers, to my surprise. "There are some people flying for the first time and it is important that everyone understands this routine. It's always the same though."

One of the crew has to tell a chap to take his headphones off, which he does a little churlishly. The luggage-lugging man looks quite pleased that his wife has been asked to stop talking, but knows his respite will be all too brief. Two minutes after we are airborne comes the next announcement:

'Ladies and gentlemen, we are delighted to offer you our in-flight bistro service. This includes teas and coffees, alcoholic drinks, and a tempting range of food items that can be found at the back of the in-flight brochure. And today's hot snack is the delicious WW cheese and ham toastie.'

"Are you tempted?" I ask.
Stevie turns up the corner of his mouth. That's a *'no'* then.

♦

Fortified by the unshakeable belief that a harmless WW coffee would soon be within reach, Stevie offers to explain to me a second theory of scheduling in the manufacturing world, a theory which is fundamentally different to the first. Rather than starting with the due date and working back with an assumption that there must be sufficient capacity in the system to cope, the second approach is almost diametrically opposite.

The opening assumption was one of finite capacity. When a new order came in, the order was broken down into the relevant sub-assemblies and components, and a schedule was built by sequencing the production of these components and assemblies through the next available slot-in time. This was based around the finite capacity of the resources. If the resources were already full, then the customer order was simply pushed out into the future until resources became available. So the due date was an outcome of these calculations. It might initially look less customer-centred but in many ways more realistic.

But just like the first school of thought, this required a significant amount of data and difficult calculations. The calculations were made more difficult by the need to know the exact capacity available for each time period now and into the future. When the lead times were finally calculated they were sometimes unacceptable to the customer, which is hardly surprising. This caused a never-ending cycle of adjustments to try to meet each customer's requirements. But if you move a customer order earlier to try to meet their due date, everything else would go later. The schedulers would try to establish which resources needed to do overtime or which components could be offloaded to other machines, or which customers could be delayed with least damage to relationships and ongoing business, which is always a difficult call to make and one that is fraught with danger. What's more, if there were a change in availability of capacity this would have major ramifications on the customer due dates and would necessitate recalculations.

'Ladies and gentlemen this is your captain speaking. Unfortunately, due to our slightly late departure we have missed our predetermined time-slot into Schiphol. Flight control has informed me that there will be a twenty-minute delay before the next available slot. I apologise for this slight delay.'

Stevie sighs.

"That was almost inevitable. When anything unexpected happens, you will always have a delay in the schedule which cascades through the remaining steps."

The cabin crew announcer attempts to soften the blow:

'*Ladies and gentlemen, as you sit back and relax we are now able to extend our onboard shop, where you can continue to purchase a number of quality items at less than high street prices. We have ladies' and gentlemen's fragrances, watches, children's toys, sweets and goodies and our own WW teddy bear, an ideal gift for your children or loved ones. And we expect to confirm our time-slot shortly.*'

Stevie's frustration is reaching new heights.

"We're going to miss the train."

I don't think an army of WW teddy bears will be able to do anything about it, but the announcer continues with admirable air-headed spirit:

'*Ladies and gentlemen, we are pleased to announce that we have a special arrangement with our local car hire company for discounted rates on today's airport prices.*'

To my mild amusement Stevie is quickly becoming apoplectic.

"How stupid do they think we are?"

I'm slightly concerned that he's about to put that to the approaching flight attendant, but he continues to vent his spleen in my direction.

"Admittedly our senses have been dulled by the whole WW flying experience, but even the half-dead luggage-carrying man knows that airport prices are way higher than if you had ordered your car hire in advance. You're getting a ten per cent discount off a rip-off price. Fantastic!"

I must say I really can't blame the flight staff as they have been polite and attentive throughout the journey. It's the management who need to realise. I notice an advert on the back of the chair in front making the same car hire offer. I carefully peel the advert off the seat and place it in my unused sick bag. Hopefully a vigilant steward will alert somebody in WW marketing, who will make the connection and realise that all Stevie and his fellow passengers really want is a safe, secure and pleasant flight, and not to be bombarded with marketing materials and sales chatter – which I suspect nine out of ten of their valued customers would prefer.

Hope springs eternal and we are buoyed as we joyfully land. There is only a small queue through arrivals and, having resisted the temptation of a hot cheese and ham toastie, we have time for a late breakfast before waiting for the next train.

Once on the train, we have the opportunity, while travelling at 150km per hour, to start to think again about the underlying principles of managing sequences. Stevie recalls the one outstanding lecturer from his MBA programme many years ago. I never met the fellow as he lectured on a different part of the programme. But Stevie recognised that the theory, introduced to him by that visiting lecturer, was a breakthrough relative to the previous two approaches, and it has helped to shape his own modus operandi from that day.

◆

As I nurse a coffee, Stevie tells me of this newest theory and his belief in it.

"In essence, it's this," he begins. "In any goal-oriented system there are only relatively few constraints. And often, the more complex the system appears, the fewer the underlying constraints."

Wow! That's a statement if ever there was one – inherent simplicity does exist. Stevie explains that a consequence of this statement is that a goal-oriented system must therefore consist of relatively few constraining resources, and many other non-constrained resources. The breakthrough came from the realisation that under this mindset it was relatively straightforward to adopt the approach of forward scheduling to finite capacity. It simply required one to pick the most constrained resource and to schedule each order through that resource against that one resource's finite capacity. Because the due date is determined by the most constrained resource, it is safe to assume that all the other resources can cope. Also the problem of schedules requiring start dates in the past was sorted out. It did not eliminate the calculations but massively simplified them. If all other resources were not constraining, the principles of backward scheduling to the assumption of infinite capacity could then be adopted.

As he talks I listen intently. And the one thing that really resonates with me is that, when using this theory, there is less need for exhaustive data accuracy and calculations. The capacity of the few constraining resources will be the overriding determinant of the due date of the order.

"This really is quite a simple breakthrough in a sense," I observe.

"Yes it is," he replies, "and it's one that you and your colleagues back at the hospital need to apply to your own predicament. The throughput of any entire chain is determined by the throughput of the weakest link. So improving the performance of other links is, frankly, a waste of time, and can even do more harm than good."

But this breakthrough relied on upfront knowledge of the many resources to ultimately find the ones that were constraining performance. In the hunt for the true bottleneck in huge manufacturing plants, the early attempts were based on analysis of capacity and load, and it soon became obvious that this was fraught with the same difficulties as the finite capacity scheduling models. And then came the next breakthrough.

Stevie's guest lecturer, incidentally the inventor of the theory, decided that identification of the constraint was the crucial factor, and so he proposed that the first step must be to slow down the release of raw materials into the plant. This decision would have two major benefits. Firstly, with less work on the shop floor, the work would have more access to the available resources and would flow faster through the plant, increasing throughput and reducing lead times. Secondly, it would identify the constrained resources much more easily, as the non-constrained resources would soon show free capacity, as they could not just keep working on things to look busy. The few underlying constraining resources would soon become obvious as they would quickly have a queue of work in front of them.

The next step was to create a simple list that sequenced the orders through the most constrained resource. The resource then works on the first order before moving on to the next one and so on, according to their due date. Stevie explains:

"It's vital to resist the temptation to jump up and down the list, and to stick to the sequence religiously. This sequence is not only followed by the most constrained resource, but it also becomes the drumbeat for the whole factory. By everyone following the same list in the same order, the flow starts to improve. It is by controlling and smoothing the flow that we can increase the speed of every order through the plant."

Everyone understands the system and adheres to it. So when a new order is won, rather than releasing it on to the shop floor the moment it arrives, the order and all the associated raw materials are only released at a rate that the most constrained resource can cope with. When a certain number of hours of work is completed by the constrained resource then the same number of hours of drum work are released into the plant. I'm keeping up.

"But doesn't this mean that some of the non-constrained resources will start to have excess capacity?"

"True enough," says Stevie. "They only looked busy before because they were doing work way before it was needed, soaking up raw materials, frittering cash and distorting priorities at the same time."

So it becomes clear that the plant must never become flooded with work again, which also necessitates a simple and practical method of determining if orders are being released too late. A risk of starving the most constrained resource would be unforgivable, and at the same time, if there is still too much work in the system, orders will start to collide as they try to pass through the constraint. The system must monitor the orders to ensure they reach the drum resource on time. And crucially, by discovering which task carried out by which resource most often causes the most disruption, you can also focus improvement efforts.

♦

"When you first asked me to help you find a solution for your hospital I must admit I approached it with some trepidation."

Stevie makes this candid admission as we near our destination.

"It didn't appear that way to me," I reply. "Why the trepidation?"

"I knew you were in a difficult position to say the least, and the last thing I wanted to do was implement an experimental approach only to find it didn't work. But I wanted to see if I could use the applications that I'd learned previously and apply them in the healthcare environment, and it wasn't long before I became totally blocked."

Stevie explains that the first step of the process is to control the release, or freeze some of the current work in process in the system. After visiting the hospital and speaking to the team it quickly became obvious to him that the most dominant and troublesome stream of care in a health system is the emergency care stream. So controlling the release is immediately impractical. Asking a patient with their leg hanging off to delay their arrival at the hospital was simply not an option.

What's more, in healthcare every patient is different, their individual care pathway emerges as the diagnosis unfolds, and recovery time is highly dependent on each patient's condition. The time for an elderly person to recover from an illness can be wildly different to the time for a young, fit person. The available capacity is not machines, as in the manufacturing world, but highly trained staff whose experience enables them to make judgements about each step in the care process.

"So you see the dilemma," he continues. "Drawing on the teachings, how could I present a solution for the healthcare sector? I needed to develop one that did not rely on controlling the release of patients as the first step."

"So how did you apply it?"

"Well," he says, "a breakthrough came when I realised it might be possible to achieve benefits by focusing on directly improving the system without controlling the release of patients."

His guiding principle was that a patient-centred system must be one where no patient's length of stay is a minute longer than their actual clinical recovery time. And so a purely clinically based discharge date, constantly updated as the patient's recovery progress changed, was the starting point.

"Rather than building an upfront plan for each patient, we should allow the plan to emerge as the patient's journey unfolds," he says. "It just needs staff to give us their latest understanding of outstanding tasks."

He realised that a simple priority list would be sufficient to overcome the worst causes of delay and disruption. And there was an underlying assumption that a combination of individual cherry-picking and rampant bad multitasking was creating much of the disruption and delay. By identifying which resource was most often causing the most delay, we would have sufficient data to start to identify and resolve the few underlying constraining resources.

♦

As we check into our hotel, a short walk from the university, I can see that Stevie has shed his grumpy persona of the early morning and is quite pleased about this trip. Our discussions on the flight helped. One thing he thrives on is intellectual challenge and he enjoys explaining the theories to me. And for my part, I'm keen to learn.

Stevie's ready for the local pharmaceutical business event he's facilitating tomorrow, but less so for this afternoon where he's giving a lecture at the university. It was a late invitation from a former colleague of his to their undergraduate operations management course. Apparently he was tempted to decline graciously at first, looking forward to a relaxing evening in his hotel – a steak and glass of Rioja – but eventually he was persuaded. Maybe when he invited me along he thought it'd be a good experience for me too. I actually think he's looking forward to it now.

"This is a chance for me to try out my new lecture on the theories of scheduling complex systems," he says with palpable excitement. But I'm not so sure.

"To a bunch of students?"

"A raw and forgiving audience will be useful to practise on before my big presentation to my client tomorrow," he smiles.

Ah – there's method in his madness.

His contact at the university, a chap called Jan, has sent some preparation notes for the afternoon. He's asked the students to say what they'd like Stevie to talk about.

"Only in the Netherlands would this happen. In the UK they get what they are given," he says.

"Do you know what they've asked for?"

Stevie scans his notes for a moment and then, with furrowed brow, holds up a sheet of paper.

"On second thoughts… we need a Plan B."

"We? I think you mean you."

He shows me the suggestions and it's clear that the students are looking for examples of the practical implications of everything they have learned, and not more theory. One of them is particularly forthright, saying: '*Please, please, please* (polite at least) *no more lectures on the theory, forcing us to sit through endless slides and killing us by PowerPoint?* A bit harsh. But Stevie does indeed need a Plan B.

"How big is your PowerPoint?" I quiz him with a smile.

"Not big at all," he replies rather defensively. "Anyway, I'm not going to use it; I'll just have to do something else. Come on, let's get some lunch."

"Don't you need to prepare your lecture?"

"I've a few hours yet, and lunch will be less than two of those," he grins. I suspect he has already hatched the alternative plan.

◆

"So that's it: *Achieving a Breakthrough at a Hospital Near You.*" Stevie beams as he refills my glass of water. "I'll just rehash your email to me with the latest results and analysis from your hospital and call it a live case study. Brilliant, eh?"

"Absolutely," I say. "I look forward to seeing our dirty linen washed in front of the young academic brains of Europe."

"They won't know it's you: we're in the Netherlands, so I'll translate all the numbers into kilometres – you'll be unrecognisable. I promise there'll be no trace. Then I'll just read out a brief and the supporting data and get the students to discuss it with me. No death by PowerPoint, plenty of real-life application; it's just what they asked for."

Stevie's looking his smuggest. But fair play to him; in the space of one hour and a chicken sandwich, he has hatched a participative lecture which he is convinced will look like a well-considered and topical format rather than a last-minute seat-of-the-pants get-out.

"I'll show them the reworked email and a few graphs and then ask them to discuss what to change and how to go about it. It will engage them in how to change the world they're about to become a part of. Vokes, you're a genius."

"If you say so, Stevie... if you say so."

◆

When we walk into the lecture theatre at 3:30pm we're met by thirty or so students who look like they should still be in school. It reminds me of Mum when she used to say '*Don't police officers look young these days?*' or something like that. I take a seat at the side of the room (nearest the door) as Jan introduces Stevie and explains how lucky they are to have him here. The students look distinctly underwhelmed. I look at Stevie, who's scanning the room. I suspect they are wondering why this guy has flown over from England and what he can teach them. I'm pretty sure they're not thinking how young Stevie looks and how stylishly he's dressed!

On his request I dutifully give a pile of handouts to the boy at the front to pass round and then he starts by reading the brief. It explains that the hospital in the case study has been missing its emergency target for the last two months and patients are backed up in the department waiting for a bed. A&E staff spend a lot of their time making calls to other parts of the hospital. Many of the emergency patients are admitted to general medicine whose length of stay is six days, which is significantly higher than the regional average. Sounds hauntingly familiar, but then so it should, and I suppose it's pretty generic.

Next Stevie shows a graph detailing how many patients stayed at the hospital and for how long. It shows a skewed distribution, with many patients staying for a day and then a long tail with a small percentage staying over twenty-one days. And there were a few who stayed for seventy-five days or more.

Stevie explains how the hospital assigns each patient a planned discharge date (PDD). If they stay longer than that then they are annotated '*in delay*'. He highlights that approximately twenty per cent of all patients present on any day are in delay, and it is steadily increasing. He uses another graph to illustrate the data and trends as he continues to explain that one ward surveyed has seven patients in delay. I'm guessing this is a key discussion prompt. All the patients are fit for discharge, but for four of them the ward has been unable to get a social care worker to attend. The other three are waiting for the discharging doctor. There is a similar story on other wards. All this familiar detail makes me feel like I'm looking in a particularly unflattering mirror: one of those at the fairground which makes you look fatter than you are.

Stevie summarises by asking them to consider how much extra revenue the hospital could earn by stopping this type of delay.

As he pauses I look around the room at the group, some open-mouthed, all, thankfully, open-eyed. And then he asks for questions. After a moment's contemplation one young lady speaks up:

"Do all the patients who come in to the hospital need urgent treatment?"

Not a bad start. She's clearly looking for ways of reducing the flow and it's not a daft question. Stevie explains that not all are urgent but generally they still need treatment for a serious problem. Often this treatment is to have some surgery on a part of their body, and they will be given an expected date for surgery. While the situation may not be urgent, it could become so if treatment is not applied.

After a couple more clarifying questions, the students start to formulate their ideas. Some want to redraw the graphs and create other versions of the data, looking at the length of stay graphs by age, sex and illness type. They proceed to ask Stevie for all manner of data, and I smile to myself as he answers everything they ask for in excruciating detail.

"Where is the hospital?" asks one keen soul, and Stevie embarks on an impressive ramble.

"It's based in a large town, not quite a city, in the UK. It is a new town built after the Second World War and has a typical population with the normal range of illnesses. There are higher than average mental health issues in the region. Access to the hospital can sometimes be difficult as it sits in the edge of a new one-way system which has been growing over the past five years.

"Often there are road works within half a mile of the hospital which have been a feature for two years as the development was stalled following a change of contractor." He pauses for dramatic effect and increases the intensity level of his voice: "The initial contractor had insufficient indemnity cover when the newly installed council leader insisted on an increase. Then with the insurance industry facing challenges and the cyclical hardening of premiums, the policy became prohibitive as well as affecting new health insurance policies."

Stevie glances over at me and then visibly smirks as he notes at least five of the students scribbling furiously, the rotter. A few of the others look mildly irritated, and at least two bright ones are smirking along with Stevie.

Clearly enjoying himself, Stevie proceeds to give long, drawn-out descriptions of the strength of the management team, the make of furniture in the hospital and the percentages of patients over the age of fifty-five with blue eyes and brown eyes. By this stage all but a lad wearing an **I'm with Stupid** T-shirt has realised he's teasing and another girl asks:

"If you had one question you could ask what would it be?"

"Excellent," replies Stevie to the girl's delight, before diluting her joy, "but I'd actually ask more than one question."

He then suggests to the still-attentive throng that the first thing they need to do is to appreciate the difference between data and information, and that in this instance the data is only useful if it helps them to answer four questions.

Firstly, *why is there a need to change?* We have to identify the negative aspects of data relative to the overall goal. Then *what to change?* He explains how big organisations are sick to the back teeth of change initiatives and employees become cynical about the latest claims of what is wrong, which is invariably a long list that periodically changes order. The third question is *what to change to?* Proposed changes must stand a good chance of working. So how do they know there will be no new, unintended outcomes of their attempts to improve things? The change-advocates must show why the proposed changes will deliver the results proposed, and this has to be a logical derivation. You can't just say, '*it worked somewhere else*'. Finally, *how should you go about it?* You need to quickly spin the wheel of inertia in the right direction, particularly in environments brimming full of professionals. The 'white knight' model of change which implores all to follow someone over the horizon to a new, brave world is not good enough; neither is the 'trust me' model.

The group has remained attentive and all appear to be following Stevie's lecture, and then another brave character sticks his hand up.

"Surely it's pretty straightforward to say *why* they need to change? It's because they're crap!"

While the boy looks confident that he's right, I'm sure there are better ways of putting it. Stevie speaks to his audience:

"You know, we should really assume that the task of changing successfully is not easy, rather than that the people are just no good. It's always best to start from that standpoint. But building rapport can be time-consuming. How can you gain attention quickly?"

"We are Dutch," explains one. "We just say it how it is," confirming that the first lad's assessment would actually be quite popular in the room. When Stevie asks them to tell him how they're going to go about deciding what is most important to change, one student suggests he would build a matrix with a list of the problems on the Y axis and senior staff names on the X axis, then ask them all to rate the problems from one to ten, to come up with a statistically backed consensus.

"If I'm one of your senior people, what happens if my favourite doesn't make the top?" Stevie asks.

"Tough. You have to accept it's fair," comes the reply.

"Really? Why should I throw myself into a solution that I don't believe addresses my own dominant problem? I'll probably just try to solve my problem on my own."

After a little more to-ing and fro-ing Stevie explains to the students that we know there must be a connection across the problems and we need to identify the core issue. The students have identified the poor-quality care, lack of beds and money, and haphazard scheduling. After he explains the idea of undesirable effects he asks them to define a problem. Then after much discussion he guides them to the understanding that a problem is a long-running unresolved dilemma that creates a series of undesirable effects. I think he's pleased he's reached this area of discussion and he'll rate it as progress indeed within an hour.

He continues to explain how when you solve one undesirable effect it can come back to bite you, while the others simultaneously get worse. I am listening intently as he tells the students that if you put in more beds, the finances will deteriorate. If you close a ward the patients will wait longer. Whichever side of the dilemma you pick, you'll experience a bucket-load of undesirable effects on the other. But try a compromise and you'll get the worst of both. I'm enjoying listening to him too.

A keen film buff, Stevie indulges himself by asking if the kids can remember in *Star Wars* who is in danger when the walls close in? He asks them how they'd react in the knowledge that if they do nothing, things will deteriorate as the walls accelerate towards them. I continue the theme in my own head, recalling how, in *Skyfall*, James Bond says that '*youth is no guarantee of innovation*' or something like that, as I wait to see what the students come up with.

But this is a brave new world. And the students in the lecture theatre are the future of the Netherlands. Once they get over their youthful energy, focused on quick resolution with a no-nonsense approach, they begin to show how good they are at practical ideas and fearless at implementation. They work their way closer to resolving the underlying causes of delay by debating with some vitality the benefits of changing policy without actually knowing what the problem is. One girl says:

"Wasting energy trying to improve things that are working well is foolish. In a hospital where a number of departments need to do their bit to see a patient through, you'll only do as well as your slowest function."

"Give that girl a cigar," announces Stevie with his broadest beam yet.

As the session draws to a close, Stevie asks the group what they want to do with their lives and they tell him about the horrendous process of job-seeking they are all going through. It's refreshing in a sense to hear about their creativity in managing the big corporates who mess them around. They each apply to one of the big guys, suss out the process and then take it in turns to apply to the good ones. One of them asks Stevie what he looks for in a new recruit and he answers, relatively honestly.

"Someone I can happily work with on a difficult job for a week, someone who is capable of thinking differently and someone who can have some fun."

"How much will you pay us to solve your problems?" asks the lad next to **I'm with Stupid**. And in a moment of wild bonhomie, Stevie offers two hundred euros to the one who comes up with the best answer to their next assignment, which is based on this evening's lecture. At which point Jan thanks him for offering to grade them and Stevie looks instantly crestfallen.

"How long do we have to complete the assignment?" asks one girl.

"Two weeks," replies Jan.

"If this is an important one then can we put the accountancy mock exam back to the following week?" asks the arch-negotiator of the group.

"Nope."

Cue a disquieted murmur and I hear one lad say: '*Well, I'm not starting tonight... I'm meeting friends and they'll already be partying*,' and another adds: '*Not tomorrow either... It's Barcelona and Man United – on live at The Walkabout. We could go there now to get a good seat!*'

Stevie's acutely aware, as I am, that any class of thirty students will range from the diligent and enthusiastic to the '*I think I'll skip it*' contingent, passing through the talented group who leave it to the last minute before winging it with the help of their diligent friends in a late-night library session... before heading to The Walkabout.

As they troop out of the lecture theatre three of them make a point of walking over to thank Stevie, one asking how he plans to evaluate the assignment. No prizes for guessing which group she belongs to. A boy behind her listens while pretending not to. She has a rival, I think.

Chapter Nine

One more roll

A month or two is long enough to test a theory. Well, particularly when you only have a few months to save your backside. After we return from Amsterdam I have another look at the figures and send Stevie an email telling him we're certainly having some success. Since we introduced the planned discharge dates and a common list to work from in three wards, we've seen a reduction in length of stay of almost twenty per cent in one ward. Twenty per cent! I am delighted, but Stevie seems to be non-committal. He just replies, '*Good for you. Interesting though... I'll have a think – S.*' I should really remember he has his own business to run and he's helping me out as a mate. I can't expect him to be at my beck and call. But I ring him anyway.

"Hi, Stevie, how's it going?"

"It's going," he replies. "How are you?"

"Well, pretty good. I told you it worked. The three wards we focused on have made a big improvement. What do we do next?"

"Have you spoken to your team?"

"We're getting together after the Monday bed meeting."

"Good. Well, let me know what you come up with."

The way he speaks doesn't exactly feel like he is abandoning me but he does seem preoccupied, so I guess we need to get on with things ourselves. And with some tangible success in the bag we can move forward with more confidence. I'm certainly not taking anything for granted, but things have been going better. We can build on small successes.

And thank heavens Dee's brother Carl is getting better, although he is now on a long and arduous road to recovery that'll be tough on him and his family. He's so lucky to have Dee on his side. I haven't seen her for a couple of weeks but we've spoken a lot on the phone. After the evening when I'd chastised her for making fun of my work colleagues, before finding out that Carl had suffered an overdose, I was terrified that I'd been a bad friend. And the fact that Carl is improving doesn't alter the fact that I'd probably picked the wrong evening to come on all 'Miss Sensible Career Lady'. But Dee, being Dee, has forgiven me.

♦

Charlie's in a good mood. Either that or he's missed breakfast, because he's brought with him a bag of croissants. Jo and Mo are already with me, having returned from the bed meeting together. And that was a historic meeting in itself, because at 9:00am we had enough beds; certainly enough to see us through the morning. But let's not run away with ourselves. A cursory glance at the pile of patient complaints I have yet to deal with tells us that any progress we've made is minute, and can be snuffed out in a second. But I'm determined to seize on the first piece of positive performance I've seen in an age. I won't let this be wasted.

There's no back-slapping, but Charlie opens by saying how impressed he's been by Staulous' wards working on the list and the response from each of the dependent departments, from A&E to radiology and physiotherapy. We've had some frustration coordinating discharges with social services but on the whole we've seen enough to encourage us to persevere. I discover that Staulous had even taken the time to meet with all the clinical support teams before the process began so that they could understand the approach. So far so good, but I'm painfully aware that we need to get on.

"We're close to having a minor triumph on our hands. But if we carry on at this pace it'll be the next millennium before we've implemented successfully across the whole hospital."

Mo reminds me of my clumsy attempt to get things going at the bed meeting a few weeks ago.

"We can't just ask or tell people to do this stuff. They have got to understand it for themselves. Getting people on board isn't down to luck. It's down to how we approach it. Getting an understanding is one thing but it can still be a long road to a change in behaviour."

But time isn't on our side. We need to get everyone, or almost everyone, doing things this new way in a matter of days and weeks, rather than years. I confide in the team that I've decided I want the CEO job after all, and if I don't get big results everywhere within the next few months I don't stand a chance.

Charlie adds a note of caution.

"My only concern is that we've seen progress on the three wards where the other departments have focused. But other wards are saying that these three have been helped at their expense. It's fine to do a small, controlled experiment, but could it work on a bigger scale?"

"I don't know," I say. "But we won't have a chance to find out if we don't get everyone on the bigger scale to go along with us. And the next million-dollar question is: '*How do we do that?*'"

"I'm sure we talked about this before," says Mo, "and Stevie said something about getting everyone in a big room and treating them like adults."

We agree to ring Stevie to find out what he meant by that. As ever, he's available. He explains that his idea involves getting as many as possible of the hospital staff together for half a day, all in the same place. We'd need four video cameras and two giant screens to project on to, as well as a stage in the centre. It sounds like we're about to put on a rock festival, which is clearly disturbing to Charlie, but Stevie says he'll facilitate the whole event. He'll call a few days before to run through it with us, and all we need to do is get five hundred influential people there!

Well, if we're going to do it then we may as well do it properly, and over the next half an hour we formulate a plan to fill a conference room. Getting a date in an individual doctor's diary is almost impossible, so imagine trying to get all of them for half a day within the next six weeks. We decide to plump for a week on Saturday, which means many people coming in when they're not at work. That'll take some doing and we can't use the normal tactics. But first things first: we book the biggest available room at the hotel which is less than a five-minute walk away. It's important to run the event offsite.

We agree on a strategy to get the numbers up. Each of us will personally invite, cajole or pull every trick we know to get ten people in the organisation we believe we must have on board. We must be well organised to ensure we all invite a different ten. Jo volunteers to coordinate this, which is a big relief! Secondly, we agree to tell each of those people that they need to bring five more and without five they won't be allowed in the room. The hook we're going to use is that we're inviting all the people we need to form a group which will help us make the most important decision this hospital has ever faced. Apart from that we'll tell them nothing. If they can't come for personal reasons that's fine, but we'll make it clear that this is a once-only event. Mo suggests we all call a Tweet Up as well, urging our internal Twitter followers to come to the event and to retweet. Charlie volunteers to orchestrate an insidious whispering campaign, a tactic we all agree he will excel at.

The plan on the day is to lay out the room with one boardroom-style table on a raised stage in a prominent position, and five hundred seats all around, no tables, just chairs. We, the executive management team will sit at that table and the five hundred will see everything that happens; every flicker of emotion on our faces and every word we say. The topic will simply be: '*Should we implement the suggested approach across the hospital immediately?*' We're after a '*yes*' or '*no*', and a '*no*' is better than a '*maybe*'.

♦

Stevie comes to the hospital on the Thursday before the day of the event. We all meet in my office, where Charlie tells us he is confident we'll get near to the five hundred figure.

"The word out there is that we're going to talk about cuts and announce a round of job losses. Nobody will want to miss that!"

It was hardly the objective to scare them witless into turning up, but Charlie doesn't see the problem.

"They'll be so relieved that we're not cutting jobs that they'll go along with everything we tell them."

Mo counsels that we don't want to drift too far from the objective of winning hearts and minds, which I heartily agree with, considering my previous failures. Stevie explains how he envisages the morning going.

"In the opening session we'll explain the dilemma we are in with no holds barred. I can talk about the crocodiles and the pot of gold and when we ponder how to approach the cliff face we'll play the dice game."

Ah yes, the dice game. Stevie had asked me to get hold of a hundred dice and thousands of counters. Sam has obtained the dice and counters and drops them on my desk, much to Charlie's amusement.

"I see. We're going to increase revenue by opening an underground staff casino."

Stevie smiles and continues:

"Trust me. This will work. After the game Linda will stand up and explain the proposed direction of solution to everyone. Each one of you will sit within a group and seek out their major reservations. We can then run a discussion to deal with every reservation until we have a positive agreement."

"Simple as that," says Charlie.

"Yes," says Stevie. "It's as simple as that. We don't leave until we have one hundred per cent '*yes*' in the room."

Stevie is pretty clear on this point. But I'm not quite as confident. In less than forty-eight hours I'm going to take the biggest leap of faith in my career so far, in front of five hundred people. Five hundred people who all see me as the face of management in the hospital, and a good proportion of whom think they're about to lose their jobs. This could all come crashing down around me, which I suspect Ashcroft would love. I start to feel my inner panic gathering pace at the thought. How on earth did I get myself into this situation? What am I even doing here as CEO? I wasn't ready for the job. In fact I was completely unprepared. So what do I have to lose? Ashcroft probably thinks I'm crazy anyway so I may as well just go for it. We agree to meet at the hotel on Friday afternoon to have a dress rehearsal.

♦

On Saturday I arrive at the hotel at 8:45am and have to park on the road outside. Promising. It looks as if we might almost get the five hundred we're after, but as I enter the conference room I'm pleasantly surprised.

"Hi, Linda." It's Jo.

"Wow, Jo, how many people are in here?"

"Over five hundred. In fact five hundred and twenty-three at the last count. The rumour mill has worked in our favour. There are a lot of people here who weren't invited, but Twitter's gone mad and Charlie's nudge and wink approach has been effective."

"Told you it would," smiles Charlie. "Is anyone here from Health and Safety?"

"No," says Jo.

"OK."

There are still people coming in. Luckily some of them can stand in the gallery above, but a shiver works its way down my spine as I imagine the newspaper headline if we have any sort of incident: **Healthcare Boss Crushed as Nurses Stampede**. Oh for goodness sake, Linda, get a grip of yourself. This is exactly what we wanted and Jo has done a fantastic job, taking it very seriously as I knew she would.

The place is set out like a bullring with the raised centre stage and she's in the process of getting us all microphoned up. There are two giant screens at either end of the room so everyone will be able to see and hear all that goes on. Well, if this healthcare lark doesn't work out we could always go into event management!

Stevie and his team are here, not three but twenty of them. They have organised ten tables equally spaced around the outside of the room and the dice and counters are set up ready for the exercise. Tim and Sam have prepared a presentation full of fantastic graphics. I've never seen crocodiles with such sharp teeth! Everybody is talking and the noise is incredible. The rumours have reached new heights with some credence attached to the one Charlie seems to have encouraged. I'm tense enough already when I notice Charlie has brought some of his GP colleagues along with a few other folk from the local community hospital and social services. Stevie goes to the main microphone, asks everyone to quieten down, explains he's going to facilitate the event and hands it over to me for the introduction.

Gulp.

The microphone does its customary squeak as I cough nervously. You can hear a pin drop. I thank everyone for coming and then, with Stevie's briefing running through my mind, I begin:

"Our objective is for our hospital to be an ever-flourishing hospital. A hospital that is respected throughout the country for the highest quality of care. A hospital with a solid financial basis, ready and able to invest in research into new clinical practices, invest in its staff, and be the pride and joy of the community in which we sit."

By the looks of incredulity I can see on the faces nearest to me I seem to have taken them by surprise, so I continue:

"To achieve this we need to dramatically enhance both the quality and the timeliness of care. And from where I'm sitting it looks like we'll never do this without more resources. When I walk around the hospital I don't see many people standing around with nothing to do."

And that does the trick. There is a spontaneous cheer from much of the crowd. So I feel able to present the dilemma.

"But we also have to be financially viable. For the last few years we have made a loss and it is almost like we have come to expect it. These days are over. We have to breakeven as a first step. That is just the start if we are to flourish; we have to be profitable to reinvest. Currently, the only way to break even is to reduce our operating expenses."

And that draws the first note of malcontent as a chap standing behind the nearest table asks if the present throng includes the first to be made redundant.

"No, that's not the plan. I have asked you here to help me make a decision as to whether or not we can find an alternative. I want you to help me make a decision on behalf of the whole hospital. Over the past month we have tested a new approach and today I want to check out whether our proposal is, as we hope, a way of simultaneously improving the quality of care for all our patients and puts us on a road to financial stability."

I then share the grim reality of our performance against operational targets and our financial position, and I remind everyone of the recent clinical failings. We need to discuss this and I don't believe we should wait for any decision about a new chief executive. We need to discuss it now.

I'm pleased to see people nodding and it looks like I have the first signs of a shared understanding of the difficulties we're in. Admittedly, a lot of our people have been beaten into submission by the relentless tide of recent years, but there remains strength of spirit, and as I explain the new approach I read the positive vibe as some recognition that this is a different approach, a fresh way of tackling the issues we face from day to day.

At this point I introduce Stevie as the facilitator of the morning, and he in turn introduces Tim and Sam, who open their presentation with a brilliantly bloodthirsty graphic of the crocodile, pot of gold, mermaid and crutches. If there was any doubt at all that we are breaking new ground in our efforts to solve our problems, that has dissipated it. As they begin the analysis that we completed over a month ago, I look around the room and they have the undivided attention of everyone present, many wide-eyed. All the way through Stevie takes on a role of interviewer, stopping them to ensure the audience has truly understood the implications for quality and timeliness of care, financial and human relationships. With some brutality he hammers home the fact that the less than harmonious relationships we've all lived with over recent years are caused by one core problem. And as Tim and Sam close he makes the hypothesis clear. The only way we can alter the devastating situation where medical costs are rising faster than revenues is by finding a dramatic improvement in patient flow across the whole system. On this cue his team leaps into action to prepare the tables and Stevie explains what's going to happen.

"Ladies and gentlemen, around the room you will see ten teams of ten people. The teams will each represent a stream of care within the hospital. There is Medicine, there is Paediatrics, there is Orthopaedics, General Surgery and so on. The relevant doctors, nurses and managers for each department are sitting at each table. The first point to remember is that each table represents the flow of dependent events that a patient needs to go through in the hospital. Every team member has a die, and on my call will throw the die. The resultant number on the die represents that individual's performance on any one day, in other words how many patients they have successfully treated. The second thing to note is that there are already patients in the system and these lucky people are represented by the four counters sitting between each member of staff."

As Stevie speaks there is a murmur of excitement as the competitive members of each team, either watching or playing, realise that they're about to be in a race. And some are even looking around their table to see whether they're happy with the make-up of their team. Stevie explains that on his count everyone in the ten teams will throw their dice simultaneously. Each person will then move the corresponding number of patients through to the next step of the system. If they throw a six but there are only three patients in front of them, they can only move the three on. That would mean they are having a great day but the person before them is having a bad day. The performance of the team will be determined by how many patients are discharged out of the end of the team at the end of each throw. Everyone else gathered around the table is to observe, and provide whatever motivation they can for their team to outperform the other nine.

At this point a round of applause spreads across the room and a few shouts of '*come on!*'. And when Stevie signals for all to make throw number one, the place erupts. This makes me smile. It's a while since I've seen so much unbridled energy in these people.

As the rattles of the dice are drowned out by cheers and groans, Stevie's team is ensuring everyone follows the rules and they each signal to Sam and Tim how many patients have been discharged at the end of the process. The results are then instantly displayed on the screens at either end of the room. Throw number two heralds more cheers, more '*ooh*'s, more '*boo*'s and more laughter. After throw number three, Cooper's team is already lagging far behind and someone has just thrown two ones on the trot, much to Cooper's disgust. Paediatrics are in the lead and looking smug. But not for long as they only discharge one patient on throw number four.

Back on Cooper's table, the look of determination on his face is priceless. If he didn't have high blood pressure before, he has now. He's willing his team to throw better. Willing is not really the word. He is screaming at them to throw better before he himself throws a one. At the end of the throw for day five Staulous' team has come from nowhere with an outstanding day. Even though the scores are instantaneously updated on the big screens, some of the observers are moving around the room to see what and how their competitors are doing. How on earth is that chap on the A&E team throwing five or six every time? Incredibly, a small group of supporters from other tables are watching him intently and urging him to fail. On throw number six he throws a five again but around the room on the other tables fingers are pointing, largely in the direction of the hapless players who have a backlog of patients building up.

At this point, amid increasing banter and in some cases accusation, Stevie stops the game for a moment and asks everyone to notice the variation in performance across the ten teams. In fact the only thing that *is* noticed is who the winners and losers are at this stage. Somebody shouts '*I told you it was all Cooper's fault. Those surgeons are always drinking coffee!*', which prompts the loudest cheer of the day, and a hilarious scowl on Cooper's face. Stevie walks over to Cooper, puts his hands firmly on his shoulders and says:

"I'm from management and I'm here to help!"

The laughter subsides and Stevie continues.

"It seems to me that your recent performance is quite frankly poor but I think I have a solution." Cue more laughter. "I've been on a management course and learned to assume that it might not entirely be your fault! Maybe the equipment you are using is the reason you are performing so badly. So I've bought you a new, special machine."

He motions to Tam, who brings across a die which is ten times bigger than the previous one. Even Cooper laughs now.

After the throw for day ten the scores appear on the screens again while Stevie's team quickly counts the number of patients that are now waiting in the system. It's noticeable that some people have very few patients in front of them and other people have a pile. The numbers of patients stuck in the system for each team appear on the screens. Keeping to the script, Stevie walks up to John and asks how we are doing against target. John, seizing his opportunity to impress the local amateur dramatics enthusiasts, of which the hospital boasts a good few, plays his part.

"Hmm, according to my calculations each person with one die is capable of treating, on average, three point five patients per day. With the use of our new patient administration system I can calculate that after ten days we should have discharged thirty-five patients from each team." He frowns, overacting spectacularly and seemingly forgetting that his face is on both of the large screens. "Disappointingly, none of the teams is on target. If it carries on like this the only option is to realign resources with output. Furthermore, our revenues are lower than expected and our running costs are not in line with the lower revenues. Heads will have to roll."

The crowd, clearly enchanted by John's pantomime display, boos. Stevie pretends to draw a sword from his side and, without John realising, he stands behind him and motions to slice our FD's head off, prompting a huge, if slightly unkind, cheer and several shouts of '*he's behind you!*'.

Calm restored, Stevie signals for the throws to recommence. After fifteen throws Cooper's team is still struggling and so Stevie reaches into his bag to hand Cooper an even bigger foam die, the size of a football! As Cooper grimaces, Stevie walks over to the table headed by Staulous and picks on the matron who is struggling with a major backlog of patients in front of her. He says:

"Let's try a different tactic this time. Maybe it's not the die that's the problem, maybe it's you. Let's swap you with someone else."

He picks on someone from the crowd who happens to be one of the junior nurses who works for the matron. As the matron gets up she kindly says:

"I always thought you'd make it to the top. Let's see if you can do a better job than me."

As throws nineteen and twenty pass, the cheering from the various parts of the room gets louder and louder and it takes almost five minutes before everyone stops talking and a winner is announced. Stevie beams.

"Congratulations to Elderly Care, who have come from nowhere to cross the line first. They have managed to treat fifty-eight patients in twenty throws."

Cooper's team has recovered to come in second. He's an ex rugby player and hates losing but it looks like he's relieved to have climbed up the table and, more importantly, to have beaten Staulous. He celebrates by throwing the foam die at his defeated colleague.

Stevie lets the room calm down again before asking the five hundred plus present, every one of whom is now hanging on every word, to have a good look at what has happened. On average, each person has the capacity to treat seventy patients: twenty throws with an average capacity of three and a half per throw. The very best team has managed fifty-eight and some have not even made it into the fifties. And if we look at the number of patients now in the system, not only is it more than when we started, it is more than after ten throws. It is increasing with every throw. Logically, if we look at how long it would take for a new patient to go through the system, now the queues are higher it would take much longer. We started with thirty-six counters in the system on each table (ten steps in the pathway so nine gaps each with four patients), and in one instance there are now nearly seventy counters in the system. The total time for a patient to go through the system, or their length of stay, would be nearly double. Stevie explains that in reality some patients may hang around significantly longer, as each counter which was worked on by each player was just a matter of choice from the pile in front of them.

I'm mightily impressed by how Stevie has run the morning. We had the apprehension and intrigue, followed by the action and fun, and he's engaged the audience for us now to be able to have a vital and transparent discussion with over five hundred people. Amazing. He continues as if he was one of us.

"I hope this exercise has helped us all to review our understanding of the way these seemingly complex systems operate. We have the capacity to treat seventy patients and yet we have not achieved this. But, more importantly, if we are going to ensure a change in understanding results in a change in our behaviour, I would like to summarise the implications of this exercise on how we ensure a rapid improvement becomes a reality.

"From this exercise we can all see that increasing the flow through the chain of activities in the hospital is a primary objective for us all. However, this must be translated into a practical mechanism that can guide us all every day. I hope this exercise has brought home to you the absolute futility of maximising the local efficiency of each step in the chain; my attempts to exhort Mr Cooper to work harder were futile. I stress this point because I want to be clear how important it is to abolish local efficiency measures if we are going to achieve real improvement across the whole hospital.

"Moreover, Linda has asked you all here to help her decide if the approach I am about to explain will help achieve this, and rapidly. Are you ready to consider this?"

There is a resounding '*YES!*'

"If we are going to improve patient flow through the hospital there are two things we must do. Firstly, we need a patient-centred priority system that everyone can trust and everyone follows; an approach which takes account of changing recovery rates for each and every patient. More importantly, the approach must help us identify which resource is most often causing the most disruption to the flow of the most patients. The game we played today was a big enough trial for many of us and showed how the delay accumulates, but imagine if, rather than working as ten independent teams, there were some resources that you shared across teams. There would be people who had to run from team to team each and every day. Imagine how everybody would be screaming and shouting at those resources to treat their patients next. That is exactly what is happening in your hospital every day."

A woman from radiology stands up and shouts across the room.

"You know what my life is like all day every day. It's ridiculous. I'm expected to scan many patients from many different streams at once and it's just a matter of who screams the loudest."

Then the head of physio speaks up.

"I know exactly what you mean. We're supposed to provide our services across all the patients as well."

Mo, who has waited his turn, asks Stevie a question.

"As I walked around the room I noticed that in almost every case there is a large queue between the first and the second step in the process. Why is that?"

Mo has no ambition to enter the dark world of amateur dramatics but Stevie builds his role.

"Mo, what is your job in this hospital?"

"I'm the clinical director responsible for our A&E department. We're the famous group of reprobates who can't hit a four-hour target."

"But your situation is much worse than we see in this game, isn't it? You can't just push patients out of A&E and let them wait in an ever increasing pile somewhere else. They stay with you. For you to hit your four-hour target you need other departments to be keeping up with the pace."

I can see Cooper nodding. He knows what Stevie is getting at. Moving a patient from A&E through the hospital is everyone's responsibility. Every patient is everyone's responsibility. The Hippocratic oath may be in the past, but it's still in Cooper's blood. And he isn't alone. So Stevie seizes the initiative.

"Linda told you her dream for this to be an ever-flourishing hospital that you can have pride and joy in. One that is successful. One that is growing. So let's have a show of hands? Who in this room agrees with Linda's dream? Who thinks this is worth going for?"

I steel myself, briefly looking at my shoes before I look up to see slowly but surely more and more hands go up. Soon enough everyone in the room, even the usually reserved John, has their hand up. Stevie smiles.

"Well, we'd better find a way then. But if we find a way that we agree on, then each and every one of you must do what it takes to implement it across the hospital immediately."

◆

As a practised presenter, Stevie manages to communicate the full details of the proposed approach to a room of over five hundred: the same message and starting strategy that he spoke to us about all those weeks ago. People are listening very carefully. He talks about the criteria against which he wants everyone to judge and invites any others, at which point one of Charlie's GP guests speaks up:

"We need a solution across the whole system, not just the hospital. Everything you have talked about is also happening in our community hospitals, our mental health services and in my own surgery."

One of my guests from the mental health service, who only came to support me, not really knowing what the event was, confirms that everything we have talked about today is happening in his environment, and almost every patient requires the co-ordinated efforts of numerous stakeholders. These stakeholders don't even work for the same organisations. A decision about one patient's next step can easily involve ten different groups of people. I remember Stevie's assertion that the apparent complexity of the hospital made it more likely that people had focused on improving the part they were responsible for. As a result, the more likely it is that local optimisation and distortion exist. This makes the potential for improvement greater, and I wonder about the size of the scope there.

Once Stevie has explained the proposed approach he adds that if the approach is going to be patient-centred then it must be doctor-led. There is no choice. Without every doctor taking the responsibility for ensuring the planned discharge dates and that the sequence is followed all day every day, the size of the prize will be considerably diminished. He lays down the challenge.

"Ladies and gentlemen, if you're not prepared to take the lead on this, then say '*no*'."

Then he suggests a decision of this magnitude is best made over a cup of tea. We have a thirty-minute break, during which every one of the management team is out talking to anyone they can, trying to work out if the vibe is as positive as it has felt so far. Stevie smiles at me, which makes me think he is confident that we're near to a resolution. I feel like a parliamentary candidate on election night as the returning officer says: '*Monster Raving Loony Party… 9742 votes!*' At least I'm not at risk of the humiliation of losing my deposit, but if we've misread the situation I could lose a lot more than that.

Once everyone has returned to the hall there is a hush as I get to my feet, searching for some inspiration.

"Whatever we do, whatever we decide, this is our hospital. Whatever we do, we do it together. Nobody can do this on their own, so we need an agreement. We need a '*yes*' or a '*no*', not a '*maybe*'."

A guy towards the back of the hall puts his hand up. I look at Stevie and he nods before gesturing to Tam to take a microphone to the man, and she asks him to introduce himself. He nervously takes the microphone and says:

"My name is Matt. I've been a porter at the hospital for over thirty years and this is the first time I've seen a Chief Executive, never mind been spoken to by one. Before we played the game, all the things you and these people said about the mess the hospital is in is right. The reality is that it's actually much worse. My answer is '*yes*'. It has to be. How on earth can any of us say '*no*'?"

You can hear the wobble in his voice. After a short moment he continues:

"Look, I retire from this job in six months and I want to retire on a high. I want to be proud of where I've worked. Whatever it takes, I'm in."

"Thank you, Matt. I promise you I'll give it my best shot."

Then a young lady on the other side of the room puts her hand up and Tam quickly walks over with the microphone.

"I've only been in this hospital for less than a year. I have my whole career ahead of me and I promise you I love my job. I love being a nurse; it's all I've ever wanted to be. But after a year I've been ready to give up. Working in this hospital has sometimes been a nightmare. I know nothing about running a hospital but even I can see that what we're doing now can't be right."

Stevie asks her what she thinks we should do, and she pauses for a moment before answering.

"I don't know if what you've said and done today is anything special. I've never seen a game like that, but what you've said seems to be common sense. I don't really care what everyone else says today. This is how I'm going to do my job tomorrow."

Mr Cooper stands up next.

"I think it's a daft idea. It'll never work!"

I look anxiously across at Stevie before Cooper continues.

"Only joking!"

Thanks!

Then he says:

"Linda. Thank you very much for showing us all such courage. This is the first time I have ever seen doctors and managers unified on an approach. We're going to do this."

Stevie has heard enough to conclude.

"OK, folks. We've heard from a tiny sample. But we could go on all day. It's time to make your call. Does anyone disagree with Matt?"

Instantly there's a loud roar of '*NO!*'.

And this is a seminal moment. The honesty and straight-talking at the start of the day took some by surprise. The dice game was fun, really got the message over and lifted the whole atmosphere. And the three who have already made their vote tugged at everyone else. But this wasn't just about smart communication. To get that response from over five hundred people, the vast majority of whom felt battle-weary and devoid of hope, is amazing. We've tapped into a real desire in everyone here to make the change. The pride has never been completely extinguished. All we need to do now is to find the joy. I feel like we have a resolution and announce:

"OK, now we're all in agreement we're safe to speed up the pace across the whole hospital."

◆

The buzz of anticipation hasn't died down as the final hour of the morning is spent agreeing the first steps, and the communication process for the rest of the staff. That will be led through informal discussions and rolling out the dice game to every member of staff as quickly as we can. But we already have a critical mass, and with total commitment from the first five hundred we have a real chance. Tim and Tam explain to everyone how they're going to start to implement the proposed approach in A&E, the assessment unit and on all the wards.

Stevie is talking to a group of visitors from the community hospitals and mental health when Charlie and Jo come up to me. Jo gives me a big hug and Charlie's excited.

"That was amazing. And hey, I've been talking to one of Stevie's boffins and they've given me a link to play the dice game. Look, it's *www.the-dice-game.com*. A bottle of Bordeaux, a packet of pistachio nuts and the laptop. I have a wonderful evening in store for my lady wife."

Jo laughs.

"Well, Linda, I think we all deserve a pat on the back!"

"I think you deserve more than that. You organised the whole thing. Thank you so much."

"That's kind of you." She turns to Charlie: "OK then, I'll have a cup of tea."

Chapter Ten

Looking in the mirror

Three weeks have passed and I'm sat in my office on a Friday evening with Mo. Cath pops her head round my door to wish me a good weekend and tells me that Stevie has arrived. I can't believe we're doing this. The only time Stevie could meet up with us was at the weekend and so we agreed to start with a briefing of our progress so far on the Friday evening. And we have some good news to report. We have concerns with the assessment unit but some huge success on the wards, and Mo believes he's halfway towards solving the problem in A&E: Sam created a list that simply gives everyone in A&E the remaining duration to a breach and we have this up on screen all day long. We then have a navigator in place on every shift to ensure we follow the list in sequence, but always allowing for clinically urgent cases. The patient closest to breaching is at the top of the list. This has had a great impact. Sam also got the software guys to change the colour of the patient's name to amber at one hour twenty minutes, to red at two hours forty, and black at four hours.

During the first week every time someone went from red to black we recorded the outstanding task and resource responsible for completing the task. In the second week we did the same every time someone went from the amber to the red zone. It soon became clear we had three key issues to address. The first was where we'd successfully assessed a patient and made a decision to admit them well within the four hours but there was no bed available. The second group had patients who were not going to be admitted but still breached. This became much worse when we had more patients in the first category: the more waiting for beds, the more the department became blocked up. The third category was a very small group of patients where it was clinically impossible to carry out the diagnosis within the breach time.

Once we realised this, the navigator focused on ensuring the tasks and resources causing the most delay were notified early and regularly escalated. And we came up with some innovative tricks to keep the process moving smoothly. Rather than waiting for a batch of tests, we sent individual tests immediately; and equally, the same results were returned patient by patient. These improvements have enabled us to greatly reduce the numbers of breaches in the second group. And for the first group we're actually requesting a bed as early as possible within the four-hour process. This was a little counter-intuitive as it meant the number of beds required initially grew, but we realised that the earlier we knew, the more time we had to react. We not only notified the bed team but also the assessment unit and in some instances the appropriate ward so they were aware of their impact on the four-hour target as well. Another trick was to put one of our top consultants at the very front of the process. Mo took the lead on this and acted as the first point of reference for all patients in A&E. Consequently there was a good number he sent home without any further treatment. He'd reduced the second group by about two thirds, but there remained some breaches when the department was overflowing. Mo has concluded that unless we find an answer for the first group he'll never hit ninety-five per cent. This is exactly what the dice game had shown back at the hotel.

The assessment unit was proving to be trickier. We quickly discovered it was used as a temporary ward where some patients' lengths of stay were close to the average length of stay across the whole hospital. I'd phoned Stevie about this while he was in China – not realising the local time was 3:00am – and I received short shrift!

So in the absence of my mentor I asked for piles of data about our assessment unit and received about two kilos worth! When I started looking through it all it was just bewildering. The team had sent over a hundred graphs and I was searching for the needle in this haystack. After many hours I formed an analysis which I want Stevie to look at now to see if I'm on the right lines.

♦

"I have a gift for you." Stevie smiles, sits down and hands me a small box. I open it to find a tiny, smiling pottery Buddha.

"So you think I need to search for inner calm?"

"No. It's just to remind you that if you make a mess of this you may come back as a slug."

Mo smiles as he shakes Stevie's hand. We all note it's 7:00pm and resolve to make a productive start, with the secondary aim of grabbing supper somewhere before 10:00pm. So I start my analysis with A&E. I hand Stevie a graph that shows we've missed our target on days with both low and high volumes of attendances.

"So there is no evidence that the issue is just volume related," he observes.

"If there was then we'd have a clear explanation."

I push another graph in front of Stevie which shows the hourly variation in the arrivals at A&E from midnight onwards. The numbers are low at first but then it shoots up rapidly through to mid morning and stays at a peak for most of the day to about 8:00pm where it starts to drop off again. On some days there is a spike after 11:00pm, when most of the pubs shut. The next graph I present shows the outcome of visits to A&E. Roughly eighty per cent go home and twenty per cent are admitted. The interesting point is that of the hundred and twenty that are admitted about one third of them breach the four-hour target. But this doesn't tell me whether they breached because it took longer than four hours to see the patient in A&E, or whether the process had been completed within the four hours and then they hung around waiting for a bed to be admitted into the rest of the hospital. Stevie nods his agreement so far, so I carry on.

The next step for most of these patients is to be admitted to the assessment unit for further diagnosis. At least this is what is supposed to happen but in many instances the AU is full and so a fight starts to find any bed the patient can be placed into. It could be any bed in any ward. If the patient waits longer than twelve hours in A&E all hell breaks loose as we have a real incident to report. So as time ticks by any bed will do. I tried to find out the split between patients admitted to the AU and directly to the ward but this wasn't easy. I could find out how many were admitted to AU and therefore estimate the number going direct to the ward, but this doesn't tell me how many patients were missing the AU stage as for some patients, such as stroke where diagnosis is obvious, it's appropriate to go straight to the ward. I present another graph.

"I think you'll find this one interesting. Remember we typically have one hundred and twenty admissions a day with little variation. Look at this."

The graph shows AU admissions averaging thirty-five but on some days it's as low as five and other days more than ten times this! It could actually mean that the volume of patients who do not need an assessment through the AU and go direct to the ward also varies by this amount, but I doubt it.

"You must have some more graphs you want to show me," says Stevie.

So I oblige and hand him two more. One shows the length of stay in the AU and the other the occupancy. The length of stay is like a yo-yo. Many of the patients stay just about one day, but sometimes it goes up to three, four or five days, and one poor patient spent six days in AU. How come? And occupancy is bouncing around one hundred per cent, with periods of no admissions for over twenty-four hours.

"I suspect when the assessment unit fills up everyone goes directly to the ward," says Stevie.

"Exactly. And this is when the fights start. Do we give the next free bed to someone in A&E who is about to breach, or the patient in AU waiting for a bed on that ward? The targets dictate that our bed manager will always go for the A&E patient to save the breach."

Stevie raises his eyebrows.

"And I suspect the story doesn't stop here. What happens to the patients that went straight from A&E into the hospital without going through the AU? Presumably some of them go to the wrong ward. Is this why the doctors complain about their safari ward rounds?"

That was exactly my own train of thoughts. And this is where it gets horrible. I have discovered that length of stay of patients admitted to the wrong ward is considerably longer than if they'd been sent to the correct ward. On a bad day many patients who should have been assessed in the AU go direct to any ward, and inevitably end up as outliers. Being an outlier can add forty per cent to length of stay. It's a nightmare. We end up in a massive negative loop. Over the subsequent days bed availability becomes tighter and tighter and the effect accumulates. The system-wide impact of the lack of bed availability in the AU is now clear for all to see.

"You have done well, Grasshopper," says Stevie, still clearly immersed in the Far East. "When we were on the MBA you always made me do the analysis and you wrote the report. How times have changed."

"Thank you, Master," I indulge him. "We need a bigger AU. It seems to me this is not just another battle between the need to improve quality of care and finances, but it's at the heart of the war. But how big should our assessment unit be?"

"Tell me how paranoid you are and I will tell you about how big the AU should be," he replies. Then he offers some guidance.

"I presume some of the patients going directly to a ward are assessed and a proportion of these went home relatively quickly. Look at the length-of-stay spread of the ward. There's a very interesting bi-modal distribution with about half of the patients admitted being discharged within two days."

A light comes on. I'd always seen this as a positive but now I realise these are probably patients who should have gone through the AU but couldn't when it was full. If they had gone on the AU they would almost certainly have been out within a day.

"So the dilemma is clear," says Stevie. "On the one hand we need a bigger AU, but increasing capacity in one of the most expensive steps in the whole system is not going to be easy."

"So what do we do?"

"The way I see it, the AU has two distinctive functions. Firstly, the vital role of clinical assessment of patients to decide if they need an admission, but equally it has a logistical purpose which is central to the flow of patients, not just through the whole hospital but probably across the whole health system. We must ensure we have enough protective capacity at this step in the system. This is not excess capacity, as its role is to provide a logistical sponge between A&E and the rest of the system. We need to ensure we have enough protective capacity but we must not be paranoid. In the theory I have been talking to you about we use the concept of a variable space-time buffer to address this."

Mo has been listening intently and now decides to speak up.

"Looking at these graphs, there is a fundamental difference between the speed and time with which beds are required throughout the day for patients being admitted, and the speed and timing within the day of patients being discharged from the wards."

"That's right," says Stevie. "The logistical purpose of the assessment unit is to provide a successful mechanism for coupling these two links of the chain together."

He goes on to explain. While there is relatively little variation in the daily demand for beds, there is great variation in the mix of patients. On one day there can be a demand for many similar beds but on another day the demand can be for many different types of beds. This means that without this protective capacity the only way we could guarantee bed availability for every different type on every different ward would be to hold enough protective capacity at each ward to cope with the maximum potential demand on that ward. But from a logistical perspective, the AU aggregates the variation in demand of all of the different patient requirements. So in total there is much less overall capacity required. This logistical function is vital, and when it's too small you'll have to carry protective capacity on each and every ward, which, as we already know, increases operating expenses and inevitably results in some wards on any one day having too few beds/staff and others too many.

"So saving a few beds in the assessment unit is costing us many more in the rest of the hospital," says Mo.

This also shows up the fruitless endeavours to solve our problem in the past by pushing to increase the number of pre-11:00am discharges using a cavalcade of supporting measures. The efforts required to create the right bed on the right ward through ensuring 'pre-eleven o'clock' discharges everywhere are enormous relative to ensuring one hundred per cent bed availability in the AU.

"But how do we calculate the number we need in the AU?" I ask.

Stevie says there is a mathematically correct answer, but suffice to say that if we do establish the correct size of the AU, it will free up a lot of capacity elsewhere, with a positive impact on quality of care, not to mention improved patient flow and less fluctuation in the demand for resources at the ward level.

147

◆

As we help ourselves to a coffee I tell Stevie of our results on the wards. Using the software provided by his team we've been able to create a planned discharge date for each admission, monitor it daily, escalate outstanding tasks, and resolve causes of delay. It hasn't been easy to implement but it has been simple to follow. The results vary across the wards as some are further down the track than others, but overall so far the number of daily discharges has increased by six per cent and both the length of stay and delayed days have come down in line. While six per cent is good, it's not been good enough to resolve the bed availability issues. The wards we started with have already averaged over fifteen per cent reduction in length of stay and some more than twenty.

"If we look at one of the surgery wards, how long did this take to happen?" asks Stevie.

"Three weeks."

"Has the financial throughput in surgery also gone up by six per cent? Everyone, please remember financial throughput is defined as revenue minus totally variable costs."

I look for the figures that John has prepared.

"Erm… no… it's actually gone up by nine per cent." Mo and I both smile.

"So how has your financial throughput increased by fifty per cent more than your discharges?"

Suddenly it feels like I'm back at school in one of those moments where you give the teacher an answer you're happy with, only to find there was another question that you completely missed. I feel like an idiot that I hadn't questioned this disparity, but Mo jumps to my rescue.

"I think I might know, Stevie. You've met Mr Cooper, our head of surgery. If you give him one sniff of a chance to increase volumes and reduce the backlog, he'll go for it. Before you arrived Linda and I were looking at the figures John prepared. He's followed your model of identifying the financial throughput per patient, but taken it a step further by comparing the financial throughput per bed day of the extra patients treated with the hospital's average. The extra patients do have a considerably higher financial throughput per bed day. Mr Cooper may not be an accountant but he is very quick at spotting a money-making opportunity."

John has provided this calculation across many different patient types, illustrating a variation between £200 per bed day for some patients and up to £1000 per bed day for others. Stevie looks uncharacteristically shocked.

"Do you have any idea of the implications of these figures? I can hardly believe it myself. It looks like I have grossly misrepresented the opportunity that exists for your hospital. Remind me, Linda, what is your current revenue?"

"Four hundred million."

"And how much are you going to lose this year?"

"Fifteen."

Stevie taps his pencil on his forehead for a moment. I can see his mind whirring. And I think I'm keeping up! We can produce extra capacity by reducing length of stay, and if we firstly hit all our targets and reduce the backlogs we can then use this capacity to not only meet all the current demand we have, but grow our revenue in a targeted way. We should grow where we can demonstrate real, high-quality clinical excellence, and be more conscious of the financial throughput per bed day. I'm right, but Stevie throws something else into the mix.

"You should also look at unfulfilled market demand, and please don't just consider your local market. Look for clinical areas where you can become a national centre of excellence."

Whoah! *A national centre of excellence*! I know we've already come a long way but my first target was to stay out of prison, then stay in a job. But hey, let's aim high. Stevie's talking about turning some of the precious reductions of length of stay into an opportunity to simultaneously transform the clinical and financial performance of this hospital. Can you imagine that? I'm bought in.

"How do we become a centre of excellence?"

"Two things," says Stevie. "We must find a solution to the assessment unit issue and we must also find a way of resolving the ongoing remaining breaches in performance. Can you ask John to redo the numbers for us to show what happens if we reduce length of stay by ten and twenty per cent across the hospital and use this capacity to firstly ensure one hundred per cent bed availability in the assessment unit, then eliminate the backlog and then start to use this free capacity to grow revenues? John will know that with this extra work there will be extra totally variable costs, but the increase in operating expenses will be minimal. Do you think he can have this ready for a discussion on Sunday morning?"

"Consider it done."

Stevie is right. Somehow we need to find an approach that will be welcomed by all. And we want to maintain the momentum of change that emerged on the day of the dice game, so we mustn't pursue an unpopular route. We need to get the most out of this weekend. So I ask Stevie for his guidance on how to ensure we really get to the bottom of the weekend problems. He replies:

"OK, but allow me to delve into this topic in a little more detail. It sounds so straightforward to ask the question '*What is the problem?*' but first I would like to get agreement on the definition of the word 'problem.'"

I know Stevie well enough to realise this is not just a theoretical exercise. He is also keen to ensure we are successful in our weekend endeavours and so I give him the nod to continue.

"Let's start by suggesting that a problem is only a problem when we don't know what to do about it. If we have a solution or a direction of solution then it is only a matter of obstacles to implementation slowing us down."

"That makes sense," I say, "but it sounds just like my maths teacher who told me not to bother to do the questions I could do and only do the ones I couldn't."

"You had a good maths teacher. But my starting point is that a characteristic of a problem is something that won't go away and is stopping us achieving our objective. Our job is to identify the core problem: one which is directly responsible for all, or almost all, of the undesirable outcomes in the field of our investigation and which without resolution will block us from achieving our goal."

"So how do we go about firstly finding, then articulating and finally resolving one of these core problems?" Even as I say it I notice my mistake and quickly add, "The core problem."

"Our starting point will be to identify what I am going to call long-running undesirable effects, UDEs. These begin to help us articulate the core problem. For instance, you have already explained there are many patients who could be discharged home over the weekend and who are not discharged until Monday at the earliest. We need to check if this is a long-running effect. In other words, did it just occur last weekend or is it a common outcome of almost every weekend? Is the number of patients who could go home and do not go home significant? Is this undesirable for the patient and for the hospital? These questions will help us determine if this is a significant and long-running undesirable effect."

Mo speaks:

"This has been going on for as long as I have been here and it seems to be getting worse. It is clearly undesirable for the patient and also for us."

"OK, so we have our first undesirable effect."

Mo is on a roll:

"I can give you a whole load more if you like. For example, mortality rates are higher at the weekend."

"Actually, no. We only need one to start the next phase of our analysis, which is to try to understand why good people who have been trying hard have not managed to resolve it. Mo, what action do you believe would resolve this UDE. Forget whether it is achievable or not: what simple action is required?"

"We just need more resources. For example, more decision-making doctors at weekends. It is as simple as that. If we had the same cover at the weekends as during the week we would achieve the same number of discharges and keep the hospital flowing."

"So what you are telling me is that in order to keep the hospital flowing through the weekend we need more doctors working weekends with the appropriate staff to support them and act on their decisions."

"Yes I am, but it is not that simple."

Stevie is very fast to interject.

"Mo, I absolutely agree. Can you tell us what would be put at risk by simply increasing the numbers of doctors and appropriate support staff at the weekend?"

"Well, the first thing is John's blood pressure. We all know this is just not affordable and would potentially cause a riot among staff if you asked them to do it on top of everything else."

Stevie walks over to the flip chart and asks us to check if he has understood correctly.

"So, my understanding is that we are here this weekend to see what it would take to improve the performance of the hospital at the weekends. Now, on the one hand, in order to achieve this you are clear we need to ensure a substantial improvement in patient flow at the weekend, and the action required to achieve this is to increase expenditure on resources at the weekend."

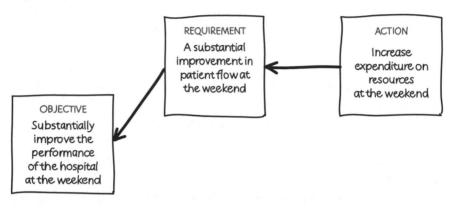

Mo confirms and Stevie continues:

"And yet, in order to improve the performance of the hospital at the weekend, we must also accept this includes the financial performance, and based on your current position there is still the need to curtail, if not reduce, further expenditure on resources at the weekend. To achieve this we must not increase staffing costs at the weekend. The reality is we should cut them even further."

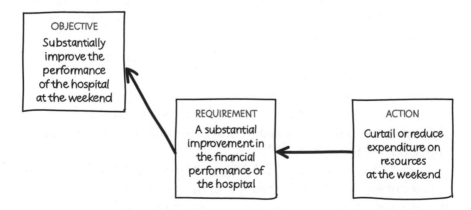

Stevie pauses for a moment and then adds one final arrow to the diagram and looks at me.

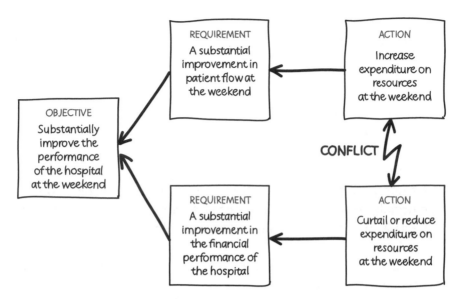

"Can you see how we have turned the long-running unresolved undesirable effect into a true problem statement: one which enables us now to explain why even with the efforts of great people this has not been resolved? This is a dilemma.

"It seems we are stuck between a rock and a hard place. On the one hand there is a clear requirement to add more staff at the weekend and on the other there is an equally valid requirement to reduce staff at the weekend. This is an example of a problem, a seemingly unsolvable dilemma. It is not a matter of choice; it is not a matter of one opinion winning over the other."

I think I get this now.

"We have been fiddling around trying to find a tolerable compromise, but how do I know it's my core problem?"

"I didn't say it was your core problem," comes the reply, "just an example of a problem. We will only be able to confirm we have understood the core problem when we can demonstrate that the unresolved dilemma is responsible for all, or almost all, of the undesirable effects we see over the weekend."

Mo is clearly on board and wants to push this further, but Stevie asks for everyone's patience for a little longer.

"I am sure you all have suggestions for how we could overcome this particular dilemma. But before we attempt to I want to explain another important step in the process of finding an agreeable solution."

I sense the mood to move to solution creation but also that Stevie is going to hold us back until we have understood and agreed on his next step.

"What I want to do is define the criteria against which any solution should be judged. Some of these are now obvious to us. Any solution must simultaneously help us achieve the overall objective of a more productive weekend, in terms of substantially improving the flow of patients at the weekends without increasing the overall resource budget. But as Mo knows, this should be done in a way that does not threaten but hopefully enhances quality of care, as well as the broader working conditions of our staff. Adding these last two criteria is important to avoid half-baked solutions."

Mo agrees:

"Exactly. We need a solution that does not simply demand everyone works harder."

"So, does anyone have any further criteria?"

After a silent pause Stevie continues.

"Let's start to look at it together. Firstly, there is no need for us to challenge the objective and the requirements. The dilemma only exists because of the conflicting actions. This means we should focus our attention on the assumptions under the following three statements."

Stevie goes back to the flip chart and rewrites each of them.

To ensure a substantial improvement in patient flow at the weekend we MUST increase expenditure on resources at the weekend.

To have a substantial improvement in the financial performance of the hospital, we MUST curtail or reduce expenditure on resources at the weekend.

Increasing expenditure on resources at the weekend is in direct conflict with curtailing or reducing expenditure on resources at the weekend.

He continues:

"Now comes the fun part. We have to try to challenge the assumptions upon which these statements are based and see if we can find a new way forward that meets all the criteria we have developed.

"My suggestion is that we can start to do this by attending each of the key management and clinical meetings that happen throughout the weekend and keep our eyes and ears open."

Mo adds that in the first instance we could focus on what is happening in the assessment unit. This is a good plan. If the AU functions effectively over the weekend and is able to ensure no patient is waiting for a bed from A&E, and if a patient never stays in the AU longer than is necessary to complete the assessment, then we will know this pivotal point of the whole system is functioning well. It will also be an excellent place for us to identify at the weekend which ward most often puts the most patient admissions at risk, because if we can't place a patient in AU it's likely the reason is because we couldn't discharge another patient directly home or to a specific ward.

It seems to me that if we're going to find a resolution to this situation we're going to have to take very seriously the question of which resource or lack of resource, or policy, or behaviour is most often causing the most delay across the most patients across the weekend.

In some ways, undertaking this analysis at the weekend will be much simpler than trying to do it during the week. I have a hunch that anything we uncover will help us solve the weekday problems too. Before we get going Stevie reminds us that it's important we distinguish between special causes of the weekend only and the more common causes throughout the whole week, and although both are important, it's the latter we're really after in our analysis.

♦

It's 8:00am on Saturday, and it's the start of the weekend. We are all in my office and Stevie is quietly sitting at the back of the room yawning. I know he's spent the week away and I'm asking a lot for him to be here this weekend. And while he looks like he could drop off at any moment I have no doubt that he'll propel a series of pertinent and direct questions just when I don't want to hear them. But it's all part of the journey, I suppose. Mo is looking pensive. He has a deep intelligence and breadth of view and he's now directly managing and intervening in both the clinical practice and operational processes of the rest of the hospital. It hasn't escaped his notice that this is another moment when true leadership is required. In a way, for him it's a dream come true. He can influence behaviour throughout the hospital, but knows that he doesn't have the clinical expertise of every area of the hospital – he's a generalist. I'm a little pensive too, wondering what we will find. Maybe I'd rather not know. We're joined by one of Stevie's younger protégés, Singh. He's done the work in preparation for the weekend and is armed with his list and spreadsheets. Everything is ready to carry out the analysis as the weekend unfolds.

Stevie, Singh and I walk into the handover meeting where the on-call consultant is waiting. We're ten minutes early and Singh hands him the list showing all the potential discharges over the weekend. It also looks like it's going to be one of those weekends where attendances are high. Ten minutes pass and only two people have appeared. Slowly, very slowly, more arrive and it's impossible to start the meeting until twenty minutes after scheduled. The consultant starts to go through two lists: the patients who are very sick and will require ongoing monitoring and treatment over the weekend, and patients for discharge. As he begins to allocate resources it strikes me that some people who are in attendance shouldn't be, some that should aren't, some are even finishing their shifts. I'm embarrassed. Amid the shambles the consultant tries to keep his cool as he allocates resources to the tasks.

It soon becomes obvious we're also short-staffed as some people have already reported in sick. One of the most senior matrons will spend her weekend trying to find short-term resources. Every weekend there are sicknesses and yet it's only when people report in sick that we start to try to solve the problem. It's actually quite staggering when you think about it. No wonder our bill for agency staff is so high.

As the consultant explains we have only thirty discharges planned for Saturday and four for Sunday my heart sinks a little. In a hospital of nine hundred beds this is woeful. Does nobody ever get better on a Sunday? As the assembled group shuffles out I feel a tinge of despair. Stevie asks if Singh can shadow our consultant for the day and he agrees. We don't know which resources are most often delaying the discharge of patients over the weekend. We only need to worry about those patients ready to go home late on the Friday or on the Saturday or on the Sunday, and identify what limited resources would be required to ensure the continued timely discharge of clinically fit patients. Stevie explains to Singh that our aim is to systematically identify the most common resources causing the most delay and to work out what level of resourcing would be required at the weekend to eliminate these delays.

◆

Youth may not always be a guarantee of innovation, yet it should always be a supply of energy and excitement. And by the time we meet Singh at lunchtime he has the look of a child having very recently discovered a chocolate coin manufacturing plant and is unable to decide whether to tell anyone. Stevie mischievously asks whether he has learned anything of interest and he looks like his head is about to explode.

"I've seen five cases where patients in the assessment unit could have been discharged earlier if they hadn't been waiting for a specialist review. Delays have been caused while waiting for specialists from neurology, cardiology, haematology, radiology, and orthopaedics."

He then tells of examples of central departments causing delay, including one case where a patient was waiting for a simple piece of paperwork from the occupational therapists describing future exercise required. Although there were OT staff available they were not rostered to work in this department at a weekend. As a result, at least a dozen patients were delayed. We gather around the coffee machine and Stevie says:

"I suggest we review the patients that are experiencing delay and see if we can identify any special causes relating to the weekend, and then any causes independent of the weekend that would happen any day of the week."

"But it's pretty obvious that a significant number of patients have been delayed due to a lack of OT assessments at the weekend," says Mo.

And I'm embarrassed again. There are OTs in the hospital but according to the rostering system they are allocated to A&E and nowhere else. Singh adds:

"I listened to the AU department phone them up three times and ask them to help. They pushed it as far as they could."

The solution is to change the rota and broaden their responsibility at the weekend but I know they'll ask for more staff. Stevie speaks.

"Is the reason they said no because they were working non-stop all day or was it the policy? You may not need someone from OT available throughout the weekend, just when you need them. We can't solve this sort of problem by adding capacity. We have to identify if the OT staff really are a bottleneck or if it is the inflexible policy that is causing the problem. Let us not blame the OT people, let us seek the policy causing the problem."

He asks Singh to check the top ten patients where OT is an outstanding task then he turns to Mo who has been looking around as well. He tells of a lady he calls a 'frequent flyer'. She came in Friday morning and was ready to go back home Saturday lunch time. But we couldn't re-activate her social care package as we had passed through the twenty-four-hour window in which the package can be restarted without further paperwork. She was actually ready to go within the twenty-four hours but we had not got round to completing the forms. So now it requires two further forms, and the staff to do this are not available at the weekend. Mind you, this sort of stuff also happens during the week as the backlog of forms often means that the re-enablement window passes without us getting to the paperwork in time. If we miss this window the amount of work we then need to do is probably fivefold. Mo has discovered more examples of this during the morning. Stevie returns to his previous point.

"So is this a lack of resource or a lack of availability of resource when we need it? If I am one of those staff, of all the patients I could be working on, how do I know which one to work on next? Are my priorities clear?"

Mo then tells of another group of patients who do not speak English and are not registered with the health service. Many of them are transient with no fixed abode. For this group we're the only port of call for healthcare. Often they're working all week and will turn up at A&E on Saturday morning. We know if we admit them they're likely to be stuck in the system for days, but if we don't admit them the chances of them getting an outpatient appointment next week without the paperwork is zero. They know this as well and they know trying to be admitted is their fastest route.

All the time I'm listening intently and looking at Stevie for signs. But I'm still second-guessing what is going on in his head. While I work on this, Singh tells of a number of patients waiting for radiology.

The department isn't busy, but policy dictates that a specialist referral to radiology can only be made by a consultant. We did this in an attempt to reduce the number of unnecessary requests. But at the weekend there are very few consultants around and the poor guys in AU can only just keep on top of it. So inevitably the referral is delayed and the patient waits in the AU until the consultant gets a chance to do the referrals. Radiology stop their normal service at 4:00pm and so any unattended patients will stay another night. Stevie asks the same question again.

"So is radiology a bottleneck or just a lack of availability when we need it? It's also clear that our response to this type of issue is to come up with a policy of declaring resource availability. Even with a relatively stable demand there will inevitably be big fluctuations in the requests for these specialist services. Trying to solve this by working out the average demand and making the resource available to meet this average demand will result in no resource available at times when the work is there, and plenty of resource when it isn't. At times of low demand service levels will be fantastic, and in peak demand periods service levels will deteriorate. You need to find a different way of solving this problem."

We decide to go to the bed meeting to see what's happening there. As we enter the room we immediately see on the screens that there are already five patients who have breached the four-hour target. One patient is fifteen minutes short of a twelve-hour delay. This patient must have spent most of the night in the emergency department. The problem is intensified by the fact that the next available bed is on the wrong ward and is designated for the other sex. The bed manager can't put this male patient in a female bay. In an hour's time it looks like four female beds should become available so another option might be to wait, redesignate the four female beds into male beds and then place the next male patient in one of these four beds. But a glance down the list shows the subsequent patients requiring admission are all female. Bloody typical! I pace up and down the back of the room for a while, listening to the conversations and telephone calls until I can hold back no longer.

"Liz, just get hold of the consultant, tell him I sent you and tell him to do an emergency ward round and to see if he can find patients to be discharged immediately. If there are any, get the matron to transfer the patients to the discharge lounge and get the porters to push the patient in A&E who is about to breach to the ward... please."

She takes a deep breath and says:

"Linda, I'm afraid four porters reported in sick this morning and the only ones we have are already engaged."

I sit down and put my head in my hands. Then it comes to me. I look up at Stevie and say:

"Mr Vokes, you're about to learn the skills of a porter. You and I are going to push this patient who has been waiting nearly twelve hours, up to the ward!"

Stevie sighs and gets to his feet. Two minutes later we're with the patient who has been waiting for a bed for almost twelve hours. The old man has no idea he's being pushed to the ward by the CEO of the hospital, and Stevie is amused by the looks on the faces of the staff holding the doors open as we push the patient through the corridors, up the lift and to the ward. When we arrive on the ward the nurse sitting behind the desk jumps up in surprise at seeing the CEO pushing the bed. And within five minutes the patient is in the allocated bay. As we walk around the rest of the ward I'm horrified to see two more empty beds. The nurse in charge tells us these have only just become available and are about to be reported to the bed office, but I can't wait.

"Do it now please."

The nurse settles in the patient before hurrying away, and I look at Stevie who smiles at me and then sighs.

"What?" I ask. "What?"

"Let's go for a coffee, Linda."

As we sit nursing our cardboard cups he looks at me and says:

"You know what? I've seen a different side to you. Your bed manner is amazing."

"Surprised?"

"Frankly, yes." That makes me smile, and then he continues: "And I understand your frustration and completely agree with the stance you took. It is unacceptable to hold back an empty bed when the bed manager is juggling with human lives."

"But I was too sharp with the poor nurse. Sometimes I think they see an empty bed as breathing space before the next sick patient arrives," I say in a moment of empathy. I'd noticed the nurse in charge was the only trained member of staff on the ward and a new, sick patient is more demanding than the patient who is ready to be discharged. But from the perspective of the whole hospital that bed is worth its weight in gold.

I resolve to visit the ward later to thank the nurse. She was trying to do what made sense from her local perspective. So we have to find a way of engaging every single member of staff with an understanding of the performance of the system as a whole. Something that they can understand. Something that they can base their local decisions on. Something that connects them to the bigger picture.

Simple.

♦

It's 8:00am on Sunday and Stevie and I arrive at my office to see Mo, Charlie and Jo already installed and John fiddling around with a projector. Charlie gestures us in and says:

"You'll have to sit down for this, chaps. John has paid for the coffees and pastries!"

"Well done, John," I say. "Are we celebrating or are you softening a blow?"

"You'll just have to wait and see."

Once we're all settled Stevie starts by reminding everyone of what we discovered on Friday. Which was that there is a considerable variation in throughput per bed day for the many different treatment types. He was surprised to see there was so much difference and is keen to hear from John the impact this may have on the hospital's financial sustainability. He stresses again that without a reduction in length of stay as a first step this is all meaningless, and that we all need to be clear that this reduction in length of stay is built on identifying and removing unnecessary delay. The delay is consuming both time and bed capacity, and both stop us providing higher-quality care to the current patients and more timely care for those waiting to be treated. With more time, all clinicians can give better and more compassionate care. Yesterday has also made it very clear to me that delay soaks up additional resources and unnecessary operating expenses. Delay is costing us money we could be saving. He also reminds us that without immediately using some of the free capacity created to improve the quality of care, staff training and bed availability in A&E, AU and the wards there can be no growth opportunity. Patients will only be attracted by rapid access to high-quality care. One without the other is not going to work.

John jumps in to say that he spent some time with Stevie last night, preparing a few slides for us to go through together. I've never seen John quite so nervous – well not so much nervous, more like animated. Actually, he just looks more alive than I've ever seen him, which is a little disconcerting.

It becomes clear that they've prepared a double act for us and Stevie is going to use his preferred questioning style to reveal the story for us all.

"So, John, can you start by reminding us the current predicted revenues of the hospital this year?"

"£400 million."

"And do I correctly remember the totally variable costs to be twenty per cent?"

"That's right: around £80 million."

"And with £335 million in operating expenses you are currently estimating a loss of £15 million this year. Correct?"

John confirms and shows us his first slide revealing these numbers which are now etched in our consciousness before Stevie continues.

"Now, Jo, in your opinion, if – and it's a big if – the process we have been using does deliver, say, a ten per cent reduction in length of stay across the hospital, how much of this capacity would we need to use to ensure one hundred per cent bed availability with a suitable level of paranoia?"

"Well, a ten per cent reduction in length of stay on nine hundred beds should give us ninety beds."

"And how many extra beds do you believe you would need in the AU to ensure one hundred per cent bed availability without allowing paranoia to slip into hysteria?"

Jo ponders a while before saying:

"Based on this weekend's analysis, if we used fifty per cent of those extra beds for ensuring bed availability it would have to be a very bad day for us to fall over."

Stevie turns to John:

"So if we ring-fence half of this initial freed-up capacity and designate it as 'protective capacity' to ensure one hundred per cent availability that would leave us the other five per cent to increase volumes. Yes?"

John nods and Stevie continues:

"How long is the waiting list for patients who need an inpatient treatment?"

"It varies considerably across the specialties," says John, "and I'm guessing it relates to about £50 million of future revenues."

"And these are patients where there has already been a decision to treat," says Stevie. "This is not attracting new patients, just treating the current patients in the system faster?"

John agrees again and then Stevie asks whether our revenue would grow from £400 million to £420 million if we could also free up a similar level of capacity across all our other activities and use this free capacity to treat five per cent more patients. John agrees that it would. Then he shows a slide which reveals that our totally variable costs would also go up by five per cent from £80 million to £84 million and our throughput up from £320 million to £336 million, but operating expenses would stay the same at £335 million. This is only true as long as we are able to treat more patients within the freed-up capacity. The next column is the killer. With the increase in revenue of £20 million and totally variable costs up by £4 million, and with throughput now at £336 million and operating costs at £335 million, we would... wait for it... BREAK EVEN!

There is a stunned silence. A beautiful silence in many ways as we drink in the sweet realisation of how close we are to the first big steps towards a return to justifiable pride and welcome joy. Mo breaks the quiet:

"So what you are saying, John, is that with only a five per cent increase in revenues we can completely eliminate our losses?"

"Yes, provided the five per cent is carried out within existing capacity."

"And only if that existing capacity is created through a reduction in length of stay and an equivalent improvement across the rest of the hospital's activities first," adds Stevie. "If we just try to force five per cent more patients through the current system we will not just have a bottleneck in AU but will create interactive bottlenecks everywhere else. That will simply accelerate your downward spiral of poor results. You'd actually push this hospital over the edge."

Charlie is amazed that such a small increase in volumes could remove our losses, so Stevie asks John what would happen if we freed up twenty per cent capacity. He reveals a third column of the slide which shows revenues growing by £60 million (fifteen per cent, as five per cent is used to solve bed availability) to £460 million. Totally variable costs grow by £12 million to £92 million and throughput grows to £368 million. With operating expenses staying the same, net profit has gone from a loss of £15 million to a profit of £33 million per year.

We all look around the room at each other, speechless, for a good thirty seconds. If we have no backlog and recoup the first £50 million, we'll be in the incredible position of winning back work that we've recently lost to other hospitals in the region. This would be one hell of a result if we could turn around the finances within a year. I realise it isn't going to happen in the short time I have left in the temporary role, but this is without doubt the best way forward I've ever seen. Once he has given us time to absorb the opportunity and the size of the pot of gold Stevie hammers home that without these improvements, and without firstly improving quality of care and removing the backlogs, none of this is a reality. Charlie has been listening intently and now he speaks up:

"But what happens if we overlay the old Cooper trick of changing the mix on this as well, ensuring the new business has a higher throughput per bed day?"

John explains for everyone's benefit that the throughput per bed day can vary by a factor of five, but to be conservative he's assumed in the next two scenarios that the extra volumes average out at only double the throughput per bed day. He reveals two more columns which show that if we were able to correctly target our growth we could be making anywhere between £17 million per year with an initial ten per cent reduction in stay and a whopping £81 million per year with a twenty per cent improvement. Once again, this is always dependent on our building this approach around high-quality care delivered with rapid access times and through current capacity.

Table illustrating the impact on profitability of eliminating delays, freeing up capacity, increasing volumes and changing patient mix

Scenario	Revenue (£m per year)	Totally variable costs (£m per year)	Throughput (£m per year)	Operating expenses (£m per year)	Profit (£m per year)
Current situation	400	80	320	335	-15
10% freed-up capacity: 5% used for protective capacity and 5% for extra throughput	420	84	336	335	1
20% freed-up capacity: 5% used for protective capacity and 15% for extra throughput	460	92	368	335	33
10% freed-up capacity: 5% used for protective capacity and 5% for extra through-put with double the throughput per bed day on extra throughput	440	88	352	335	17
20% freed-up capacity: 5% used for protective capacity and 15% for extra through-put with double the throughput per bed day on extra throughput	520	104	416	335	81

What fascinates me is that delay in the system has always been the most annoying thing for all of us but we've never before considered the full impact of not addressing it. As well as being potentially life-threatening for the patient, it is also destroying our finances. I want to share this with the whole hospital but Stevie counsels caution.

"When we're sitting on such an opportunity we must approach it with care. There may be some unintended outcomes of the approach that we need to think through. For example, we may need to increase operational expenses a little bit to deal with the extra volumes."

John adds:

"The initial leap is because we currently have a backlog, and only if we can convince our masters we can reduce the backlog without any more resources will they be willing to pay for the extra volume. They have already agreed to pay as these patients are on the waiting list, but on these figures it will mean them paying earlier than expected.

"The second jump is our gain but another hospital's loss. We would have to make sure everyone understands we're now able to treat more patients within the same resources and that this is the basis of our increase in productivity."

I'm finding it hard to contain my excitement.

"You know what I really love about this? It starts with improving the quality of patient care and simultaneously focuses on freeing up front-line staff to treat patients and to improve access times. It's got to make sense as a good way forward."

The fact that John has embraced the proposals speaks volumes. He agrees to prepare a briefing document for the executive team and specialty leaders before Stevie refocuses us on the ever-growing pot of gold.

"With this level of profitability you could leapfrog your way into the top twenty research hospitals. If you just invested a fraction of this level of profitability into research then you could attract major investment from the drug companies. More and more of them are looking for a joint deal."

A broad smile is spreading across Mo's face, and Charlie leans back in his chair and bites his top lip before saying:

"What are we waiting for?"

Stevie asks for caution again.

"I'm sorry to deflate the euphoria, but what we are actually waiting for is patients to be discharged on time. What have we learned from our analysis this weekend?"

I decide I want to take a lead.

"First of all, spending these two days analysing the hospital and seeing weekend working for ourselves has been a real eye-opener. It's now really clear to me that we should not assume that adding resource at the weekend will increase operating expenses. Yes, it may increase the weekend operating expenses very slightly in a few areas, but I think we have seen enough examples where it's possible to find a situation where the additional weekend resource actually reduces the total operating expenses across the seven days. It may be that when we cut resources at the weekend we actually cut the available capacity of those few critical resources that govern our entire throughput. We have been assuming all resources are equal and yet we've learned that in a goal-oriented system this is one of the most devastating assumptions we can make."

Stevie nods his approval. And at last I am confident we have more than enough to find a real win–win solution for the hospital, the staff and the patients. It is now clear to me that resolving our financial difficulties is in our own hands. Once we are profitable, we can further reinvest in our staff and improve our quality of care.

Chapter Eleven

An unrefusable offer

I get a nice surprise on Wednesday morning when Stevie calls to ask me to dinner this Friday at the Reform Club in the West End. He's invited some people from his pharmaceutical client. It'll be a pretty impressive meal if nothing else, but I wonder why he's asking me. He knows this industry isn't my favourite, to put it mildly.

"Well, I could take a couple of my colleagues, but I think you'd find it more interesting. And why don't you bring your friend Dee along?"

"You do realise Dee isn't an escort."

"I'm quite aware of that, but I'd like you to be there. The other three on the table are guys and I thought you'd like a friend there to redress the balance a little. And why not Dee?"

"Well, mainly because if any of your clients have questionable dress sense, dull conversation or, even worse, a stutter then you may well lose them."

"The answers there are possibly yes, yes and no. But I think you do Dee a disservice. I'm sure she can be perfectly charming when she puts her mind to it. Anyway, just let me know."

Admittedly, Dee is pretty good in these situations, and it would be a great chance for us to catch up. Apart from that, she would cut me off forever if she found out she'd been invited to the Reform Club and I hadn't told her. Her brother Carl's on the mend. He's receiving treatment and responding well. So I ring to invite her and she replies immediately.

"He does realise I'm not an escort?"

"Probably not. You must admit you've always been rather attractive to certain men."

"Attractive to certain men – you mean like an escort! Oh well, that's brilliant. Thanks very much. Tell him I'll do it for two grand and a year's supply of Dom Perignon and Minstrels."

"So you'll come?"

"Do I have a choice?"

"Not if you're a good friend, no."

◆

We leave our hotel at seven in search of the private members' club just off Pall Mall.

"Do you know where you're going?" asks Dee, rather abruptly.

"Well, I'm positive it was the fourth street after Chumley's."

"That was the fifth."

"There it is."

We spy the grand Reform Club, a four-storey Georgian building, the type inhabited by lords, landowners, financiers and captains of industry for over two centuries and latterly also by Premier League footballers, the ones who haven't been barred. Dee is impressed.

"Bloody hell! How is Stevie in here?"

"His dad's a member."

She raises her eyebrows as an attendant takes her coat. We're led through an oak-panelled room, populated by gentlemen sitting in leather armchairs reading the *Financial Times* and sipping malt at £30 a dram. Dee nods towards one chap and says:

"Is he alive?"

We arrive at a small private room to be met by Stevie and his three guests. He introduces them as David, Piers and Scott, the senior team at his client, then he introduces us. As she shakes Scott's hand, Dee says:

"I do like your suit. It's beautifully styled and perfect for you. I think more people should make their own clothes."

My eyes widen and scan across to Stevie, who looks faintly stunned, before, thankfully, David and Piers burst out laughing, although sadly not to be joined by Scott. We sit down around the table, attended by three waiters, and we all order an aperitif. I'm relieved that Dee doesn't order a pint of bitter and a rum chaser.

As the dinner progresses everyone relaxes into conversation.

There's some business talk but interspersed with all manner of subjects. Scott becomes increasingly impressed by Dee's encyclopaedic knowledge of Wittgenstein, Euripides, twentieth-century existentialism and the World Wrestling Federation. I'm impressed, too, as a matter of fact. After a truly delightful menu Stevie makes a toast of thanks to us all as the coffee arrives. But as ever he has his mind on work. After thanking the pharma guys for giving him the opportunity to carry out a more detailed analysis of their organisation, he asks if they mind if he has a few more questions. No one has an objection so he begins.

"My understanding is that you asked me to carry out this analysis to see if my claim that it was possible to accelerate your profitable growth in these challenging times had some proper substance. Am I right?"

"Well, it was a pretty bold claim," says Piers. "Lovely venue as it is, Stevie, if it was not for the huge benefits we have seen in our production and supply chain using your advice I would never have persuaded David, our corporate growth director, to join us for dinner tonight."

Dee bursts out laughing but Stevie continues unabated:

"For Linda and Dee's sake, can you explain how you have managed to ensure the right drugs are available at the right time, neither too early nor too late? And then how much free capacity this has revealed?"

"Sure," says Scott. "At the outset Stevie got us to do a proper analysis of availability. According to all our standard measures the availability was close to one hundred per cent, but when we got beneath the detail it soon became obvious that we were kidding ourselves. Availability was much more of an issue than our measures were telling us."

He goes on to tell how Stevie explained that the core reason for lack of availability was not the changes in demand in the market but actually their company's mode of operation which was based on forecasting the demand. Switching from a forecast mode of operation to a consumption-driven mode enabled them to reduce shortages and with less inventory. Dee speaks up.

"So you improved availability by producing a particular product more often. Why weren't you doing that in the first place?"

"Fair question," says Scott. "We didn't think we had the production and distribution capabilities. This strategy required us to be able to respond immediately and reliably to a demand composed mainly of smaller quantities. We thought this would destroy the efficiencies in our plant and in the distribution system."

Piers interjects.

"But we had failed to understand that when we started to run our operations according to actual consumption rather than batching the orders, not only were we able to provide higher availability with lower overall inventories, but we also exposed substantial free capacity. This was the biggest shock to us."

They hadn't realised how much capacity in production and distribution they were wasting by making and storing things before they were needed and were also pushing through rush orders to ensure availability was maintained.

Dee smiles.

"And it was Stevie who pointed this out to you."

"Yes," says Scott. "We were a little sceptical at first, and it was only when we actually took the described steps that we saw just how much capacity was freed up."

Dee winks at Stevie and says:

"Who's a clever boy then?" And I cringe. Then she turns back to Scott:

"So what have you done with this free capacity?"

Scott hesitates for a moment and then says:

"Well, that's interesting. The traditional approach would be to shut down some plants and consolidate on a smaller base. But Stevie has brought us here to ask us to consider something different."

He explains how the ramifications of making to forecast turned out to be further-reaching than they had suspected. When they had too much inventory of one product they put pressure on the sales force to offer deals, and this often resulted in pushing too much stock on to customers. An unintended outcome of this was that when they introduced a new drug or new variant it often meant initial sales were dampened down until the customer had used up all the old stock. On top of that, too much of one stock also resulted in too little of another and this was causing the poor availability and lost sales. Dee is fascinated.

"Hang on, though. Why should too much of one product cause too little of another?"

"Well, a combination of the forecast and our eagerness to fully utilise all resources resulted in there being too many orders in the pipeline. Many more than we needed to match short-term demand for those products. The resulting traffic jams meant it took longer for every product to be made and not only caused the products already in production to be late but also meant capacity was not available to make other products as well."

The company found itself in a situation where it was taking so long to produce that they brought forward future orders for the same product to try to improve availability and this just made the situation worse. They normalised this behaviour by calling it a campaign, but the effect was devastating.

"How come everything was not always late?" asks Dee.

Scott's impressed by Dee's question and is happy to oblige.

"It's a little embarrassing. It was only when we changed to producing to demand that we realised just how much excess capacity we had built into our system to cope. The excess capacity was stopping everything being late. Once you have built these plants you are sort of stuck with them."

I'm as intrigued as Dee.

"How much free capacity did you actually create?"

David, who is responsible for sales, doesn't really want to answer the question.

"We now have very close to one hundred per cent availability and are looking for new markets that would enable us to increase sales by at least twenty-five per cent without the need for any additional capacity."

I'm just about to ask how they identified the parts of their process that were holding them back when Stevie suggests we talk about increasing sales. He checks some starting points from his analysis.

"My understanding is that with the high speed of entry of generics into the market and the increased risk of a competitor launching a better-performing product, there is less time for you to exploit the competitive edge from the drug you have developed and that you have invested so much money in. This must have a detrimental effect on your return on investment in R&D."

Piers confirms that not only has the window of protection itself shrunk, but the average cost of developing a new drug has risen year on year. In consequence, investments in R&D are rising every year relative to sales growth. The only options are to increase prices or increase sales within this smaller window of protected opportunity.

For a brief moment I feel sorry for them, but then remember how John's figures showed how drug costs as a percentage of our own revenues have also grown.

"So is that the end of the corporate jet, then?" asks Dee helpfully.

Stevie stays focused.

"If the cost of your sales force has risen as well, then this is why you claim a common cry is to push for increased prices."

He then turns to me.

"Can you explain to the guys how your finances at the hospital work?"

"Sure I can," I say through slightly gritted teeth, not having expected to be put on the spot. But as requested, I explain that after an unprecedented number of years where the total spend on health rose year on year, more recently the growth has been limited to inflation. And medical costs are still rising faster than revenues, so the hospital is running at a loss. I explain that Stevie has been helping us.

"I didn't know you were in the hospital market," Scott says to Stevie.

"Neither did I. Actually, Linda heard about the work I was doing with you and asked if I could help her in her hospital. In all honesty, I had no idea what we faced when we started, but we are having a go. And just as you are reducing your work in progress and production lead times, Linda has been reducing her length of stay by similar amounts."

I explain that with revenues not increasing as in the past, we have to be more careful with our costs.

"And your drugs make up about twenty per cent of our costs. The rest are mainly staff wages. So faced with your increasing drug costs the only option I have is to reduce the front-line staff and the consequence of that is reduced quality of care, longer queues and overstretched staff."

David's eyes have narrowed. Maybe that was an easy swipe, but in the early days of my career I had a stomach full of drug reps constantly trying to persuade me to buy the latest and more expensive drugs. Stevie intervenes:

"So on one side the only way a pharma company can protect its return on investment in R&D is through increasing prices and pushing volumes during the shortening window of opportunity. And on the other side your customers are under increasing pressure to reduce their spend on the new drugs you have been developing."

Dee looks as though she thinks Stevie is planning some sort of cross-sector love-in. But I'm interested in what he's saying and have another point to make.

"And we're in a postcode lottery. Some regions pick some of the drugs and others pick different ones. And we get ever more complaints from patients where we will not provide the drugs they're after."

Stevie then asks me to share our recent analysis on the throughput per bed day. So I do, explaining how we recently did an exercise whereby we looked at each stream of care and calculated the sales price minus drug costs and a few other variable costs, and divided this number by the average length of stay. That gave us a way of comparing the throughput per bed day across the different treatment codes. We did this because we were discussing how best to use the free capacity we'd created by reducing length of stay. In the first instance it was straightforward as our head of surgery, Mr Cooper, had caught on to the opportunity immediately and simply started selectively working through the backlog, which resulted in our financial throughput increasing by fifty per cent more than our increase in discharges. There was a huge variation in the throughput per bed day, and when we discussed this with Stevie he showed us Mr Cooper was right to work through the backlog; but once we have eliminated the backlog, if we choose carefully how we fill this capacity, we can dramatically change our profitability. The pharma chaps have been listening carefully and David speaks up.

"When you say '*huge variation*' what are you talking about? Twenty per cent?"

"No. Some were five times others."

"Have you checked these numbers, Stevie?"

Stevie confirms he has double-checked them and the range is from £200 to £1000 per bed day, and then he drives the point home.

"Linda's hospital is sitting on a financial knife-edge, but if she can shorten length of stay by eliminating unnecessary delay then quality of care and improved finances follow. But at the moment every penny she saves simply goes to reducing her losses. If she could treat more patients with higher quality of care through the same resources, she could improve her profitability dramatically and the system as a whole would be better off. More patients would have been seen within the same operating expense window. But without these improvements and with increasing drug costs the hospital is facing a downward spiral."

"How long has it taken to achieve these improvements?" asks Piers.

"It took about a month to get everyone to agree, and we've been working on it for a few further months," I say.

Stevie then turns to David.

"What market share do you have in any one hospital?"

"Stevie, it's very small."

"How often is a particular drug only supplied by one company?"

"Hardly ever."

"So there's a battle for market share in an industry where the pie isn't growing."

There's a moment of quiet as Scott refills Dee's cup and we all consider what has been said. The current situation won't lead to a sustainable way forward for either the hospital or the pharma company. There isn't enough revenue to go round. The pharma boys have realised that their policy of upping prices and pushing volumes is intensifying the hospital's problems. Piers looks at Stevie.

"You're a clever sod. You're telling us that we should focus our efforts on helping to solve our customer's dilemma. If we do that they can create their own process of ongoing improvement, which in turn will help us to flourish."

"Until you admit you are part of the problem you cannot be part of the solution. That's probably a good first step but there's something else I'd like you to consider, something which could be a win–win. You have an issue that if you roll out the work we have done so far to all your factories around the world, the excess capacity is vast. We need to build you a decisive competitive edge and the capabilities to capitalise on it, in sufficient markets, without exhausting the company's resources and without taking real risks."

David doesn't believe there is a market big enough to soak up all the free capacity. Even if new product development is accelerated it will never be able to fill all that capacity quickly enough and the pressure to shut down the plants is enormous. He looks at Stevie.

"I can't see a market big enough available to us. You're not asking us to consider entering the generic drugs market, are you? That is a daily fistfight, and we're just not geared up to deal with that sort of battle. Those people have built the leanest and meanest factories and supply chain models in the industry and we'll never be financially viable in that space."

Stevie asks:

"What would happen if you already had the capacity for free?"

Nobody speaks. David looks at Scott, who is looking at Piers. Dee catches my eye and we all want to know what's coming next. Stevie doesn't keep us waiting.

"Imagine you put together an offer for the hospital that covers a wider portfolio of drugs they need. And rather than selling the drugs to them you agree an upfront percentage of revenues adjusted for patient mix and only invoiced once consumed. How much market share could you gain with this approach?"

The truth of it is, if this is provided through the excess capacity, almost all the increase in sales would go straight to the bottom line. Profits would accelerate rapidly. Stevie says that the numbers will show that even when the pharma company needs to reduce the overall expense to any one hospital its overall growth will still mean growth in profits are outstripping the growth in sales. Then he looks at me.

"Linda – would this kind of offer be of interest to you?"

"Of course."

◆

Once the pharma guys have gone Stevie orders another coffee. It's been a good evening and I say to Stevie:

"They were alright."

"You mean they only had one head each," adds Dee. "You were quiet tonight, though."

"Compared to you maybe," I reply. "I was trying to keep up. I must say much of the discussion got me thinking."

My mind had been flicking back and forth all evening. While I had been listening to the pharma chaps' explanations I had also been distracted by constantly thinking about the hospital. Now the pharma guys have gone it gives me the opportunity to bend Stevie's ear about another topic. One of my current preoccupations is the never-ending stream of complaints from the outpatient environment at our hospital. The chance of us actually seeing an outpatient when they should be seen is almost zero. New patients wait on a waiting list, and even when a patient is seen it can take ages between follow-up appointments. I decide to seize the moment.

"I could do with more help, Stevie."

I'm almost imploring him. I know he's done a lot already, but I also know this would really help me as our outpatient department gives another very tangible measure of our performance and one that we are also struggling with.

"Look, I'm really busy over the next two weeks. I have two client meetings and I'm way behind with my book. But I can lend you two of my people to help you. How about that?"

"You're a gem."

Dee's been fascinated by the evening and, on the whole, has been on impeccable behaviour. I was truly surprised by how engaged she was in the conversation, but I guess I shouldn't have been. She is nobody's fool. She pushes her coffee cup away and eyes Stevie.

"So what's in all this for you?"

"Well, the truth of it is, Dee, that Linda is a very dear friend and I think the world of her. And if I needed her help, she would be there."

I look at Dee and she says nothing for a moment, and then, almost predictably:

"Does he have a brother?"

Chapter Twelve

Sorcery or science?

"Andreas, I have a question for you. You've been in charge of medicine as long as I've been here. Do you see anything in common between medicine and management?"

Dr Staulous peers up at me over his Costa cup and says:

"Sure I do. They both begin with M."

"I was hoping for something a little more insightful than that."

"Hey, Linda, I'm sorry. I've spent the whole day in clinic and I can't begin to tell you how frustrated I am."

"Go on. Try me."

I need Andreas to give me a perspective. Cath spent a day last week reviewing the complaints we've received in the last few months, and many are related to outpatients. So I want to explore this together from both a medical and a management viewpoint and see if we can figure out how to improve things. I ask Andreas to go first.

"No, you go first."

"No… you go first."

"OK, Linda. What I find unbelievably frustrating is that I spent seven years at medical school and I've been practising for fifteen. I lead a team of consultants and we've achieved regional specialist status. We are constantly adding research. And in a lot of ways we're punching way above our weight for a hospital of this size." Then he pauses, steals himself, and exclaims: "And we can't even run a bloody outpatients clinic!"

Anecdotally I've heard that the issue is simply a matter of starting on time, and I put that to Andreas.

"I suggest you think of another idea unless you want a very short conversation, Linda."

Oops. I got a reaction but not quite the one I expected. While I've been desperately trying to lead improvements in the hospital I've often noticed how difficult it is to get people to face up to reality. And the one thing I like about talking with doctors is that they say it as it is. I have a lot of sympathy for Andreas. It's ridiculous that we have doctors who are so knowledgeable and talented and yet the seemingly simple task of running an effective outpatient service is proving to be so difficult. I know that Andreas and his peers think that, at best, management is a dark art, practised by sorcerers, whereas in medicine they base their decisions on scientific analysis.

"It wasn't always that way. But we've learned how to identify and validate the cause of a patient's illnesses as a first step. That is at the heart of what we do on the first patient visit in outpatients."

"What do you mean, it wasn't always that way?"

Andreas explains.

"In the early days of medicine before they were able to identify the causes of some diseases doctors limited themselves to simply trying to stop the spread of the disease. Some diseases spread through human contact, and medicine did nothing more than isolate them. Medicine only moved into the world of prevention and elimination of diseases when more sophisticated forms of immunisation were found.

"In the management world you have your business gurus, but in medicine we have the likes of Edward Jenner, who discovered if serum is transferred from an infected cow to the human body the human will not be infected with smallpox. At that stage, it was unclear why but we knew the treatment worked. The holy grail in medicine was to understand the actual cause of diseases, and Louis Pasteur's leap of imagination achieved this."

As Andreas talks it's impossible to deny his passion for medicine and his suspicion of the value of management. And I realise that management doesn't seem to have all the necessary answers to what is causing an organisation's poor performance, or even good performance. Management books often adopt an evocative title like *Seven Steps to Eternal Prosperity*, and they often propose a cauldron of ingredients to solve any corporate conundrum. I'd love to find a book, a small book, which could remove our frustration with the performance of our outpatients system. I pose another question.

"Imagine the hospital is a patient. How can we identify the cause of illness?"

"We can't treat a patient like we treat the hospital. Our actions are always driven by the latest crisis or initiative. If we treated patients like that we'd kill them all!"

"Just bear with me. Why can't we look at the outpatient problem like diagnosing a patient? Let's see if we can identify the cause of discomfort and come up with a medicine that will work."

I tell Andreas of the dinner we had with the pharmaceutical chaps and how their approach to getting the right product to the right place on time made me try to understand why it was so difficult to see the right patient at the right time. I also explain how by changing some of their policies they had changed things in a remarkably short timescale, with better than expected benefits. I'm all too aware that in both our cases early success is essential to keep everyone in the improvement cycle. In the hospital we'll never convince people we're doing the right things unless they produce results and quickly. It's like turning a liner around. Andreas speaks.

"I thought leadership was all about setting visions and saying: '*Follow me, all will be wonderful in the end, the pain on the journey is worth it.*'"

"I'm not a white knight, Andreas, nor do I have a white horse. So I'd rather be a little more robust."

"And how will you do that?"

"Actually, I'm not going to, Andreas. If I arrange it, are you willing to sit down with two of Stevie's colleagues to try to see if we can develop a simple solution to help us?"

"What, now?" Andreas looks around as if they've been hiding under the table.

"Not while you're so cross. How about tomorrow afternoon, after clinic?"

♦

Andreas greets Tim and Tam with a warm handshake and welcome.

"So, Linda, here we have the two hot shots who can tell me how to run my outpatients department."

It seems his mood hasn't lightened noticeably. No matter. Tim, who's already spoken to some of the patients and observed a clinic, is the first to speak.

"Sitting in on the clinic enabled me to see why you are so frustrated."

Tam had interviewed some patients and experienced their angst too. She met one lady who'd waited four weeks in some considerable pain for her first appointment. She had an appointment at 11:00am and was obviously stressed by the whole thing, arriving at 10:40am. By the time she was seen at 11:50am she was virtually panic-stricken. The delay was caused by patients arriving late earlier in the day. The appointment itself took about fifteen minutes and she was in some despair when she learned that her repeat appointment with Andreas was going to be six weeks away.

Another patient who was coming for her last appointment consoled her with the fact that she had similar symptoms, and although it had taken four months to identify the problem, she was now feeling much better and without any pain. Another patient Tam saw had been told by his GP to arrive before the clinic started to see if Andreas could see him as an extra patient. He'd been fasting for twelve hours before the appointment. But unfortunately the clinic didn't start on time as Andreas was attending to an emergency. By the time he got to clinic the waiting room was already full and booked patients were running late. The clerks were looking for a slot to put him in but it was 1:30pm before he was seen. By this time he'd gone over seventeen hours without food or drink, apart from a biscuit Tam saw him sneaking mid morning. Andreas recalls this case.

"Well, the blood tests were probably a waste of time. He'll have to come back and we'll have to start again."

Another patient had to see two specialists with two different sets of tests and come back for a joint consultation, but one of the consultants was not available on time.

"There's a huge inconsistency between when you want to see the patient and when you actually do," says Tim. "Some of your new patients had only been waiting a few days. Others had been waiting weeks. Some of the ones seen quickly weren't urgent."

"We slip them in if we see a gap, or sometimes we do a favour for one of our GP colleagues and just double book," admits Andreas.

This irregular pattern of booking and treatment also affects repeat patients who are invariably seen on a different day than that suggested by the consultant; some earlier and some later. Those who find no space in the booking window sometimes have to call back in a few weeks when the horizon next opens up. Andreas defends the booking clerks. He explains most doctors see how far into the future appointments are available and try to match that against when it's appropriate to see the patient again. Then he describes a policy that leaves both Tim and Tam with a look of confusion.

"We have a six-week rule, which means we can't book appointments more than six weeks in advance because I have to give six weeks' notice for my holidays and if we book them in we then may have to rearrange them all."

"From a clinical perspective, how do you decide when it's most appropriate to see the patient?" asks Tim.

Andreas describes a number of criteria. For new patients he aims to beat the four-week service level and never turns an urgent patient away. For repeat patients where a treatment has been prescribed, it may be days, weeks or months before he can judge if the treatment is successful. The third group requires diagnostics and so the date is set after their diagnostics are completed, which is reasonably easy to judge. And then there is his own availability.

"This may sound daft," admits Tam, "but in the case of a first appointment would it not be better to see the patient straight away?"

"It may not be clinically necessary," replies Andreas, "but, for the patient, waiting can be stressful and painful. In the cancer stream it is important to see the patient as soon as possible and this is why we have higher service levels there."

"And for those waiting for diagnostics, if the diagnostics could be completed immediately, when would you want to see the patient?" asks Tim.

"Well, as soon as possible," comes the reply.

"And if there isn't a slot available in your diary?"

"That's often the case. Otherwise why can't I see every new patient tomorrow?"

I come back to a conversation I had with the pharma guys the other evening. In essence, Stevie had asked them to look at and quantify the things they should have been doing but weren't and which resulted in shortages, and the things they were doing that they shouldn't, or shouldn't have done yet – this leading to the unnecessary stock in the supply chain. They highlighted the issue and expense of things not being on time. Just like us, their factories have finite capacity and the reason some orders were late was that they had used the finite capacity to produce orders against a forecast which was inaccurate. So they made too much of other products too early. By doing some things earlier than expected, other things were being done later than expected. But rather than bemoaning the accuracy of the forecast, Stevie got them to focus on making sure that the limited available capacity was used to ensure what was recently sold also remained available and that this drove their schedule of orders. As a consequence of this approach they uncovered internal policies and procedures that had been put in place in the past to optimise various elements of their supply chain. By analysing the early and late orders they were able to systematically address the resources whose lack of flexibility was causing the most disruption and the internal policies that were driving local optimisation. I tell Andreas that I think we can learn from this.

Naturally, he isn't ready to jump in with both feet. There's already a distortion when he asks for a repeat patient to be seen, depending on his own availability and expectation of how long it will take for diagnostics to be completed. And on clinical grounds alone there's considerable variation in the time intervals of appointments. Identifying whether patients are being seen in a timely manner is not as straightforward as seeing whether a drug order is delivered on time.

"Do you have any idea how many patients we see in this hospital a year?" he asks.

"Over six hundred thousand in the last twelve months," says Tam after a sneaky look at her pad. "And that does not include more than eight per cent of patients who had an appointment but didn't attend."

She then talks Andreas through her early analysis, showing that the waiting time for a new appointment has an average of six weeks. Apart from emergency cases and outliers, the time oscillates between two and eight weeks. The mean time between appointments is six weeks, and again there's enormous variation from two weeks to six months. I ask Andreas what he thinks.

"I can see there's a problem and I don't know how big it is, but I'm struggling to see if there is anything we can do about it."

Tam tries to help. She explains how she worked on the pharmaceutical project and that they had a similar issue. They knew they had a big problem by the number of rush orders that were being placed on the factories around the world. In some instances they were flying packages from one country to another where stock was unavailable in one country and there was enough for generations to come in another. In the hospital some doctors have a waiting list much longer than others. Many doctors feel they're working harder than others and still cannot keep ahead of their workload. This may just be down to variations in the type of patients they are seeing, but Tam has checked and this situation exists between doctors who are seeing the same sort of patients. The pharma industry and the hospital have many differences but issues can be approached using the same analysis.

The starting point is to identify what is limiting performance. And the bigger the size of the limitation, the more value a new approach can potentially bring. Tam goes on to highlight the non-attendances in outpatients, running at eight per cent. While this may not seem a lot, she confidently predicts that if we could get eight per cent more patients seen through the same resources this would improve availability and could add tens of millions of extra revenue with no significant additional operating expense. Andreas is incredulous to say the least.

"Are you joking?"

"Not in the slightest," says Tam. "You and your team are always ready and willing to work but not always able to work because… eight per cent of patients don't turn up. It's a big opportunity."

Tam goes on to explain that these non-attendances are not only a waste of time and capacity, but they also have a negative impact on the service offered to other patients. And while eight per cent is the average, the range is between four and sixteen per cent across clinics. Furthermore, the number of unused slots where no patient was ever booked in runs between three and twelve per cent. The frustration grows when you consider further slots are double-booked when patients have been waiting too long. And with the restriction of the six-week booking window there are literally thousands of follow-up appointments not yet booked. So somewhere between seven and twenty-eight per cent of available capacity is being wasted while Andreas is being forced into double-booking and has a rapidly increasing backlog. Andreas has a furrowed brow.

"There's not a lot we can do about the eight per cent who don't show, but when you're in it every day it is difficult to see how big these issues are. The numbers make sense, though, and that brings it home."

He admits the situation is worse than the bare statistics. As well as double-booking, there are times when not all of the diagnostics are in when the patient arrives and so there is some guesswork. If the guess is wrong, the result is more appointments for the patient and doctor. Tim makes the point that all of these formal and informal practices have been developed over time with the express purpose of making the most of the available capacity.

"We need to understand these historical approaches and see why they were put in place. Maybe they once served the hospital well but have now turned into a major limitation. But we should come back and consider the things we don't do that we should, and the things we do that we shouldn't or shouldn't have done yet."

But there aren't many variables to play with. We can try to reduce non-attendances. We can try to reduce unused slots. We can increase capacity by running more sessions or recruiting. We can review the number of repeat sessions that is clinically appropriate. And we can seek out best clinical practice across a group of doctors. We could even ask each other which of us is working the hardest. But all of these ideas are just shooting in the dark if we don't know what impact they have on the quality and timeliness of patient care. Andreas has reached the stage where he's ready to ask for help.

"How difficult could it be, Tim? You're the whiz – what do we actually have to do?"

Tim raises his eyebrows and touches his nose with his pencil.

"Here's an idea. This may seem a bit odd, but why don't we forget government targets to start with?"

"Hear, hear to that!" For the first time Andreas is grinning broadly.

"Let's aim to do something that will be patient-centred," continues Tim. "Something that is doctor-led and clinically excellent." Andreas stops short of shouting '*Hallelujah!*'

"And let's set ourselves a challenging time within which all new patients should be seen to maintain our clinical excellence. Then for repeat patients I want you to forget any perceptions of how long diagnostics will take or how full your diary is. I want you to state, purely from a clinical perspective, when the patient should be seen next. If it's in a day, it's a day."

"We can't do that," says Andreas, suddenly deflated.

Tim reassures him:

"I know that, but if we have a go we can measure deviation from this point and identify the most common cause across the most patients. We can also look at it by doctor, by patient type and by most common resource."

With this information we'll be able to establish the size of the deviation and find the most simple and practical change required. I think we should start this as a controlled experiment. If it works we can get others to follow. It's a hell of a leap of faith but is consistent with the principles of improving patient flow and ethics that every doctor in the hospital holds dear. And if it does work we will do much better than the targets anyway. Andreas stands up.

"What are you two doing tomorrow? I have my monthly meeting with the team and I can get us through the agenda in record time so you can explain this to everyone."

"How about you give us the first hour and we promise not to overrun?" suggests Tam.

"It's a deal. Linda, will you come along and do an introduction to add the weight?"

"Of course, and I will then leave it to you, Tim and Tam to tell the same story as we have today and you to ask your team to help with the experiment we are proposing."

◆

I'd agreed to meet Dee for a quick drink on Wednesday evening and as we sit in the back room of Trippiers Pub she is, uncharacteristically, moaning about work.

"You know what, Linda. The VC's on Planet Zog! We were down twenty-five per cent on postgraduate recruitment last year and he thinks we can recover it next year. And the Health Faculty dean wants eight more professional doctorates next year. Have they had their heads in the sand for the last five years?"

She's twiddling a cocktail stirrer between her fingers – something she started doing when she gave up smoking last year – which is a decent barometer of her current level of annoyance. As I hone my body language analysis skills she speaks again:

"Are you listening?"

"What?"

"I knew it."

Then my BlackBerry winks as a text comes through. It's from Andreas and reads: '*Thanks for today… good job from Tim and Tam… everyone on board.*' That makes me smile. Dee leans into view.

"I had another offer, you know."

"No you didn't."

"How do you know?"

"I can tell when you're lying."

And then it strikes me. For goodness knows how long Dee has been my keeper and restorer of sanity. During the last few years I've saddled her with problem after frustration after worry and she's always had a way of putting them into context. Now it's my turn and I can hardly believe it. I'm not under any delusion that the hospital is on a clear and distinctive path to recovery, but there are certainly some encouraging signs. Not least the fact that we've won the hearts and minds of well over five hundred of our people and a good number of the most influential. And we have some plans in progress.

As I ponder, the room is filling up quite quickly, which is no bad thing because we were previously accompanied only by a peculiar looking man sat in the corner, wearing a long brown overall-type coat and with very greasy hair. A couple of smarter characters wearing blazers, one with a rakish moustache, arrive and then a small group of relatively normal-looking people – aside from the fact that one of them has a cuddly toy parrot – sit on the table adjacent to us.

After this temporary distraction, I decide it's my turn to cheer Dee up:

"Carlucci's or cinema?"

"What's on?" she smiles.

"You have a look while I nip to the bathroom." And I leave Dee scrolling on her iPhone.

But when I return to the room the door is closed and on it a small sign which reads:

Southern Counties Monty Python Fan Club

AGM

7:00pm to 9:00pm

I feverishly look around and there's no sign of Dee. Oh crap, she must still be in there and the meeting has started. I wait for a couple of minutes before leaning over to listen at the door. I can hear talking and then a few people saying '*ni*' in a squeaky voice. This goes on for a short while before it dies down and then it sounds like someone is reciting a poem which seems to last forever. I wander around for a few minutes more before stooping at the door to listen again. It's now 7:10pm. Soon I can make out some sort of mumbling, and then a raised voice which I recognise, and chairs scraping on the floor. I stand back as the door opens. It's Dee. She closes the door behind her and, unable to contain myself, I burst out laughing. She accuses:

"You knew, didn't you?"

"No, I promise I didn't."

"Do I look like a Monty Python fan, for goodness sake? What a set of freaks! I was the only girl in there, but not the only one wearing a dress! And that guy in the blazer kept winking at me and nudging me in the arm."

As I feverishly try to recover my composure, my efforts are thwarted by a chap who emerges from the room, wearing a T-shirt which says: **HE'S JUST A VERY NAUGHTY BOY**, and makes a beeline for Dee.

"You're not leaving already are you?" he implores in his high-pitched faux cockney tone.

I smile at Dee.

"Aren't you going to introduce me to your new friend?"

She glares at me.

"This is John."

John, inspired by the barely believable notion that his new girlfriend has remembered his name, continues confidently.

"But, Dee, are you not staying for the buffet? There's a good choice... spam and egg; spam and cheese; spam, egg and cheese; cheese, egg and spam."

Dee grabs her bag, smiles sternly at John and says:

"It's been lovely but we have to go. May the force be with you," and she pushes me towards the door.

"May the force be with you?" I say, "Dee, I don't think that's..." She glares again... "Oh, never mind."

Chapter Thirteen

Setting the rhythm

The next day I want to catch up with Andreas about his conversations with Tim and Tam and have agreed to meet him at 6:00pm in the coffee lounge. As I approach I see he's talking to his good pal and colleague Mr Cooper, so I get a cappuccino and settle down in a chair next to them. I've always been confident and comfortable with these guys but over the past few months I've felt a greater level of companionship and trust. We're happily on first-name terms now. But the thing that tickles me the most is that even though the two of them are close friends, they still refer to each other formally. I suspect it's a form of mutual mickey-taking. Cooper, or Chris to his friends, speaks:

"Hi, Linda, Dr Staulous is telling me about the idea for outpatients. It makes some sense to me but it'll be interesting when we start to get a handle on the various causes of disruption. Let's see if they get any results."

Andreas says:

"Well, we've got to try to catch up with you surgeons somehow. The extra throughput your team is delivering is clearly helping the backlog and the finances – not quite the way the finance boys thought though, eh?"

Chris, as ever, is still somewhat frustrated though.

"Look, once Linda's mate Stevie identified a vast difference in the financial throughput per bed day and we had used the idea of a planned discharge date to work on reducing the length of stay, it was the most obvious thing to do with the capacity we had created. I have looked at the numbers, and our inroads into the backlog of patients are making things better but we're still only just about hitting the access target."

Chris knows there's more to be done and I tease him that he must be delighted how much more time his surgeons are spending in theatre treating more patients. He's not greatly amused.

"Fair enough, Linda. We are able to treat more patients, but only by running more theatre sessions. The sessions themselves are still in dire straits. I've spent most of today in there – we started late, there were too many delays and overruns, and I have had to cancel the last patient on the list."

"What sort of problems did you have?" I ask.

Chris tells me at the beginning of the day they were all ready and keen to start on time, but although the first patient was checked by the anaesthetist some of the results from the preoperative assessment had not come through.

"We discussed it as a team and decided it was too risky to go ahead without them," he says. And then he explains how they tried to bring the second patient forward but the ward wasn't ready as they were not expecting a call for another hour.

"So we sat around for forty-five minutes while they rushed him down. This had a knock-on effect throughout the day and the morning list wasn't finished before lunch. So we started the afternoon with hardly a hope in hell of getting all the patients seen in time."

Chris' frustration was compounded mid afternoon when he tried to replace a faulty piece of equipment with a second unit but it was being sterilised, causing further delay. Even though a few operations went faster than expected it was still impossible to finish all of them in the allotted time. He sighs.

"It is ridiculous. All those resources – me, the anaesthetist, the theatre staff, the theatre itself and the equipment – and yet we're all standing idle as one piece of the jigsaw is missing!"

Andreas peers at his friend.

"You know, Cooper, I really wonder if the approach we have been using on the wards might help with some of this problem. Rather than a planned discharge date, in your instance you have got an operation date you are trying to meet. Once the operation has been decided, why not use the green, amber, red time buffer system to highlight if any of the preoperative tasks are putting the theatre set-up at risk? If you work out the task and the resources carrying out the task, you could probably build a template for each operation type, or at least the most common ones, and then they could be ticked off as the date approaches."

I agree.

"One of the other things we've learned is that when you have everyone working towards the same date we reduce what Stevie calls mis-synchronisation and bad multitasking. Everyone can work according to the patient that's nearest their operation date and we can escalate when things get in the red."

Another complication is that general theatres have a mix of planned and emergency cases, and this creates further tension in the system. Surely we need to give ourselves some real protection here, and I suggest that if Chris agrees to look at this idea, we set the target date one or two weeks before the operation date, so that everyone in theatres is absolutely clear, up to two weeks in advance, exactly who we're going to be operating on. Chris isn't convinced.

"Linda, do you have any idea what you've just said? When I got in this morning the theatre manager had only just seen today's list ten minutes earlier. If we had this list and it was right even a week in advance I am sure it would eliminate many on-the-day cancellations."

He concedes that, in theory at least, it sounds like a sensible idea but counters that often there just isn't enough time between the decision to operate and the access target.

"The way we are running at the moment there is no way we can get patients through the preoperative clinics in time."

"Yes," says Andreas, "but if we apply the new outpatient approach to your clinics then maybe we can solve this at the same time. The first thing would be to reduce the number of patients that cannot be operated on because a preoperative task hasn't been completed."

"That's all very well," says Chris, "but sometimes we have to cancel due to the lack of a bed."

Andreas isn't having any of that:

"Come on, Coops, you know those days are long gone. When was the last time I had medical outliers in your wards? Since we have reduced our length of stay those days are mostly over. And don't think I haven't noticed some of your surgical patients recuperating on my medical wards. So you can't claim a lack of beds any longer."

Chris makes a small concession.

"OK, maybe that was just living in the past. But even if we did have theatre sessions where everyone turned up, that only deals with half the problem."

He then talks about his access target where currently ninety per cent of patients must have their operation within a fixed number of weeks from referral by the GP. Recently he's been hitting the target most of the time and, concerned that it looked a little too neat and tidy, he decided to investigate further. He discovered that because the measurement does not actually happen until the operation is carried out there are many patients beyond the access target who have not been operated on and so not recorded. He talks of one example where someone had been waiting two years. With some shame, he then admits that to hit the target his team has planned for only a limited number of the patients in the backlog to be put on the operating list. I'm incredulous.

"WHAT! You're joking aren't you?"

"Nope. And if we stop doing this now you can kiss goodbye to meeting your own targets, and that is not going to do your job prospects a lot of good."

That does little to curb my annoyance. It's a ridiculous practice and I'm determined it doesn't happen on my watch. But I don't want a row. I just want to get to the bottom of it.

"Can we get some real numbers which show just how bad the problem is? We can't let this carry on."

This is yet another example of *'tell me how you'll measure me and I'll tell you how I'll behave'*.

Chris is not at all confrontational.

"I am right with you on this one, Linda. If there's one thing I like about you it's that when you turn over a stone and see something you don't like, you get hold of it. I know it's wrong. Let's get it sorted together."

He knows the practice is a direct violation of the rules, but his desire to get something done runs deeper than that. Happy to have got his first worry out in the open, he goes on to talk about another concern.

Each surgeon is given a certain number of four-hour sessions to operate in a week and we need to maximise the value of this time.

Surgeons approach it in different ways. What Chris calls the bold pilots tend to plan to operate on slightly more patients than the available time, hoping that some operations will take less time than they estimated. Inevitably, though, some sessions finish late and that annoys theatre staff. The staff have been brilliant, staying late and cancelling personal arrangements. Chris tells us that last week the theatre manager missed her daughter's school play. They're willing to do this when necessary but hate it when a consultant is repeatedly late.

Then there are the old pilots, among whom Chris counts himself, who are more cautious. They accept that some operations will take longer than expected and it's not just the patient that causes the delays. It also depends on the combination of the surgeon and anaesthetist.

"I've been working with my current anaesthetist for fifteen years and it works like a dream most of the time," he says. "But even we can get caught out. Of course, sometimes everything goes better than expected and we finish early, although you will never see this on the performance sheets as it would look like we were being unproductive."

This is yet another example of how measurements are distorting our behaviour. Chris continues:

"As you know, there are old pilots and there are bold pilots, but there are not many old, bold pilots! I'm not sure how your time buffer ideas can help us here."

Andreas wants to assist.

"Come on, Cooper, slow down and explain the problem to us."

Chris ponders a moment and then says:

"Let me give you an example. If I am planning one of these sessions and I am placing patients in the session, then on any one day I might have a number of simple operations that typically take half an hour, but also some complicated ones which may take an hour or an hour and a half. I like to do the most complicated one first, so say in my four hours I plan two operations which I think in total will take three hours, if I try to slot two more half-hour operations in I am right against the wire and if anything goes wrong I will overrun. It is even worse the closer I get to the four hours. I can't fill the remaining time with half an operation."

"Isn't this why we agreed to do all-day sessions?" I ask. "So you could run late in the morning without disrupting someone else in the afternoon?"

"Yes. But there are other issues. An all-day session once a week, rather than two half-day sessions equally spread throughout the week causes peak loads in the support services carrying out the preoperative tasks, and spikes in demand for particular beds on a particular ward."

Then he looks at Andreas.

"The reason I have been using your beds is that when I do one of these all-day lists my ward quite often cannot cope with the demand, and that can cause us to spill over."

Andreas smiles:

"Don't worry, my friend. We are on the same team, and at the minute we can cope thanks to our reduced lengths of stay, but we all know it is not ideal. Clearly, the risk of cross-infection grows."

As I listen I start to wonder whether using the time buffer system is the real answer here, but the problem lies in the series of dependent events – one operation cannot start until the last one is completed – and statistical fluctuations. Although there's an average time an operation takes, there must be a skewed distribution around how long it actually takes. Trying to come up with a schedule saying exactly what time an operation should start and finish within the four hours simply cannot work. Chris continues.

"As the day unfolds there's almost zero chance of the operation finishing and starting as planned. But we have to ensure that everybody else is flexible enough to work with the changes in the schedule and understand why things take longer than expected."

It strikes me immediately that Stevie would tell us planning the start and finish times according to the averages is ridiculous. If one finishes early and we cannot use that time, and then another finishes late and bumps the next patient, there's no wonder that even though there are some earlies, every session will finish late. This is why the old pilots have learned not to be bold pilots. I want to know what the potential for improvement is.

"Chris, just between you and me, how much time do you think there really is left for us to improve this process by?"

He thinks for a moment.

"Honestly, Linda, it must be at least twenty per cent."

"Well, if we could only get our hands on half of that, with ten per cent more capacity in theatres, and the free beds we're creating on the wards, there may be a chance that I can go to regional office, explain the hidden backlog of un-booked patients and ask for a period of amnesty to eliminate the backlog without being penalised."

Surely they'd understand, particularly because we wouldn't increase our operating expenses during this period of catch-up. I want to make a move on this straightaway, and I give Stevie's mobile number to Chris to see what advice he can give and Chris agrees to phone him this evening. And with that I bid them goodbye. I have to make a run for it as at 7:00pm I'm giving out the prize for the best project that our graduate trainees have submitted. This is a nice job to do and I'm looking forward to it. Some of the projects are really very impressive and it's good to see what the future of the health service can come up with.

On my way home that evening I ring Kieran to give him the heads-up, but I don't think I've caught him at a particularly good time.

"Do you have a minute to speak?"

"Not really," comes the reply. "Can't it wait?"

"Well, I guess so. Shall I call you tomorrow?"

"If it will wait until Monday we can talk about it then. And I was going to call Cath to book myself in for a visit. I want to come down there and see for myself what's happening."

"Er... sure."

Fantastic! I just call to try to smooth our path for the coming weeks and end up agreeing to a regional visit to our hospital. The team will crucify me! But then I am overcome by a welcome surge of self-belief. Kieran can't be coming down to haul me over the coals. We've been showing good signs in recent months. Maybe he's genuinely coming down to see if we're doing something that could be passed around. And in any case, the silver lining to what I initially thought was a cloud is that I'm positive he didn't mention that Ashcroft was coming. Hope springs eternal.

♦

It's 7:30am when I arrive at my office and Chris is already standing outside.

"Morning, Head Mistress," he's already mocking me, "I used to have to do a lot of this when I was at school, but happily this time I have some good news. You didn't tell me Stevie was in the Far East by the way. He gets about, doesn't he? Anyway, we had a brilliant discussion about the problem and I can see the start of a way forward. It is all about aggregation."

"Aggregation of what?"

Chris is animated.

"Let me explain."

"Well, let's at least sit down and get a coffee." I usher him into the office but haven't taken my seat before he begins.

"We know that the time to complete every operation will fit some sort of skewed diagram. If the average is one hour, it is unlikely that even I can do it in less than forty minutes… but with complications it could take up to two hours. So inevitably, when we are estimating a time, us old pilots tend to be a little conservative. But the chances of five operations in a row all taking longer than expected is very, very low."

He makes me smile as he refers to the dice game, recalling that sometimes we will throw a good number and sometimes a bad one. Stevie suggested Chris should plan according to a challenging but achievable timeframe and use this throughout the session to calculate the start and expected finish time of each patient, AND leave a time buffer at the end to soak up the variation. Stevie has further explained to Chris that this overall time buffer can actually be considerably smaller, probably as small as half of the total protection embedded in each of the individual estimates. This is known as aggregating the variation.

"In other words, we're planning as though things will go well, or at least reasonably well, and providing protection at the end of the session in case they do not. I now understand it is extremely unlikely they will all take longer than expected so the total protection needed is less. All we need to do on the day is teach all the teams involved to have everything prepared according to the schedule but also to be prepared that things may slip as the session goes on."

Ever the sports fan, Chris says that this being prepared means behaving in the same way as the pit crews of a Formula 1 team: they are permanently ready just in case, and when called upon will do everything they can to minimise any delay in the schedule. In fact, they practise it time after time, and Stevie told Chris that his teams should do exactly the same.

"We should treat every minute as if it was the most precious minute of all. If you think about it, Linda, every minute we waste here is like wasting a minute across the whole of this planned care pathway. It is just like everyone involved standing out in the car park for a minute."

I don't want to stop Chris in his flow. The sheer enthusiasm in his voice is diametrically opposite to the tones of cynicism that have echoed through the corridors of this hospital for far too long. That's not so often the case now but it's still great to hear him. He continues:

"The other thing we talked about was my preference for doing the most complicated operations first. Stevie asked me to take into account the likely variation in time to complete the operation and he talked me through the advantages of doing the short operations with the least variation first. This will give us the best chance of minimising the number of cancelled operations when things go slower than expected."

Chris admits that it isn't entirely straightforward but it's got him thinking. He thinks it's a good idea to use the time buffer system on the planning.

"Linda, these actions should create considerable extra time within a session but I need help to get this to work. If we just save a few minutes we will not be able to safely insert an additional patient into the schedule. The session has to be made up of a discrete number of patients; I can't start and not finish an operation! I'm more than happy to be the pilot but I need some help with the planning systems. I think I know how to do it but I need someone to help me sort out the practicalities. So if you have a bright spark available I'll be delighted," he says hopefully. Then I have a plan.

"You know what, Chris, this might just be your lucky day. The young woman who won the prize last night certainly is a bright spark. Come to think of it, I don't know how we managed to persuade her to come and work in healthcare. She has the brains to head for a top job in the City but she seems totally committed to helping the health service. God bless her. Her name is Ruth. I'll give her a ring and sell it to her that the second half of her prize is working with you!"

"Thanks, Linda. I may be an old pilot but you never know, I might just turn into a bold pilot!"

"Actually, Chris, all I need from you is to set the rhythm. I don't really care whether you're old or bold. But a doctor-led change like this is exactly what we need."

Chapter Fourteen

Pride

It's the morning of Kieran's visit, 7:00am and we're ready to go! Well, almost. Kieran's due in at 8:00am to have a look at what and how we're doing here. And the great thing is that I've a significantly better hand of cards within my grasp than when we visited regional office a few months ago. We're by no means perfect but, by God, we can show that we're doing all we can to lift this place. The meeting is quite timely from my point of view too. In recent weeks I've clarified in my own mind that I want to stay in this job, and when Kieran spoke to me a couple of weeks ago he mentioned that they were ready to start the process to appoint a new CEO here. So I've thrown my hat in. And maybe I can show Kieran what a good job we've been doing as well as getting some of the inside track on what's happening with the appointment. The interviews are being held at the end of this week.

I can't believe Kieran wanted to start so early. He lives a long way away, but from my point of view, the earlier the better. I thought the best way was to show him round the hospital before going through the numbers, so we can have a quick chat when he arrives and when we set off at around 8:15am the hospital will be in full swing. Cath brings in a fresh pot of coffee.

"Morning," she says breezily. "You look nice… is it a new suit?"

Taken aback, I try to remember.

"Er, thanks but no. I'm sure I've worn it before."

"Well, you look very smart."

"I thought I should make an effort."

I know Cath would appreciate that. She's pretty much old school in many ways and her own standards of etiquette and presentation are extremely high; so much so that I sometimes feel positively scruffy. And she has an acute sense of occasion combined with a protective instinct towards me.

"I hope it all goes well today. Are you worried?"

"No. You know I'm not in the least bit worried. We've all worked hard and I don't think Kieran could ask for a lot more."

"You're right. Why don't you meet him in the car park so you can catch him before he enters the building? And that way you can guarantee he gets the right parking space."

She smiles her encouragement and, pep talk delivered, leaves me to it. I look at this morning's post in my tray and see a letter from regional office personally addressed to me. It's a letter from the chairman of the hospital saying I've been confirmed on the short list for the CEO job and need to be available for interview this week. Wow. What a week this could be.

At 8:00am on the dot I see Kieran walking across the car park.

"Morning, Linda, beautiful day for it."

I look up at the blue, cloudless sky. I cheerily agree and Kieran says:

"Thanks for taking the time out to show me around today. I'm really looking forward to it. You have certainly been doing something here and you must be pleased with your progress. I want to try to understand how you have done it."

This is a wonderful start. Kieran's been looking at our progress reports and, unless he's been briefed by good old Ashcroft in the art of counter espionage, he's generously putting me at ease. And so I'm confident enough to start the tour without delay.

"It's my pleasure, Kieran. I thought that before we go to the office I could show you around so that you can see for yourself some of the changes we've made. I suggest we start in A&E and work our way through the building."

"That's great."

We walk into the A&E department and through the waiting room where less than a third of all of the chairs are occupied. This in itself is a big difference for us and I wonder whether Kieran will notice. The first person we meet is Mo and, with his usual warm smile, he comes straight up to both of us and I introduce him:

"You've met Mo before at your office."

"Hello, Kieran," says Mo, shaking hands. "Thanks for coming to have a look around."

Kieran has been looking at the A&E numbers and seen the impressive inroads Mo has made towards achieving the ninety-five per cent access target.

"It seems there are now only a few days in a month that you are missing it. Can you tell me how you have done it?"

"I'll be delighted," says Mo. "Let me walk you through and I will explain as we go."

Firstly, he takes Kieran to the reception area where he can see that, rather than just taking the patient details, we have a doctor-led assessment process working. Mo explains to Kieran that if the patient is an inappropriate attendance we refer them immediately to either their GP or the local treatment centres in town.

"So has this been the major part of your solution?" asks Kieran.

"Not really," says Mo, "but it has definitely helped. Before we started this process these patients would have spent a couple of hours in the department before eventually being referred back, but actually this is not the major change."

He goes on to describe how in the past, once a patient had been registered, the majority either completed their treatment just before or after the four-hour target. Kieran knows this full well. Quite often two or three hours passed before any diagnosis happened and patients were queuing everywhere. Kieran nods at Mo to continue.

"So we've instigated a pretty simple approach. Rather than throwing more resources at the problem we worked out that we needed a better system of prioritising and synchronising all our individual efforts but, more importantly, we needed to identify what the underlying cause of the delay was across all patients."

Mo then explains how his version of the time buffer management system works.

"We have split the four hours into three time zones of eighty minutes each, and as the patient passes through the department we identify at eighty minutes, one hundred and sixty minutes and two hundred and forty minutes the task and resource that was disrupting or delaying the patient's journey."

Kieran interrupts:

"But surely there were hundreds of causes."

"Surprisingly not," answers Mo. "There are actually relatively few tasks and resources that are causing most of the delays."

He then takes us into the office and shows us, on the wall, graphs of the last eight weeks of causes of delay. Kieran scans the graphs as Mo explains that there were two types of delay: the first caused by resources within our own department and the second caused by resources outside the department.

"I explained to our staff that there was no way we would ever get the external sources of disruption resolved until we could prove to the rest of the hospital we were squeaky clean ourselves. We had to get our own house in order."

Kieran likes that so Mo continues, saying that he uncovered some behaviours where we were shooting ourselves in the foot, the first being the A&E doctors' propensity for cherry-picking once true emergencies have been treated. We were not treating patients according to a common prioritisation. In too many cases patients were first seen by a junior doctor and finally escalated through to the consultant. So we have moved to a truly consultant-delivered service with all staff now working to this common list. This also resolves the bad multitasking, which was inevitable in this environment. Mo explains that when each resource is working on patients in a different order, and when a number of different resources are required to complete the diagnosis, invariably there were one or two different outstanding tasks for each patient. He says:

"Every hour we review the green, amber and red status and escalate to the various internal resources accordingly. Everyone knows if they are the cause of a delay to a particular patient, and we also monitor throughout the day if one of our own internal resources is causing multiple delays across multiple patients. Then we can do something about it.

Mo explains the previous approach of analysing the cause of the final breach is really missing the true underlying cause.

"It is more valuable to explore what is happening in the amber and red zones. Now, every shift change we review the performance, the causes of delay and what we need to do differently, and discuss with the next shift. Then every week we sit down for an hour to review the data and identify what we need to improve."

"It's a pretty simple process," says Kieran looking at me.

"And that is its strength," I reply.

Kieran wanders up and down, looking carefully at the graphs before homing in on one of the bar charts for the last week. He points out that for one of the delaying resources the amber bar is much higher than the red bar, which is higher than the small black bar, and yet for another resource the amber is small, the red grows and then the black is the largest.

"What is this telling you?" he asks Mo.

"Well, in the first case something which was a large cause of delay early in the process has actually diminished as the journey unfolded, and yet frustratingly there are still some patients where this early disruption resulted in a later breach. Looking at the resource that was responsible as the patient went through the black zone is not really the issue. We have to tackle the problem that is occurring much earlier in the process in the amber. If we can reduce the ambers we can reduce the reds and eliminate the corresponding breaches at four hours."

Mo explains that the second case is an example of a resource outside the department.

"This is where we were waiting for an external specialist to review the patient. It did not really matter whether they were called when the patient was in the amber zone or the red zone; whatever time they were called, by the time they arrived and the rest of the diagnosis was completed almost all such patients end up breaching the target."

In reality, if we'd looked at the graphs eight weeks ago the problem was significantly worse, but colleagues in the rest of the hospital have helped Mo to resolve his issues. I speak up.

"I have to say, Kieran, without the leadership of our clinicians, particularly Dr Staulous and Mr Cooper, this would never have happened."

The remaining problems, which now make up less than a tenth of the volumes of eight weeks ago, are where the resource we require is between a rock and a hard place: needed in two places at the same time. It's become clear that we need to change the rotas to solve problems like this, but at least we now know that there are only a few key resources that we need to change rather than trying to change everyone and everything.

Kieran's intrigued by what he's seen.

"Who else sees this data?"

"Cooper and Staulous take their teams through it every week," I answer. "It has really helped to change the blame culture. We now tackle the problem together rather than spending hours arguing whose fault it was."

Kieran's clearly delighted and he pats Mo on the back.

"Well, young man, this is impressive stuff, but how many more weeks do you think it will be before you can guarantee you can consistently meet the target?"

"I'm not in a position to guarantee anything yet, Kieran, but what I can assure you of is that we have developed an evidence-based process that is driving every step of our improvement. And we are hitting the target with significantly less overtime and agency staff, and I can tell you things are different around here. People are starting to be proud of the department again."

He seizes the moment as today's navigator walks past.

"Can I introduce you to Jenny?" Jenny looks startled. "Today Jenny is the nurse who ensures we all follow the list and is pro-actively escalating disruption and delay as it happens throughout the day."

Kieran shakes Jenny's hand and thankfully she doesn't have the faintest idea who he is.

"Hello, Jenny, it's nice to meet you. Tell me what it is like in this new role."

Jenny briefly wears a look that says '*who me?*' before gathering her composure.

"The best way I can describe this job is that it's like being a Master of Ceremonies at an event. It probably looks like I do very little. But I'm acting as a human radar to look into the near future and ensure nothing goes wrong. Now and again I have to chase people down or escalate, but most of the time it's just ensuring we all keep to the process."

Kieran smiles.

"That sounds like an important role; challenging, I bet. Do you enjoy it?"

Jenny glances over at me again for reassurance before saying:

"At the start of this year I was ready to quit the job. I'd enrolled on a college course to begin to retrain. But since we brought in the new approach we know what we're doing, and so I'm happy again. The only thing that lets us down now is if we've completed the assessment and a decision to admit is made in good time, but the patient still breaches because there was no bed available either in the assessment unit or on the ward. That's when you see the screens go red and then black and it frustrates the hell out of everyone down here."

"Well done, Jenny," says Kieran. "Thank you for all the work you and the team have put into this. It really is encouraging. Would you mind if I brought some other people around to have a look?"

Jenny blushes slightly and says:

"The only time people came round here in the past was to tell us what we were doing wrong. It would be fantastic for morale for people to come and see how we're doing it right – and an honour."

Mo offers to take Kieran to the assessment unit to show what we've done there. As he leads the way I lean over to Jenny and whisper:

"What were you retraining as?"

"A welder."

As we enter the assessment unit it's noticeable that the air of calm prevailing in the A&E department isn't quite so evident here. It looks like almost every bed is occupied and there are some patients sitting on chairs. Mo is actually proud of what we've done here and isn't deterred.

"Kieran, this is really the hub of it all. This is where we get it right or we get it wrong. If this tips over then you can say goodbye to the A&E target. If there is not a bed or chair available here there is nothing A&E can do to save a breach."

Kieran looks around the unit as Mo is talking.

"If you had been here ten weeks ago this was nothing more than a spillover ward. Patients were being transferred out of A&E to the next available bed and that was the only way we could save a four-hour breach. If the available bed was here then here is where the patient landed, regardless of whether or not they needed an assessment. Often the stay in this unit was longer than on some of the wards."

He goes on to explain how we've established that this is the only place in the whole operation where we can absorb the difference between the rate at which patients are discharged from the rest of the hospital and the rate at which beds are required from A&E and direct GP admission. He provides an excellent explanation of the need for protective capacity at the vital link in the chain of activities.

"We call it the Tardis; it's our space-time buffer. It is a space buffer because it has to be of a size that can soak up the variation in requirements. It is a time buffer because, just like in A&E, we want to ensure the assessment is carried out in a timely manner. We use the same principles as in A&E but rather than having one fixed, common target we have broken it down by patient type and we now have four-, eight-, twelve- and twenty-four-hour assessment time buffers.

"The first action is the doctor decides how long, purely from a clinical perspective, it should take to carry out the assessment. Sometimes it is just a matter of getting some tests done quickly and deciding whether a patient can go home or needs to be admitted to a specific ward."

"But what happens when you need a period of observation or more detailed assessment?" asks Kieran.

"Well, by setting these different time zones and adopting the same approach as in A&E we have been able to keep the flow going through the department and, most importantly, signal to the rest of the hospital when a bed will need to be available."

A light goes on in Kieran's head and he can see how much more proactive this approach is, as Mo tells him that every ward can see live 24/7 our latest data of near-time bed requirements. He continues:

"We can also identify which ward most often causes bed shortages in the assessment unit and even through to a specific breach in the A&E. By connecting together these three important steps in the patient journey there is now nowhere to hide; everybody knows exactly what is happening all day long."

Kieran looks at me and asks:

"How do your people feel about this high level of analysis? I can imagine how someone might feel exposed."

"This isn't about identifying who to blame," I say. "It's about identifying, from all the places we could try to improve, which place to focus our efforts on. The analysis of this part of the system is now driving our improvement initiatives across the whole hospital."

I explain how in the past, to ensure bed availability for A&E, we needed to have a bed available on every ward, just in case the next patient was going to be admitted to that ward, and how we were overtly pushing for earlier discharges in the day across every ward:

"Kieran, we had this 'by 11:00am' discharge initiative, but it was like firing a blunderbuss at the problem. Much of it was wasted effort."

"I know," says Kieran with half a smile. "That was a best practice we put out two years ago. And I bet when you really pushed a ward beds suddenly became available, as if by magic."

"You're right," says Mo. "Either because there were patients who were ready for discharge but had not been discharged, or there was some hesitation by ward staff in signalling a bed was now available. Under this system we don't just know by ward but can even analyse by doctor the chain reaction resulting in an A&E breach. Beforehand, it was not simply a case of someone being stubborn or lazy; it was down to some local prioritisation in another part of the hospital which resulted in misguided priorities for the whole system. We used to see this as a bed management problem. There was a whole team trying to gather live data about bed availability across the hospital and make decisions accordingly. Our new approach of ongoing analysis and improvement means that instead of just treating the symptom of a lack of bed availability, we are treating the underlying cause."

Kieran asks:

"Right now it looks pretty crowded in here. How do you know it's big enough?"

"That's an extremely good question," says Mo, "and it's not straightforward. Rather than trying to establish the right size, we are counting the number of patients whose journey extends into the red buffer zone per day to see if it is increasing or decreasing. We are planning to use this to eventually try to establish the correct size. But I must admit my current view is that there is actually no correct size; what we need is a mechanism to dynamically adjust capacity at relatively short notice."

The trick with this idea though is to learn how quickly to open up additional capacity and also how to close it down quickly. Mo explains this was Jo's idea, and one of her lead nurses is working on the project and has already done some practice runs.

"We can now open a new bay in two hours, fully staffed; and we can close it in twelve with all patients treated safely throughout."

"But how do you staff this when your people are already running as fast as they can?" asks Kieran.

"This is the clever part." Mo looks pleased. "We don't need additional staff. We have a virtual team, trained up from across the hospital, and they come and help as required. When the peak demand is over they return to their own ward. We have made sure they understand how important this is for the system as a whole and they are proud to be part of this virtual team."

Kieran is impressed.

"This is great. But it will have required big changes in practices and behaviours of everyone involved. How have you done this in such a short period of time?"

After a long pause Mo says:

"Kieran, I couldn't have done this without Linda's help and leadership. She is the one who got everyone together and made the case for change. She explained why we needed to change and she was the one who introduced us to this simple way of focusing our efforts. She made it clear that if we worked together it was possible to achieve a major improvement in performance. She also made it crystal clear that once we have agreement on a new way forward we can't drag our heels. She has relentlessly reinforced this point ever since the day she took over. You should get her to show you the dice game. That day was a seminal moment of change in this hospital."

I'm mildly embarrassed as I smile at Mo.

"Thanks, Mo, the cheque's in the post. Is it time for a coffee?"

As we walk to the coffee lounge Kieran says:

"Impressive stuff, Linda. It looks like you stand a real chance of hitting your targets if you can keep the bed availability high across the rest of the hospital. But as we all know, you don't have any extra money for that. I'll be interested to see how you've been solving this."

I take Kieran to the coffee shop. One of the uncomfortable things about being in the health service is that as we pass the newspaper stand and the vendor cheerily waves at me, almost inevitably the headlines are saturated with stories of a hospital that's being accused of unnecessary deaths by cutting clinical staff. The brutal, if rather unimaginative headline reads:

Heads Will Roll!

Chapter Fifteen

And

I want to take Kieran to one of our elderly care wards to see the daily activity and so we head to Willow ward. We arrive just in time for their daily patient review meeting. As we walk in, one of the junior nurses asks us politely to follow the hand-cleansing process, and proudly tells us the ward has now gone fifty-two days without a breach of this practice. Very impressive. Then after introducing Kieran to Andreas and some of the ward staff, we listen to what he has to say.

"OK, everyone, let's get on with it. For the benefit of our visitors I'll start by reminding everyone of the process. We will start at the top of the list. The first step for the top patient will be to review the planned discharge date and agree if there is any clinical reason why this date needs to change. OK? So, Lizzy Trebore, seventy-two years old, and her planned discharge date was three weeks ago."

Kieran's ears prick up as Andreas recounts that Miss Trebore was actually fit to be discharged weeks ago, but she is an out-of-area admission and we've been unable to get her repatriated.

"They are claiming she was homeless," he says, "although she was actually staying with friends. She has mental health issues but we have stabilised her and after repeated calls to the mental health services in her area we were just fobbed off day after day."

A nurse adds:

"She is desperate to get out of here. The poor lady has no visitors and is feeling more and more depressed. We could have treated four more patients in the extra time Miss Trebore has been here."

I despair at this and ask Andreas to discuss it with me offline, and maybe we can enlist Kieran's help in getting some movement.

The next patient on the list is Mina Ebadi, seventy-six.

"Her planned discharge date is the day after tomorrow. Is there any reason to change the PDD?"

The physio responds:

"Actually, I think if we do the stairs test today I have a suspicion she may well run up them! So from a clinical perspective there's probably no reason why she can't go home tomorrow."

Her colleague adds:

"I agree, but I'm not sure the adjustments at her home will be completed in time for her to go home tomorrow."

Andreas interjects here.

"You know the process. The planned discharge date is based on purely clinical grounds. So if she can go home tomorrow we should bring forward the PDD to tomorrow and then deal with what's needed to make it happen. Are there any other outstanding tasks for this patient?"

"No. I spoke to Mrs Ebadi about leaving tomorrow and she would be delighted to. She feels ready to go and is excited about being home in time for her granddaughter's birthday."

"So, we all agree then. We bring forward the PDD by a day."

"Yes, and I'll ensure the adaptations are completed on time."

For Kieran's benefit Andreas explains that social services and the housing department can view this system and they will see the PDD come forward, but it's worth a call just to ensure it happens in time.

The next two patients are straightforward. Their planned discharge date is three days away and all of the current tasks are complete. It's just about waiting for the patient to clinically recover before discharge. Further down the list there is an interesting case which Andreas explains to us all.

"So this is Pavel Brovlowski, sixty-eight. Planned discharge date four days away and this patient is predicted to be delayed."

"How do you know this patient is going to be delayed when their planned discharge date is in the future?" asks Kieran.

"What we do is list all the outstanding tasks and against each task we note the responsible resource," says Andreas. "That resource provides us with a daily update of how many days there are remaining before the task will be complete. If we look into Mr Brovlowski's time buffer consumption chart we can see that there are three tasks that will hopefully be finished just in time, currently showing to be completed in the red zone. But there is one task that cannot even start until these three tasks have been completed, and on average that task takes ten days."

This man will require ongoing funding, which will not be confirmed until the patient is officially fit for discharge. So even now Andreas knows we have a built-in delay. The final tasks that are needed are predecessors and will be finished on Thursday, and yet the panel meeting to discuss the funding application only happens every week on a Wednesday, and so six days will go by with no action. I can see Kieran becoming a little frustrated with the story but Andreas is quick to add:

"They used to run the panel meeting every two weeks, and based on the data we produced, with the number of days' delay this was causing both on this ward and across the whole hospital, we were able to persuade them to run the meeting once a week. It is now only two hours rather than four but runs twice as often. I'd like to move it to twice a week but it is these sorts of policy changes that take us a while when the whole system is involved. Without the specific evidence by patient, by ward and for the whole hospital, we would never have even got the discussion on the table."

"Why were they only holding the meetings every two weeks in the first place?" asks Kieran.

"Well, it's a big decision," replies Andreas. "It's about the ongoing funding for the patient and it requires a number of people to be in the room. It took a while to persuade them that to reduce the delay we needed to increase the frequency of the meetings. We weren't asking for more time for the meeting, just more frequent meetings of shorter duration."

Andreas leads the team down the list, reviewing each patient, and within twenty-five minutes there is a specific plan updated for each one, with a to-do list that will keep everyone focused throughout the rest of the day. The green, amber and red buffer system is similar to the one used in the assessment unit but is regularly updated to take account of changing clinical recovery times. When the patients are in the green zone there is no need to review them. The system ensures staff focus all their time on the few patients in or at risk of delay. He ends the meeting by presenting a chart which shows the reasons for delay, which the group filters by task and resource, before discussing how they will resolve the most common causes.

Once everyone has gone Kieran is keen to understand how this is different from the past. Andreas explains they used to have board rounds where every patient was reviewed on a white board. This took a couple of hours and it was difficult to keep everyone's attention and attendance. Now, because the buffer system allows them to focus on the few patients most at risk or most delayed, the whole process can be done in under half an hour. Everyone sees the enormous value of it and by the end of the day the positive results are clear.

"It's a winner all round," he says. "Not only is it patient-centred, but we can genuinely engage the patient in their own recovery plan. It stops the bitching and moaning among staff and focuses on resolving causes rather than blaming resources. It is flexible and adaptive rather than controlling and prescriptive. It is clinically led and it is patient-centred. And the nurses are just as likely to challenge me as the other way round."

Kieran asks:

"What's been the impact of this on the ward's performance?"

"Well, this was one of the later wards to adopt this approach so we've only been using it for the last four weeks," replies Andreas. "That helped us because the process was quite well refined by the time this ward picked it up. We could tackle reservations with other examples of success around the hospital."

And of course, Andreas has his colleagues' competitive nature so no little part of him wanted to show everyone else that this team could improve faster than the previous wards! So far, average stay has reduced by thirty per cent, and bed availability for patients coming from the assessment unit is at ninety-nine per cent. Patients in delay is now a tiny fraction of what it was when we started. At the start, the number one cause of delay was one of his own doctors, but this no longer makes it into the top ten. The ward has recently been audited by another one of the external review bodies, which assessed a dramatic improvement in the quality of care with zero readmissions.

"We are proud of what we have done with the freed-up time, and we are trying to be an exemplar ward. We have also maintained zero infection. One of the other effects is just how clean and tidy the ward is. Using this approach has given us more time to do things right the first time and bring back the pride in our work. By the way, has Linda told you about our trip to the bakers?"

"No?" says Kieran, looking inquisitively at me.

"This ward had one of the poorest track records for cleanliness and hygiene," I explain, "and the argument we were given was that everyone was too rushed off their feet to maintain standards. And it wasn't just in this ward – it was normalised behaviour. Another day, another failure; and in the most tragic cases another day, another death."

"Linda arranged for us all to visit a bakery," says Andreas, "and at first we all thought it was a ridiculous idea, not to say a monumental waste of time, which we let her know. But we had the shock of our lives."

He explains how the morning went. Before arriving everyone had to send through their shoe size and head size, and as they entered the site it was clear just how seriously the bakery had dealt with cleanliness and safety. They wouldn't even let their own lorries in until they'd been through the lorry wash. Andreas' team was unable to walk into the bakery until they had washed their hands, put on white wellington boots, walked through the disinfectant trays and had their hair pinned into hats. And make-up and perfume was banned (much to Andreas' disappointment).

One of the bakery workers told him that anyone chewing gum would be reported as this presented a risk of contaminating the product. All the staff were acutely aware that if a customer consumed a contaminated product the ensuing publicity glare and reputational damage would cripple the financial performance of the company and put their jobs at risk. Everyone in the business recognised their responsibility and there was zero tolerance from the shop floor right up to the CEO.

"Our people spent half a day there, and that's all it took," says Andreas. "We came back a different team, and now we run quick briefing sessions for every new patient and every visitor to continually reinforce the importance of this."

Kieran tells Andreas he is mightily impressed by what he's seen. He asks him to send over the details of the patient who is delayed due to the neighbouring patch's reticence, and promises to make a call to get it sorted. We then bid Andreas farewell and I take Kieran to meet Charlie.

This will be a meeting where Kieran will see us at our worst, warts and all. We will attend the top delays meeting run by Charlie, where they discuss the most delayed patients list which continues to be a concern to everyone, despite our best efforts. He reviews the top twenty patients one by one and runs the meeting with an iron fist. Anyone who walks into the room cannot leave until there is an action against every one of the twenty patients, and nothing can be delegated to someone who's not in the room. He also reviews tomorrow's imminent discharges to look at those patients whose outstanding non-clinical tasks are not scheduled to be completed in time and to see what it will take to get it solved within the next twenty-four hours.

Despite Charlie's iron rule manner, the meeting is well attended and in full flow when we arrive; they're already dealing with patient number four on the list. After sitting and listening for a while it becomes clear to us that nobody in the room knows whether the doctor responsible for the patient has spoken to the relevant social worker team about the reason why the discharge has been delayed. Charlie picks up the phone, calls the doctor's mobile and asks him to join us straightaway. He also makes it brutally clear that he's not impressed that the doctor in question has not attended when one of his patients is in the top twenty. I look at Kieran, who returns my glance with raised eyebrows as Charlie, who's starting to sound unnervingly like Al Pacino, coldly says:

"If you don't want to come to the meeting, don't have a patient in the top twenty. And now we're all sitting here waiting for you. Sitting and waiting."

A few moments later the chastened doctor comes through the door apologising, and the discussion continues. Soon it's clear who needs to do what and who needs to phone whom, and Charlie asks the doctor to call him back at 4:00pm to confirm those actions have been taken. Kieran whispers to me:

"This all looks a little draconian but it seems to be working."

I think he half expected Charlie to start walking around the table nursing a baseball bat before kissing the errant and increasingly nervous doctor. I tell him that when we started this process, on any day across the whole hospital we had twenty per cent of patients present in delay. When we added up the total number of days these patients had been delayed, the top twenty accounted for nearly half of that. Now, the twentieth most delayed patient has only been in delay a few days, and the number of patients in delay on any day is less than five per cent. This has made a huge difference to bed availability and patient flow. We think that if we carry on we can get this down even further. This has definitely been a major ingredient in the culture change.

"Let's face it, Kieran, this is basically a list of the patients we have failed, so why not treat it with such serious intent?"

"Why is Charlie leading this and not you?" he asks.

I tell him we both led it to start with but now Charlie does it on his own.

"The massive advantage of this is we have our own senior doctor demonstrating commitment to achieving not just higher-quality care but also operational performance improvement. And to be honest, he's brilliant at it. He's better than me, and his clinical insight is an enormous help. Plus there aren't many clinicians who can pull the wool over Charlie's eyes."

As they come to the end of the list, Charlie brings up on the big screen the latest analysis of the most common causes of disruption for these most delayed patients and takes everyone through the top three to agree action points. He then represents the data showing all patients rather than just the top twenty, and it's clear to see that the hierarchy in causes of delay is almost identical. Kieran is very interested in this and at the end of the meeting asks Charlie to elaborate.

Charlie begins by explaining that this is the core hypothesis which Stevie explained to us at the outset. Stevie claimed that while the hospital is a not-for-profit organisation, it's a for-purpose organisation. In any organisation with a goal, which consists of a seemingly complex set of dependent resources, there are actually few underlying constraints. And these constraints would determine the performance, or lack of performance, of the whole system. He says:

"Where there is a lack of synchronisation of resources, some patients are seen before others while other patients end up being delayed. But these few constraints can cause delay across all patients. Some will experience severe delay but almost all will experience some delay, so we should not be surprised that the two lists are similar. In fact, if they weren't it would question our hypothesis."

"I understand the level of challenge," says Kieran, "and it is clearly working, but what's to stop a doctor simply claiming the patient isn't fit to go home and moving the PDD into the future? Then their patient won't be in delay and they won't have to come to this meeting."

Charlie replies.

"We review every ward and every doctor to see if they are simultaneously improving the quality of care, reducing the length of stay and reducing delays. You can't play that game when those three requirements need to be delivered simultaneously. All that happens is the length of stay goes up and apparently without any delay. You can be caught out. But in all honesty, this hasn't been an issue; everyone has been behind the approach since we all spent the day with Linda and Stevie."

Kieran looks at me.

"Who is Stevie? Everyone seems to know him."

"I'll explain later," I say. "There's one more person I want you to meet. But before we leave here, can you see how we have just taken the simple idea of a patient-centred and clinically led approach, and then put all our efforts into identifying why we cannot follow this through?" Kieran nods. "We've had to hold our nerve," I add, "because this also meant stopping numerous other initiatives that were trying to improve things around here."

We had come to realise that we were improving areas of the system which were not impacting the performance of the whole system. We were failing to concentrate on the few constraints that we really needed to focus our efforts on. Kieran speaks up.

"I have to say, Linda, holding your nerve is a salient point. At the centre we've been discussing how you've ignored the request to close some wards, yet you have managed to reduce length of stay and free up capacity."

"I want to take you to see the work we've been doing in surgery. Rather than closing wards, we've reallocated them to help us improve our access targets in planned care and improve our financial position."

"But you must have created enough capacity to shut down at least four wards, so why are you holding back? Why aren't you cutting costs?"

"We have cut some costs. I'll show you the numbers later. You can see for yourself our overtime costs and agency numbers have definitely gone down."

Kieran's satisfied for the time being and so we go to meet Chris Cooper.

♦

Chris and his team are down in the education centre and we find them in the midst of a heated discussion as only surgeons know how. They're an eccentric bunch. They could start a fight in a phone box if you left them on their own, and they must be responsible for keeping the local bow tie shop in business! But there is real positive energy here. Being the type of character who gets on at break-neck speed when he has a job to do, Chris has quickly completed his pilot and has good news for his team. He is in flying form, taking the lead and loving every minute of it.

"Ladies and gentlemen, we now have the early evidence we hoped for from our controlled experiment. We have already increased the number of operations carried out within the same number of sessions. Sessions are starting on time. We have fewer overruns and, even though our measurements are a little crude, more productive time."

He explains how signing off the lists in advance has resulted in a better mix of patients on the day with fewer gaps. And with all the improvement, more sessions are not overrunning; however, he is convinced there's still room for more use of the aggregated protective capacity. Then with gathering Churchillian momentum he announces:

"I am going to designate a select few of the sessions as Gold sessions, where I will be slightly more ambitious in the planning, and equally more paranoid about ensuring there is no unnecessary delay. I will work with theatre staff to ensure everything is in place for the session and we'll aim to minimise the turnaround times between patients."

He makes it clear there will be no attempt to actually speed up the operation itself, but simply the downtime between patients. He'll conduct daily reviews to identify opportunities to improve next time. And he'll explain upfront to the patients placed at the end of the session that there is a very small risk the operation may need to be postponed, but for no longer than two weeks. In any case, any patient placed at the end of the list will have their operation carried out in advance of their current planned operation date. He also makes it clear to staff that with these few Gold sessions there must be an agreement with staff upfront that there is a greater risk of overrun and they should prepare accordingly. Chris expects these two tactics should help to highlight the opportunities that still exist. Then he talks about his vision for the future.

"With the improvements we have made over the last few months, there is no earthly reason why we cannot achieve or improve against the access targets with increasing confidence. And we can also combine with the work we have been doing in outpatients to deal with the backlogs and set a higher internal service level. The analysis that Ruth has completed tells us that more than two thirds of the patient's journey is spent queuing. So if we continue on this path and reduce the queues, there is no reason why we cannot be the first hospital in the region to be offering GP referral to operation time in just a few weeks. With that sort of performance we will win back the work from our colleagues down the road and work towards our dream of becoming a centre of excellence."

Blimey! I'm not sure I wanted Kieran to hear this. Not like this, anyway. But there are discernible mumbles of approval around the room. Chris continues unabated:

"Those guys down the road have had it too good for too long. They've been creaming off all the work that we couldn't do within the access target. Listen, lads and lasses: as we speak we are running at half a million pounds a month above budget. With this extra work we can extend this to well over one million pounds extra net profit per month."

Kieran looks at me, surprised to say the least, and wondering if he is hearing right. Chris concludes.

"And let's not forget this will actually be cheaper for our customers as well, because those big city guys get a premium for their work."

Can't argue with that.

Chapter Sixteen

Joy

Back in the office Cath has coffee and biscuits ready for us. I want to make the most of this opportunity to take Kieran through the analysis and early results of our outpatient work. But first he notices my interview letter from the chairman.

"I hear you have an interview later this week. Well done."

"Thanks, Kieran. Do you think I have a chance?"

He looks into his coffee cup to see if there's a forecast in there:

"I won't be on the interview panel. But you have an interview, so yes, you have a chance. It will be a very strong field."

I could start to analyse and over-analyse that comment. Is he trying to let me down gently? Is he trying to make sure I prepare rigorously so I don't waste my chance? Or is it a brilliantly crafted, universally employed, non-committal answer? Probably the latter, so I return to the matter in hand:

"Have you noticed a common theme in our visits so far?"

"Your senior people are all treading the thin line between genius and madness?"

I decide to help.

"In the A&E department we looked at the statutory requirement to treat patients within four hours and used a time buffer management system to identify and resolve the few places that were causing our failure to achieve this.

"In the assessment unit we took our first step towards an individual patient-centred approach and categorised patients into various assessment period groupings of four, eight, twelve and twenty-four hours.

"On the wards we did the same, but rather than using a fixed time what we've done is come up with an individual planned discharge date for each patient based purely upon their clinical needs. But in essence, everything else is the same."

Kieran is following the thread.

"Yes, and in surgery you adopted the same philosophy, but based it around the operation date to ensure the preoperative tasks were carried out in time."

"That's right," I say. "For theatre slots themselves, we've modified it to aggregate the variation in operation times into one time buffer, to protect us against the unknown level of variation in individual operation times."

Now I want to show Kieran how we're applying the same principles in our outpatient departments. I open the file on my computer to help me illustrate the activity while I explain that, once again, we're basing the whole approach on the principle of defining what's clinically best for the patient. Having done that, we can then work out the cause of why we deviated from it.

In total we see over six hundred thousand outpatients a year, but the first spreadsheet I want to take Kieran through relates to one of the departments which undertakes about twenty-five thousand per year. The chart shows there's a variation from fifteen hundred to twenty-five hundred a month, and I can only show the early results because when we started the first six weeks were largely fixed and it's only after that window we can begin to make a difference.

"I want to explain to you why we think we're on the right track, and then you can draw your own conclusions about the ongoing results we'll achieve. The initial findings were quite shocking, but I want to tell you how we're going to solve it."

I show Kieran that while the department sees roughly two thousand patients a month, each consultant or registrar is seeing about five patients per hour. But when we dug into the detail we uncovered that there were more than five thousand un-booked appointments, and we estimate about half of the patients should have completed their treatment by now. In some instances we've seen a slow deterioration in the percentage of new appointments as slots are given to follow-up appointments to try to ensure we stay within the access target. As a result the time from GP referral to first appointment is inevitably growing, and I press the point.

"If we do nothing here the problem will just get rapidly worse."

Kieran looks a little perturbed to say the least.

"How come there are so many patients with un-booked appointments?"

I explain that the clock starts ticking the moment the patient is referred, but judgement of whether or not we have hit the access target only occurs when the patient leaves the system. So once they've had their first appointment the pressure is on to use the available slots to complete the follow-up appointments within the timeframe. If they'd simply filled all the available slots with new appointments there would be no hope of achieving the target.

"How long do you think this has been going on for?" asks Kieran.

"Probably years," I say, "but the moment I found out about it I put a process in place. I'm going to need your help with this one, Kieran, but before I talk about my idea for the way forward, can I share with you some other findings?"

"Go on."

I start by talking about the variation in consultants' contracts. Some are full time and some less than full time. But the number of patients under the care of any one consultant varies considerably across the team within this specialty, even when taking into account the different contracts. The current number of patients in the system is clearly going to directly impact how long it'll take to eliminate the growing backlog. So I get to the nub.

"You know we have a policy that says consultants have to give six weeks' notice for their holidays. As we speak, the average wait for an appointment in this department, excluding un-booked patients, is sitting at, or very close to, this six-week booking horizon. If the un-booked patients are included, this rises to an average of three to four months, but for some consultants it stretches to well over half a year."

I see Kieran's brow furrowing again but I continue to reveal the equally worrying other side of the coin. The number of patients who do not attend an appointment is averaging about eight per cent, but again can vary from four per cent to sixteen per cent. In addition to this, on any one day unused slots vary between three per cent and twelve per cent.

"I suspect this gave you a pretty decent hint that there must be something wrong with the way you are scheduling slots," observes Kieran.

"Absolutely; but there's more. We've also looked at the number of appointments a patient requires and compared this across consultants for the same treatment type, and there is considerable variation. I don't know whether one consultant with a higher number of appointments per patient is providing better quality of care, or other consultants with lower appointments per patients have just found a better way."

Kieran asks:

"So why do you think there is such a large variation across consultants in the time it would take to work through all the un-booked appointments?"

I show Kieran that the doctor with the highest backlog also has the highest number of patients under treatment, so he's clearly most at risk of breaching the access target. But his appointments per hour ratio is one of the best. He's in great demand and has taken on more patients than he can handle, so the chance of any one patient being seen at the right time is deteriorating rapidly. Yet he's probably working harder than anyone else to solve it. His mean time from GP referral to first appointment is now longer than anyone else's and his mean time between first appointment and subsequent appointments is also longer.

Once we had this data by consultant, we took them through the findings for the department as a whole and sat down with each of them to review their own workload and develop an action plan. I talk through with Kieran exactly how and on what basis we develop the action plan.

"Once again, Kieran, we began by defining patient-centred, clinically led times for a first appointment and for the clinically led intervals for follow-up appointments. Clearly the target for a cancer patient is shorter, but we wanted to decide a service level for first appointments that would make us better than any other hospital in the region. Now we have the ambition to see every new patient within a week, but at the outset we set our goal at half the time of the best hospital in the region."

"So how does this apply to follow-up appointments?" he asks.

I explain that the ambition is dictated by the clinical situation: if there's simply a sequence of tests to do, and if they were carried out the next day, the second appointment could follow almost immediately. In other instances there may be some intermediate treatment where a period of time needs to pass before further clinical assessments can be made.

Once a patient is booked into the system, we're measuring the deviation in time from this point to identify the most common cause of disruption. I tell Kieran that what we've found is quite fascinating. In some instances, just like elsewhere in the hospital, the local policies and practices have delayed patients. But also, time and again, the actual time a patient was booked was more dependent upon the next available slot.

"When the best time was not available, some patients were simply booked in earlier than necessary; and others, inevitably, later."

I open a graph which highlights by day how many patients were seen before or after the clinically derived date. Below the horizontal line shows patients that were seen early, and how early; above the line shows those that were seen late, and how late. Kieran looks to me for my thoughts.

"When we started this, virtually nobody was being seen on time. By using our new approach and reviewing the data with each consultant we were able to come up with a plan to improve things. Sometimes this meant offloading patients from one doctor to another to spread the load; other times it meant stopping the release of any new patients for one of the doctors into the schedule until they had worked through the high volumes. And at other times, it's meant simply running more sessions."

This has become known as the 'Elephant Project', on the basis that elephants go through a door much faster when they go through in procession. It also sparked two other interesting activities. We've been more proactive in trying to solve the non-attendants by publishing our performance to patients so they can see how much we are improving and, by not attending, how much they can damage us. We've also sparked a genuine and unprecedented level of sharing of best practice across the clinical teams. They are now fascinated by their own data and keen to work with their colleagues and learn from each other. So far we have almost eliminated double-booking and we see an increase in patients per session of about eight per cent. When we add in the extra sessions we're running, we can see a way to deliver the access target for planned care with the current patients and also bring through the un-booked patients. But this isn't the end of the tale and I want to influence Kieran.

"If we do this but fail to improve the performance in theatres, we could end up in the distorted and horrible position where we're achieving a rapid improvement in the number of patients treated and perversely a deterioration in our performance against the targets. We need you to support a new initiative and give us time to recover."

"These are all patients who have already been referred by the GPs?" asks Kieran.

"Yes."

"And if you complete the treatment of more of these current patients within the year you can see a significant increase in your revenues."

"Yes."

He pauses for a moment, and then:

"I suppose you realise there are quite large implications for the region's overall budget."

"Yes, Kieran, I do. But this will only be the case while we're reducing the backlog without adding any additional resources. Normally when the region runs backlog initiatives, the operating expenses of the participating hospitals rise as well. But in our case we can do the extra work within the current resources. The only additional expenses will be the additional totally variable costs, which in this department are about twenty per cent of revenue, so basically eighty per cent of the increased revenues will pass straight through to our bottom line."

I can see Kieran is almost with me. He sighs, taps his pencil on the table and says:

"I know what you are saying, Linda. This will give you a one-off and much needed shot in the arm. It will transform your profitability for sure, but what happens when you've worked through the backlogs?"

"The first thing I would like to do is bring back work that was transferred to other hospitals. We had to pass the work over when we were providing poor service levels. But the boot is on the other foot now, Kieran. We can cope with it and we deserve to get it back."

"And then what?" he asks.

"Well, with the improvement in service levels there's no reason why we couldn't take on more work from outside the region." He did ask. And he also knows that some of our doctors had a backlog precisely because they're so well respected within the region. "We may not be the biggest hospital on the patch, but our future could be focused on being the most respected hospital in the region. Respected for fantastic service levels, fantastic quality of care, and being the most productive. Once we have eliminated the backlogs I see no insurmountable obstacle to offering a next-day referral without even requiring the patient to make an appointment. We have the capacity and we will soon have the flexibility so we should be able to see and treat a patient on demand. Well, why the hell not?"

Kieran grins.

"Well, why the hell not?" I retort.

"You'll be telling me your local Sunday team will be playing in the Premier League next!"

But he doesn't want to pop my balloon; in fact, he's reassuringly supportive.

"Look, Linda, you have obviously taken a different approach and one that has delivered quite remarkable results in a very short period of time. And that has taken a lot of courage. But if you carry on like this it won't be your hospital I'm considering closing but I'll still have to look elsewhere. What favour does that do for the economy as a whole?"

I push forward.

"This is the way I see it, Kieran. We're living in a world where the nation is struggling to meet all the health needs of its people, and with the changes in demographics this need is growing. Current predictions are a rise of two years' life expectancy over the next ten years."

You only have to look at the weekly news bulletins telling us that a million more people are coming through the A&E doors this year than a decade ago. There are more and more examples where hospitals have been unable to meet the patients' needs. I continue:

"When this demand for healthcare can't be serviced there will be life and death and critical quality-of-life issues left unaddressed every single day. The core of the approach we've followed is being able to simplify the perceived complexity and focus on those few critical areas that are causing the most disturbances in the health system. Then we utilise these areas to improve the performance of the whole system. Now we're able to deliver a higher quality and we can turn our improved productivity into more affordable care. At the end of the day, Kieran, we can treat more patients within the current resources. This is more affordable care, and you can see for yourself how the staff have pride and joy in their work. And in time there's no reason why the patients can't as well. We're all very proud of what we've done and we have a workforce that will stick with us."

Kieran replies.

"I can see that, Linda. Everything you have shown me today is very, very impressive. You have every right to be proud."

I cut to the chase.

"I want to carry on, Kieran. Do I really have a chance of getting the job?"

Kieran shrugs.

"I honestly can't say. It's going to be tough."

"I just want to be judged on the results I've achieved and the manner in which we have worked together."

He sucks in his top lip while he searches for the right words.

"You're in the right place and you've proved you can do it, but only over a short period. You just don't have a long enough track record as a CEO, so you'll have a real struggle to persuade them to give you the job. You need to play a blinder."

Chapter Seventeen

Scrambled eggs

So I've left work and gone home to finalise my presentation for the job interview tomorrow. I can't believe it's tomorrow. I walk through my door and kick off my shoes and then into my kitchen where I stop and look around for a moment. Then I feel a little sad. I'm on the eve of the most important day of my career and have nobody to share it with. Tomorrow I'll have to perform in front of the interview panel; the good and the great of the health service will be sitting there in judgement of me. I should be very excited but in reality, now in my own home and with the chance to think about it, I'm starting to feel a little down.

What am I doing? Do I really stand any chance of getting this job? Kieran gave me the impression that I'm an outsider, but with a genuine, if slender, chance. But then do I really want this job when I think about it? It's a real quandary. The way I feel now I do. The last few months have been the most invigorating of my career, but then again do I really want to do this now and into the future?

In any case, it may be out of my hands. I'm pretty sure I'm not exactly the sort of person they're expecting or possibly even want. They set some very clear criteria, not least the requirement of having extensive experience of running a hospital. How can I turn a few months into extensive experience? And apart from that, what about the so-called work–life balance that we all believe in, or at least pretend to believe in? Apart from a few evenings with Dee, I've not had any social life at all in the last few months. And an evening with Dee can hardly be described as restful! Maybe if I don't get the job I'll just opt for the easy life.

On the other hand, I suppose it all depends on how you want to enjoy life. In many ways I've never felt so alive. We've achieved so much at the hospital and the constant challenge of trying to find and overcome the next problem has been truly invigorating. The team's been brilliant, and working with Stevie again has been fantastic. I left him a couple of messages before I left work, but clearly by the ring tone he must be overseas again.

I decide to start my preparations in the time-honoured fashion of searching for a snack, but when I open the fridge door the only offering is an unopened rocket salad, described as strong and peppery. It's a week past its sell-by date so I suspect it may be stronger than advertised. And then there's a cold pork and leek sausage from last Sunday's fry up. Says it all really. But there again, this is a great excuse to procrastinate, and so I grab the car keys and drive down to the local convenience store where I find a very healthy chicken salad – in date – and a not-so-healthy chocolate pudding. How do they manage to squeeze so many calories into such a small pot? Impressive.

On my return I pick up my phone to see that Stevie has left a message.

'Hi, Linda; sorry I've not got back to you earlier but am in the States at the moment and have just picked up your messages. I'm working on my book for the next couple of days so give me a call any time. How are the preparations going? You don't sound too chirpy. Listen, I'm sure you'll be fine; just give me a call if you want... er scrambled please...'

Stevie will remember from the old days that I always got a little tense before interviews. But then I usually managed to do OK on the day. He always told me to just relax and chill out before these big ones. Anyway, the way I feel at the moment it's all too easy just to hit the call-back option and within a minute I hear Stevie's voice for real.

"Hi, Linda, what's up?"

"What makes you think something's up?"

"I have known you long enough to suspect that if you leave me more than one message then something's bothering you. What is it?"

"It's this interview I've been worrying about. I'm not completely happy."

"I can't see why," he says. "The results within the timescale are very impressive indeed. Just make sure you show the core analysis and that what you have achieved is backed up by a process of ongoing improvement. Tell them there are a lot more benefits to come. Then if they don't want to listen to you they must be mad."

"It's not what's in my presentation that bothers me. Our rate of improvement relative to the other hospitals in the region is a killer. It's what's not in the presentation that bothers me."

"What do you mean? What are you missing?" Stevie sounds quite frustrated.

There's a long silence and then I answer:

"The bit that is missing is me. I just don't fit what they're looking for. I don't have the right image or background."

"Don't be soft, Linda. You have tackled mission impossible and everyone around you wants you to get the job. The clinicians don't want anyone else."

Then Stevie admits that when I first talked to him about the hospital he was doubtful that we could turn it around in the timescales. He says that's a compliment because we have. But my problem isn't what we've done or could do. I'm really proud seeing the joy in the faces of our staff. Almost everyone in the hospital is determined to continue to improve it. I'm just not sure I'm the person they want. As I implore Stevie to understand my apprehensions he has a real go at me.

"I hear your words, Linda, but I haven't the faintest idea what you are talking about. This is not the girl I know, the tough one from the north of England who came down to show the bureaucrats how to do it. Where the hell is that northern soul?"

"Somewhere near Manchester."

"Bloody hell, Linda – if I was there I'd give you a damn good shake. Just be yourself for goodness sake. JUST BE LINDA! You might make them feel uncomfortable, but you're fast becoming a great leader and they know it. That's why they're worried."

I'm furious with myself as I know that Stevie's fighting my corner but I find myself in tears.

"The advert clearly says candidates will have extensive experience of running a hospital, and how the hell can I claim that a few months is extensive experience? It's not that I don't want the job, you idiot, it's that I don't stand a chance."

"Well, why didn't you say that?"

"Why the hell don't you ask Socrates?" I yell.

There's another long silence and then Stevie speaks again.

"Do you have a tissue?"

"Sorry."

"I should flippin' well think so. I know very well that you are the bravest, most confident person in the northern hemisphere. But I turn my back for one day and you've turned into a blubbering wreck!"

That makes me smile. Stevie continues:

"I used to think you had the skin of a rhino but over the last few months I have learned just how much you care. I guess today I assumed that you didn't have a valid reservation, and look where that got us. If I was there now I wouldn't shake you I'd give you a big hug. I'm really sorry."

"I'll hold you to that," I sniff.

"Anyway, let's get it right here, Linda. Being a CEO and leading thousands of people is much harder than my job. I couldn't do it."

"That's as may be, but right now can you tell me what I'm going to do?"

"That's more like it. Let's see. You're right; in this situation when choosing a CEO they're usually looking for two things. Does the candidate have the vision and ability to turn around the hospital, and then is he or she a safe pair of hands? Failing is often seen as worse than not succeeding and, however well you've done, if they don't see you as a safe pair of hands they won't pick you."

"And that's supposed to make me feel better?"

Stevie doesn't answer that. He just explains that the most frustrating thing is that the other candidates may well have much more experience, but I have a few months of a different experience; one of facing up to the inconsistencies between what is common sense and what is common practice, and then leading people through the change. Somehow we've got to get the currency of this sort of experience to demonstrate that I'm the safest pair of hands. That makes sense.

Stevie talks about his own experience and how he has learned two ways to view the world. In the first way we look for things that confirm our understanding of the world. Things that, through that confirmation, help us to feel more secure because what we see is in line with our assumptions about the world around us. If somebody is bitching and moaning it means they're just that sort of person and it's a waste of time trying to get them to change. If we see a kid at school playing up it's because he has not been properly disciplined. If there's a poorly performing company it's because the management team is weak. The trouble with looking at the world through these eyes is that you can become more accepting of things that are going wrong in the world. If you're a leader, and you not only think like this but people see that you think and act like this, then it's all too easy for the next breach in your targets to become just another breach. It's a relatively short road until the next avoidable death is just another avoidable death, justified by the claim that the whole world is against us and it's all too difficult around here.

The second way of viewing the world starts with some different assumptions. Firstly, that people are good; they do not come into work to screw things up. Yes, there appears to be conflict everywhere, but underneath this seemingly complex world things are inherently simple and we need to overcome the perception that reality is complex. As he speaks, Stevie reminds us that Pooh Bear pointed out if we stop to think about things then maybe we can find a better way.

I'm listening intently as he says the first step is to commit to finding a better way. Finding a better way is to respect the knowledge you have gained so far in your life but to never say '*I know*', and to always try to seek out how the situation can be substantially improved. That leaves us with a huge dichotomy to try to understand. Stevie explains that's why he could not take on his father's business. His dad wanted to tell Stevie how to run his company, and this is why he left his brother to do it alone. I speak up:

"I'm not sure if that little therapy session was for you or for me."

"Look, Linda, what is important is that you must go for this job. Your experience is truly valid. Just imagine if what you have learned so far was more widely spread. Somebody has to go first. Somebody has to learn how to create a new approach that we can all use to jump forward. Otherwise all we can look forward to is new heights of mediocrity."

"Thanks, mate."

I do feel genuinely better. Stevie has refocused me on why things have happened as they have in the last few months. It's exactly because we had the balls to do it, and that stands for more than however many years of safe-hand work. So I let him return to his own time.

"What are you doing?"

"I'm having brunch. I missed breakfast this morning as I was in a meeting at seven, which is a rather uncivilised hour to eat."

"OK, enjoy. Hey, I bet you one hundred pounds I can guess what you're having."

"Go on then."

"Scrambled eggs."

"How the hell did you do that?"

Chapter Eighteen

Showtime

"Good luck, darling, and whatever the outcome, you can only do your best."

As always, spoken with that time-honoured parental offering of comfort, which has served well for centuries for every parent wishing, with all their heart, that their little loved one survives the ferocious challenge that looms. From the Grade 1 piano recital, the debut for the school netball team, the first daunting exam, the university finals, the appearance on *Britain's Got Talent* (well, probably not that one), the wedding, the divorce hearing, the witness statement, the parachute jump, the resulting operation and physiotherapy, your appointment as head of the UN '*good luck… you can only do your best*'. OK, I'm getting a little carried away, but you catch my drift. And you know what – that's all I need. I had the deep discussion, somewhat emotional, with Stevie last night when he impressed upon me why it's important for me to go for this job. Someone has to be brave enough to follow the path less travelled, and stay on it. And now I also know Mum's right behind me. As if she wouldn't be. Then I receive a text from Dee which says '*you'll be fine – just don't say anything too stupid x*' and I have all the advice I need. I'm feeling fine. It's a beautiful day, the sun is shining and I'm up for the challenge.

I do wonder whether I've prepared well enough though. Other than speaking to Stevie I haven't really done a great deal. I haven't tried to anticipate the questions I may face, but I think they're likely to be fairly predictable. Also, I've been working in the hospital where the job to be filled is, so that in itself is pretty good preparation and could give me an edge. Or am I kidding myself? I may be. From an early age I haven't ever been particularly good at preparing for important tests.

Having said that, ever since I was sixteen, on the morning of a big test, an interview or anything that demanded an uplifted morale, I always had half a grapefruit and a bacon sandwich for breakfast, a ritual established by Dad. I look in the fridge. The dry cured back bacon's still in there and still in date and I've a bag of bagels in the bread bin: result! The only drawback is the notable absence of a grapefruit. I momentarily ponder how important this is, and whether I should return to the convenience store to buy one of theirs. They may begin to wonder whether I shop anywhere else, so I decide it's not such a big deal. I never really liked grapefruit anyway.

This sunny morning my only option is a kiwi fruit, so I go for that. And if I don't get the job I have a ready-made excuse. But hey, what kind of an attitude is that? Why shouldn't I get the job? Like Stevie said last night, the results we've turned in over the last few months have been undeniably impressive and the interview panel can't mistake that. And as Dee says, as long as I don't say anything too daft I have as much chance as anyone. But having said all that, I don't actually know everyone I'm up against. I know of two of the other candidates as I had to show them around the hospital last week. One is a very impressive woman called Susan Mee, extremely personable but highly driven and with an excellent track record, having successfully run a hospital in the south-west for the last three years. I liked her. She knew I was applying too and she wished me luck, genuinely. The second person I showed around was a chap called Mark Heaton; he was nice enough but I can't really see him as a threat. He's currently a COO of a larger hospital but has no experience of running a hospital as CEO, so I'm already ahead on that significant front. I'm actually a safer pair of hands than him! But the fourth candidate remains a mystery. I don't know why he or she didn't visit the hospital last week. No matter how busy you are, that seems to me to be a rather risky strategy. You can ask around all you like but there is no substitute for seeing the hospital with your own eyes. So my guess is that Susan Mee is the strongest candidate and I'll need to be right on my game to beat her.

◆

My interview is at 11:00am and I'm sitting in my office at 10:00am with Jo and Mo when Charlie breezes in.

"How are you feeling, Linda?"

"I'm fine, thanks. A bit apprehensive, I guess, but that's a good thing, isn't it?"

"Nervous tension is vital," he says. "It's how you use it that makes the difference. If you can keep your head while everyone around you is losing theirs and blaming it on you, and if you can trust yourself when people doubt you, you won't go far wrong."

"That's Rudyard Kipling, isn't it?" smiles Mo.

"Possibly," admits Charlie, "but I gave him the idea."

Jo puts her hands on my shoulders and says:

"You'll be absolutely fine, love. Don't worry, just be yourself and be proud of what you've achieved. We're all rooting for you. No one else will do for us."

"In fact," adds Charlie, "if you don't get the job it will be an unmitigated disaster. It'll be hell around here again. Don't let us down, Linda."

"You're not helping, Charlie."

I know he's just winding me up but I also know he, and all the great people who have helped over the past few months, are really rooting for me. I wonder whether I'm starting to believe my own publicity, but I actually feel responsible for these people. Then Mo speaks:

"Wasn't that Ashcroft just walking past?"

"It was," says Jo.

"Oh no. Ashcroft on the interview panel. I'm doomed. I may as well pack my bags."

"How do you know he's on the interview panel?" asks Jo.

"What else would he be doing here?"

"Maybe he's lost," offers Charlie.

"I wish."

Charlie smiles.

"Anyhow – there'll be six on the panel, and they'll all have more weight than Ashcroft. You need to impress at least three of the others and preferably all five, and then Ashcroft will be impotent."

"Thanks guys. I do appreciate it."

"Well, break a leg," says Charlie, and they get up to leave.

As they wander out I hear Jo muttering '*Break a leg! Is that the best you could do?*' and then I'm left to my final thoughts. I pick up the smiling Buddha that Stevie bought for me and look for inspiration, but all I can think of is the prospect of coming back as a worm or something if I fail in this life. Not much to smile about there.

I wander over to the window. I think back to my arrival here as COO and the optimism I harboured in the hope that I was going to have some sort of positive influence on the place. There have always been things happening in this hospital that are wrong, which is in the nature of any gigantic, organisational beast. There have also been things happening that are right, and in my short tenure as CEO, with Stevie's guidance, we have actually effected a turnaround. So why can't we carry on? I don't mind admitting that when we set off down this path I didn't have a clue whether it would work or be an unmitigated disaster. But we all know that something needed to change and we had exhausted every hopeless cost and efficiency idea within our grasp. So we did it.

I look at my watch to see it's 10:45am. Fifteen minutes to go. This is it. Come on, Linda, it's now or never. My future, well my immediate future, rests on what happens in the next two hours and whether I can communicate clearly how I'm the best bet for CEO to a panel of the great and the good. Just two hours.

It's 10:55am so I set off for the boardroom. As I pass Cath's office she smiles at me and holds up her right hand with fingers crossed. Oh God. Don't blow it, Linda. Suddenly I feel churned up inside and begin whispering to myself as I walk down the corridor, almost feeling an out-of-body experience; it doesn't seem like I'm there. A rush of adrenalin flies through me as the door opens and I'm welcomed in by Mike Pitt, the HR Director. As I take my seat at the grand table and scan the panel I suddenly feel like I'm in the House of Lords or about to face Parliamentary Questions. The chairman of the panel is also the chairman of the hospital, Sir Archie Ternent, and he's flanked by Baroness Valois, who heads up a government healthcare thinktank, and on the other side sits another person I recognise. It's the CEO I met at my first regional meeting, just after Bob had been fired. He's the guy who stood up and blew his own trumpet rather loudly for half an hour, regaling all present with the incredible financial achievements of his hospital. I didn't really take to him. He probably doesn't even remember me. There are two external assessors present and then there's Mike Pitt. There's often a senior person from HR on these panels to ensure adherence to diversity considerations and general fair play.

I look again and I'm right… there's not a sign of Ashcroft. I resist the temptation to peep under the table. That wouldn't look good at all. No Ashcroft… that's pretty good news, I think. Although in some ways it could have been even better. The dynamics of the interview will be different than for my competitors because I've been working here already. In many ways it's more pressurised being interviewed on your home turf because at least two of the panel know who I am. What if they ask me something that I should know but I can't answer? The embarrassment factor is tenfold. If anyone else messes it up they'll never be seen again, but if I make a fool of myself I'll still be here, every single excruciating day. Also, it's not great being interviewed by Super CEO. I don't really fancy being asked questions by him; he's a finance expert so he'll concentrate on that, I'm sure. And even though there is a standard set of questions, the make-up of a panel can work in your favour or against you depending on where your own strengths lie. If there's an HR person you get people-related questions and if there's a lawyer on the panel, which Baroness Valois is, then you may get testing legal questions. So I have to play not only to a group audience, but also to the individuals. I need to be able to tick all the collective and single boxes.

Sir Archie introduces me to the rest of the panel and the questions begin.

"So, Linda, please outline to us the breadth of your experience in running hospitals?"

There it is – the Six-Million-Dollar Question first out. This is the question that was always going to appear. It's the one that carries the most marks, and if I fail to produce a track record then I'm surely sunk. Somehow I need to paint the picture of the hospital as it is now and as it was before, and apply as much longevity to my experience as is humanly possible. So I begin by talking about my influence in senior management roles and my appointment as COO of this hospital. Each of the panel is watching and listening intently but only

Mike is smiling as he nods at appropriate intervals. Then I lead into my survival, to date, since being chucked in at the deep end as CEO. I talk as intelligently as I can of the care and consideration invested as we, no I, have effected what is clearly a sharp turnaround in quality of care, length of stay, operational productivity and, crucially, finance. I go through the numbers which John helped me to prepare. When I pause, Super CEO interrupts my flow.

"You're talking about a very impressive few months, Linda, and the numbers certainly back that up, but it is just a few months. A new head quite often has a honeymoon period, but how can you prove that you have a sustained track record and not simply a bounce?"

The truth is, when we're talking about the CEO role I can't, and he knows it. So I respectfully say that I can only illustrate strong performance, however short, and I have no track record of failure to speak of. Baroness Valois raises her eyebrows and smiles, glancing across at Super CEO. How can it be a 'bounce' in any case? I'm not the manager at a Premier League football club; I'm running a hospital, for goodness sake. I keep that thought to myself. Baroness Valois probes.

"What have you learned during your period leading this hospital and how would you have done it differently?"

I think for a moment and then say:

"If I had my time again, I believe I would have been a better source of support for Bob when he was in the role. We have put a huge amount of effort into improving the timeliness and quality of care here, and I think we could have done that earlier."

"So why didn't you?" asks Sir Archie.

"I didn't have either the knowledge or courage of convictions that I have now. So I suppose I have learned that the personnel we have in this hospital are perfectly capable of achieving success. To do that we need every senior figure to work on the same agenda, and that can take time. The senior team here work excellently together."

I'm trying to illustrate just how the hospital is in the position we find ourselves in now and to prove that it's anything but a fluke. I'm desperate to show that this level of improvement, however early in its cycle, is a compelling argument for keeping me in place. But I don't know if I've achieved that by the time Mike asks the next question.

"You've talked a little about leadership already, Linda. When we are appointing a leader in the health service it's imperative we find someone who is fit for purpose as a public servant. Can you give an example of when you've taken a strong leadership approach?"

The best example I can think of in leadership terms is exactly what's happened right here in the last few months. There have been things I've done and achieved earlier in my career but not at the level they're looking for. I'm coming up against the same problem again. I just desperately hope it's strong enough. I think back to Stevie's words and talk about treating people as grown-ups, tapping into their consciousness and abilities, and gaining consensus. Super CEO thinks he's seen through something.

"How can you gain a consensus with thousands of people?"

I answer:

"If you have belief in your strategy, you should have the confidence to speak to all of them about it, or as many as you can get together in one place."

I talk about winning the minds of the strategic senior players and equipping them with the communication tools needed to take their own teams with them, and so on. The panel seem to be receptive to my argument that you could not effect a turnaround in an organisation of this size simply by telling people what to do, and even less so by focusing purely on costs. I'm gaining a little confidence as I seem to be getting some reasonably content vibes from my inquisitors, but I still wish I had more to talk about than the last few months. Baroness Valois is the next to ask a question.

"Linda, can you tell me about a situation at the hospital that has gone wrong, and then how you reacted to rectify or minimise the negative impact?"

I talk about the clinical disaster weekend that happened just a week into my tenure, where operational failures resulted in patient distress, complaints, blockages and a death. I explain how Charlie and Mo had worked through the weekend as a result and the effect on the staff and patients.

"How did you ensure that the patients suffered no further distress?" asks Sir Archie.

"I spoke personally to the patients and the families involved, and also to the staff."

"You spoke personally to them?" Super CEO checks.

"Yes. I believed in my role as CEO I needed to lead the investigation and assure all concerned of my commitment to providing some sort of an answer, however difficult it might be."

"I understand your motives for intervening," says Mike. "But the textbook approach would have been to stay out of it and appoint an independent person to do a thorough investigation. This type of problem belongs to the Governance Department. You can assimilate the feedback from the appointed expert and Governance. That will give you a clear, dispassionate perspective."

"Somebody has to be the judge of whether anyone has to be disciplined or even dismissed," adds Baroness Valois. "If you get too close to the injured parties you may inadvertently affect that."

"I see."

Damn it.

Sir Archie offers a closing concession.

"Well thank you, Linda. You have spoken with clarity and conviction. I can speak for the whole panel when I say that we are indeed impressed by the work you have done in this hospital over the years and particularly the past few months. Your presentation was very impressive and you have a vital role to play in the future of the health service, of that there is no doubt. Do you have any questions?"

"Yes, just the one: when should I expect to hear?"

Mike answers:

"Hopefully this evening. We have two more interviews to do and then we'll make a decision."

I thank everyone and leave.

♦

"How did it go?" Mo is sat opposite me in my office.

"I don't know, Mo, I really don't. I made a mess of one question for sure but I just need to hope the other three did the same. I think they were pleased with our work this year, but I just don't know. They kept on saying that my track record at this level was short – at least I think that's what they were getting at."

"Well, you must have as good a chance as anyone."

"I don't know about that. Susan Mee looks to be an excellent candidate from where I'm sitting."

"But you're already sitting here, which must count for something. Anyway, who was interviewing?"

"Sir Archie, Baroness Valois, a CEO from the region, two external chaps and Mike Pitt from HR. No Ashcroft… I couldn't believe my luck."

Mo turns up the corner of his mouth.

"I know."

"What do you mean you know? How do you know?"

"He's being interviewed."

"Ashcroft? Interviewed for the CEO job? Are you sure?"

"Yes, Kieran was on the phone asking to get a message to him. You were in your interview so Cath put him through to me as I was around."

Good God. Ashcroft! I don't know whether that's a good or a bad thing. Surely he can't be that strong a candidate. He'd miss the challenge of putting his paperclips in size order every morning if he came to do a real job. Surely the panel would realise that. Maybe it was just a political interview, to keep him happy. Maybe they wanted to look at someone away from the field to give a contrast. Who knows? I'm not particularly bothered that he is being interviewed and I'd like to think his fun-sapping charisma shines through. At the end of it all, it doesn't really matter what anyone else did; there's nothing at all I can do about that. I just did my best, and if that isn't good enough then so be it. Whatever the outcome I'll take it like a grown-up, and I tell Mo as much.

"I know you will. So let us know if we can put the champagne on ice as soon as you hear."

He gives a reassuring smile and leaves.

♦

It's just gone 6:00pm and I'm sharing a coffee with Jo. She's in high spirits as we've had another good day of discharges, and we have beds available on the assessment unit ready for the next twenty-four hours' admissions.

"You know what, Linda, this is a different place now. I've always wanted to work here, even in the worst times. But sometimes it almost became too much. Now I actually enjoy coming to work and I know many others who feel just the same. There are more smiles around the place. Even John's got a spring in his step."

That's an unnerving image. But I'm grateful for Jo's words. She adds:

"I do hope you've got this job, Linda. You deserve it, you really do."

I look at my watch and wonder whether I'll hear this evening. I decide to stick around and clear some paperwork, more to pass the time than anything else. Jo bids me farewell, asking me to let her know if I hear anything. As I open the door for her who should be passing but Ashcroft. He looks fairly grumpy, even for him, and I decline the opportunity to have a word. By his demeanour it looks to me like he may have had a nightmare. Hope springs eternal.

After half an hour working through my in-tray, which includes a congratulatory letter from Kieran following last week's financial return, I decide to ring Mum.

"So how did it go?" she asks.

"I'm not so sure, but I did my best."

"And that's all you can do. They'd be mad not to appoint you."

"Thanks Mum, but there was a very strong candidate from the south-west."

"He'll be saying the same about you."

"She actually, oh hang on, Mum..." My mobile is ringing. "I'll call you later."

It's Sir Archie's PA.

"Hello, Linda, I'm just connecting you."

"Thanks."

I listen to *Eine Kleine Nachtmusik* for a few seconds and then the line goes dead. Oh no. What are they trying to do to me? I sit still and silent, staring at my phone for one, two, three minutes... and then it rings again.

"Hello... oh hi, Simone. Erm... yes I think I'll be free on Sunday. That's very kind... sorry to be rude but must dash, see you Sunday."

Then I sit still and wait once more. Another minute passes, and then another, and I'm beginning to accept that maybe I won't hear anything until tomorrow. Maybe Sir Archie has lost patience. But surely he'd try to call me again. Then again, maybe his PA hadn't told him I was on the line and he didn't know, in which case he may have decided to leave it until the morning. I get up to pack my case and then my phone rings again.

"Hello."

"Hello, Linda, it's Archie Ternent here. Are you still in the office?"

"Yes."

"Door closed?"

"Yes."

"OK, I'll cut to the chase then. We've decided to appoint an alternative candidate."

I feel every ounce of energy drain from my body. He continues:

"Linda, you are an excellent candidate and your work in this hospital recently has turned heads in high places. I have every confidence that you could do a very good job for us here. You have a particularly bright future in the health service." He pauses: "But I should think you'll want to know why you didn't get the job."

"Well, I… erm…"

"I know it's bad news, Linda, but you'll gain a lot from the experience. It's often better to meet with disappointment early on, which you can draw strength from. And that's just the point. We felt this was a little too early for you. You'll be ready in two years, I'm sure. In this case we wanted to appoint someone with a longer track record, someone who has done it before over an extended period and, I'll be perfectly honest with you Linda, a safe bet."

Susan Mee.

"So I hope you aren't too downhearted. You will come back stronger, I assure you. Well then, it just remains for me to thank you for all your excellent work so far. I can tell you who the successful candidate is if you wish."

I'm happy to hear. As I said, I liked Susan when I met her. She's a lovely person and a proven CEO. I can certainly see myself working for her and I can't see why she wouldn't want me here.

"Yes."

"It's Mr Ashcroft."

At this very moment I feel like Wile E Coyote standing on a precarious ledge and with an ACME one-ton weight whistling down towards me.

"Mr... Ashcroft."

I hope Sir Archie didn't detect that I started to gag as I spoke. "That's right."

I can't think of anything lucid to say. I think I gasped an entirely inappropriate '*wow*' as Sir Archie bade me goodbye.

Ashcroft.

BEEP BEEP... SPLAT!

♦

"Ashcroft?!"

"Yup"

"You're joking, aren't you?"

Charlie can't believe it. The team has been hanging on for me to leave and as soon as I opened my door they are in to hear the news. Mo looks perplexed, Jo exudes sympathy and Charlie is pacing up and down.

"There is no way in this world that Sir Archie and his chums couldn't see what a prat Ashcroft is. He'll take us back five years. Please tell me you're joking."

"She's not joking," says Jo quietly.

"Well bugger it. I'm off, I'm not going to work for a lobotomised bureaucrat," retorts Charlie.

"Don't be an idiot."

Charlie looks at Jo and then sits down.

"So what did Sir Archie say?"

"He said we're doing a great job but he wanted someone with more experience."

"More experience of what? Attaching pens to a clipboard?"

Jo scowls at Charlie. I continue.

"They want someone with a longer track record. I guess they want to be as sure as they can that nothing will go wrong."

"It appears that their belief is that not succeeding is preferable to failure," says Mo. "I suspect Mr Ashcroft ticked a number of boxes, and they can trust him to adopt the safe management practices and to cut costs. And I think I'm right in saying he has CEO experience in the past."

"They don't think I'm a real CEO."

"Of course they do," says Charlie. "Come on, let's go to the pub. It's my round."

But I can't really face it.

"Thanks, Charlie, but I think I'll just go home and get an early night. I'm exhausted. I'll see you all tomorrow… and thanks."

As they troop out Jo puts her hand on my shoulder, smiles and closes the door behind them. I breathe a heavy sigh, pack my case and bag and stand for a moment looking at the smiling Buddha. Then a single tear trickles down my cheek.

That's enough now.

Chapter Nineteen

Reflections

1:00am. I puff up my pillow, well, punch up my pillow, and turn over in a grumpy flourish with sufficient vigour to hurl my quilt asunder. I spend the next hour or so tossing and turning. After a while I look at my clock; it's 2:22am. Maybe I should just get up and go in to work. I close my eyes and try to sleep but my mind is whirring. My thoughts flit around firstly to the tasks of the day, Friday being Regional Office Return Day, and a bed meeting scheduled with Jo. I wonder what level of admissions are happening as I lie in bed. Then I think a little further forward. What does the future hold for Linda? For me? I could slide back into the COO position with a boss I'm not altogether thrilled to be working for. I think of Bob and wonder how he's doing in Special Projects. I wonder if he'll have a job for me there. And then my thoughts drift to the weekend ahead and what I can do on Saturday. I'm not on call this weekend. And I'm at Simon and Simone's for Sunday lunch. I'd better get some flowers or a plant. Oh no... when's little Kirk's birthday... he's nine sometime around now? What's the date? It's the 3rd, no the 4th. So... his birthday is Sunday! I can get something for him later today or Saturday. Maybe a scooter. Has he got a scooter? I wonder if Bob's been watching and seeing how we've been doing at the hospital...

My eyes open. It's still dark... 5:04am. I watch the clock at roughly five-minute intervals and then decide to surface. Before I get up I look at my phone and see I have a message from Stevie. I sent a text to him before I went to bed but fell asleep before he'd replied. It says: '*Sometimes things that make you unhappy now, happen for a reason.*' I wonder what he meant by that.

♦

I get the strangest feeling as I walk through the A&E doors at 7:00am. It feels so different to a few months ago, when stepping through the doors invariably meant a day of fighting fires, lurching from one crisis to the next and leaving twelve hours later exhausted and drained. It is over a year ago that we were full of optimism at the opening of the new building. I'm struggling to get my head around just exactly what has happened in the intervening time.

It almost feels like I'm not actually here; I'm just watching myself walk through the department and towards the management corridor and into my office. The office that used to be Bob's office. Then it was my office. And now? Well, I suppose it's still my office, for a week or two anyway. Mo's in Cath's room and as he sees me approach he comes out to meet me.

"Hi, Linda. How are you this morning?"

"Come in, Mo."

We sit down and look at each other for a moment, neither of us ready to speak.

"So," I venture.

"So," he replies. And then: "Have you ever felt like you were on the verge of finding something really exciting, only to find it was never actually there?"

"What do you mean?"

"Well, I have to say, the route we have taken over the last few months, and the things that have happened here in the hospital, have been unlike anything I've seen previously in my whole career. And I genuinely thought we were about to find the pride and joy we have worked so hard for. Then the chairman makes an appointment which, on the face of it, seems to discredit everything we came to believe in. They have taken a safe, well-trodden option."

I think for a moment.

"That's a bit dramatic, Mo. How do you know Ashcroft won't carry on where we left off?"

He raises his eyebrows, and I respond with a '*hmm*'. Then the phone rings and it's Cath; she has Kieran on the line. Mo leaves and I take the call.

"Morning, Linda. How are you?"

"Fine thanks, Kieran," I lie.

"You're not really, are you?"

"Yes, really. I'm fine."

"Well, I just wanted to say hard luck with the application. I understand Sir Archie was and is impressed. Look, I know you haven't always seen eye to eye with Ashcroft." *Really?* "But don't throw your toys out of the pram. He has more about him than some people give him credit for and he's been there and done it." Mo was right. "He says he wants you to stay on as COO."

"Oh." I start by thinking, '*That's good of him*'; and then, '*I'd rather stick a pin in my eye.*' But I say neither:

"I haven't really decided what I want to do."

"Oh come on, Linda. Don't do anything you may regret in the future."

What the hell does he mean by that? Is that some sort of warning? I'm not particularly concerned by the risk of offending Ashcroft, but I suppose it might not look so good if I walked out as soon as he arrives. On the other hand, I'm not relishing the thought of sticking around while he follows the route that Mo is concerned he will.

"I'll try not to, Kieran. I just need a little time to think."

"Well, why don't you take some time off? Ashcroft has work to finish off here for the next two weeks before he arrives at your hospital. You'll need to be there when he arrives so it may be a good time for you to get away."

He may be right, but the way I feel right now, if I go anywhere I may not come back. I say I'll think about it and let him know if I decide to take some time off.

Moments later Cath pops her head around the door.

"Would you like a coffee, Linda?"

"That'd be lovely. Why don't you join me?"

A moment later she returns with a tray of coffee and a packet of Jaffa Cakes.

"Wow, what's the occasion?" I ask.

"I just thought you might need cheering up a little." Cath offers a comforting smile. And then:

"Did you really want this job, Linda? You've worked so hard and done so well, but can you see yourself here for the next few years?"

"I don't really know, Cath. I thought I wanted it, and I was upset last night, but I don't actually know how I feel about it this morning. I may not be here for a few years but I kind of expected to be here longer than a few weeks."

"Are you going to leave?"

"I don't have anywhere to go."

"You won't struggle to find a place, but it would be sad for the rest of us if you went. You're very popular here, you know."

I smile at Cath. I want to give her a hug but don't want to risk the possibility of blubbing on her smart Marks & Spencer jacket. She has been a marvellous support for me, and for Bob before me, always the personification of professionalism while never losing her warmth and kindness, and diplomatic to the last. And she's a shrewd judge of character.

"So, Mr Ashcroft, then."

"You'll be able to mould him quickly enough," I smile.

"I don't know if I'd care to, Linda. Charlie tells me he's an exceptional pain in the backside and, I'm told, his own biggest fan."

I'm surprised by Cath's frankness but quietly pleased.

"That's not like you, Cath."

"Well, isn't he?"

My refusal to answer is deafening. I'm not in the most charitable of moods.

"If there's one thing I can't abide, it's people who think they are better than everyone else," she says.

"But you can cope with anyone, Cath. You've coped with me, for goodness sake. And didn't you always say that the height of good manners is keeping quiet about other people's weaknesses or your own strengths?"

"Yes, but that may be more of a challenge if Charlie's opinion of Mr Ashcroft is well placed."

"You can't always rely on what you hear from others. You can make your own mind up when you meet him," I say in a magnanimous moment. Cath looks at me quizzically.

"So what are you going to do?"

"I don't know yet. Yesterday I thought I might be here for a while. Today I'm not so sure. Why don't we get through today and see what tomorrow brings?"

Once Cath is gone I check my phone for messages and highlight one from Dee which says: *'Unlucky yesterday mate. Lunch at Carlucci's on me. See you at 1 x.'*

That doesn't sound like such a bad idea. Then I wonder how Dee knew that I hadn't got the job. I check my phone and I hadn't texted her. Maybe she called in to the office. Dee knows Cath, and Cath knows that I wouldn't mind her telling Dee my news. That must have been it. Anyway… lunch on a Friday? I have a bed meeting in half an hour and then I want to get all our returns in to regional office by midday as we have done for the last two months, and I don't know what else will crop up during the morning. Hell, if I can't spare an hour to go to lunch with my friend then maybe we haven't made the great progress here in the hospital that we think we have. So I text my reply.

◆

Dee peers at me over the top of her glass of sparkling water.
"You mean the guy with the bad breath?"
"I didn't say that."
"Yes you did. You said his breath could turn milk sour."
Oh yes, so I did.
"I was sort of exaggerating."
"But you don't want to work for him, do you?"
"I don't know if I have any choice. I may not get anything else in time. And in any case, Ashcroft may decide he doesn't want me so it could be taken out of my hands."
"Well, you need to get it in your hands," says Dee sternly. "I know what you've achieved in that damn hospital and how you've done it. You're holding all the cards."
I don't quite see it that way.
"How exactly am I holding all the cards? I could be out of a job in two weeks' time."
"Look at it from Ashworth's point of view…"
"Ashcroft."
"Whatever. Look at it from his point of view. He's just landed a job in a hospital that has turned a corner and issued some frankly spectacular results in the last few months. But he doesn't know how.

He may hope it's a fluke, but if he has anything about him he'll know in his heart of hearts that it isn't. And the brilliant thing is he hasn't the faintest understanding of how you've done it. There's no way he could unless he was there."

I'm starting to like Dee's logic. She continues.

"And unless he's entirely numb between the ears he'll know that he needs you to get everyone in the hospital on his side. Imagine how it will look if he messes it up having replaced an unmitigated success. The stakes are very high for Ashworthcroft… and you, my dear friend, have nothing to lose. You've succeeded there and you can either help Ashcroft to do likewise or set off into the sunset. Your phone won't stop ringing."

"If the university lark doesn't work out you can always be my PR."

"You don't need a PR."

"So what do you suggest I do?"

Dee smiles and raises her eyebrows.

"Well… I still have two tickets for the Rockley Beach Resort Hotel in sunny Barbados burning a hole through my purse; flying from Gatwick tomorrow."

Oh my goodness, I'm so tempted. If ever there was a time to do something for myself then this is probably it.

"You know what… you're on!"

"Fantastic! We've just got tonight to pack. I knew you could make a sound decision if you put your mind to it."

"I could actually take two weeks off. I haven't had a holiday all year and my new boss won't be around for two weeks."

"Brilliant. The flight's at 7:30am so I'll order a taxi for 4:30am. Get an early night."

"Cool." Then I ask: "By the way, did Cath tell you that I hadn't got the job?"

Dee mischievously touches her nose, winks at me and says:

"No, not Cath. A little bird told me… I have friends on the other side you know."

♦

Once I've had the afternoon to think about it I'm really pleased that I'm going on holiday. Not only will it be a blast going away with

Dee but it will also give me a chance to get my head together. I feel as if a weight has been lifted from my shoulders. Cath is as supportive as ever saying, '*Good for you… you deserve it.*' She assures me everything will be fine for a week, Charlie will pick up anything urgent. And I call Kieran to tell him I've taken his advice and I'm going on holiday.

I suddenly seem to have heightened clarity of thought, so much so that I call Simon to tell him I'll be away for Kirk's birthday and ask what to buy him. Simon tells me that Kirk is getting into golf (I suspect Simon is getting Kirk into golf) and he recently bought him a junior half set of clubs.

"Maybe you could buy him a three wood and a four iron."

So that's it sorted. He suggests I go to his club to buy them.

"If you see Tom, the pro, he'll give you a discount."

So I do. On my way home I buy the aforesaid three wood and four iron, briefly haggling with Tom (inappropriately as I later find out), nip back to mine to wrap them in **Happy Christmas** wrapping paper and head off to Simon and Simone's. I'm greeted by Simone, immaculate as ever in her Karen Millen cocktail dress as she continues to lightly toss a colander of baby spinach while effortlessly opening the door and ushering me into the kitchen.

"I'm taking a week off so I'll be away on Sunday. I'll call Kirk but here's his present and card."

I try to unbalance her, thrusting the untidily wrapped package in her face as she drizzles olive oil over an anxious looking bowl of pomodoro tomatoes.

"Wow!" she exclaims. "How exciting… what is it?"

"It's a BB gun, the new Kalashnikov model. I know they can be dangerous but Kirk is a sensible boy. I'm sure he'll be fine."

Simone's eyes widen with genuine horror as I breeze into the lounge to give my wishes and hugs to Kirk.

Today has come and gone in the blink of an eye and I'm positively excited as I finally drive home. School's out! The goodwill and kindness I've experienced at work since the news has been a real lift and, whatever the future holds, I know I have some wonderful colleagues and friends at the hospital. And I can go on holiday happily, with the comfort of knowing that it will all run fine while I'm away.

Once I've packed my suitcase I check my phone and see a text from Dee instructing me to bring an extra sarong as she's booked us a second week! A brief moment of panic is soon overcome by a sense of joy that I'm going on holiday for a fortnight. This is unbelievable. I call Charlie to let him know, and he assures me all will be fine and that he'll pass on a message to Kieran. I text Kieran as well and he simply wishes me a happy holiday. So that's it… I'm on my way.

♦

"How did you get a second week booked so quickly?"

Dee empties her glass of diet cola as the seatbelt sign lights up above us.

"Oh, didn't I say? We're not in Barbados for the two weeks. I've arranged for us to meet a friend in Florida for the second week; he's working there for a while."

"Do I know him?"

The passenger crew prepare for landing (by sitting down) as Dee explains who we are meeting.

"Stevie?! What's he doing out there?"

"He is out there with Scott from his pharma client."

"And you know all this how?"

"He told me."

I suddenly realise it must have been Stevie who told Dee I hadn't got the CEO job. He must have got a message to her after I sent him a text on the Thursday evening. Dee continues.

"Anyhow, you said you could have two weeks off so it seems too good an opportunity to miss. Stevie has a lot of work to do, and apparently he's writing some sort of book. He's at the Four Seasons on Palm Beach, so I've booked us a penthouse suite."

"You've what? Why did you do that?"

"There's a PGA golf tournament on and it was all they had left!"

My head's still spinning as I step off the plane into the warm air and colourful vibrancy at Bridgetown Airport. The ubiquitous poster girl with gleaming smile and surrounded by bright foliage and a parrot welcomes us to Barbados. We navigate passport control and start to adapt to the leisurely pace of life as the customs officer peers at our passports for at least ten seconds then looks up with a grin, says '*Irie*' and hands the documents back. Then we spot a little sweaty man holding up a sign that says **ROCKLEY BEACH – DEE**.

It's less than an hour's journey to our hotel, through St Lawrence Gap, alive with restaurants, reggae bars and melon sellers, before we drive through the resort golf course and up to the reception. Our small, damp chauffeur disappears under the weight of my stuffed suitcase and Dee's two, and we are welcomed into the grand marble reception area which is festooned with leather armchairs and wicker seats. We opt for leather as a kindly waiter offers us a rum punch or glass of champagne. We opt for champagne. Our luggage is taken up to our room and ten minutes later we summon up the energy to squelch off the leather chairs and follow.

"This is fantastic," beams Dee as she steps out on to our balcony overlooking the golf course which stretches out in the middle distance to a glistening turquoise Caribbean Sea. I've been lying in the middle of my bed staring at the ceiling and daydreaming since we arrived, while Dee busies herself unpacking and tipping the luggage man from her stash of EC dollars. She's always savvy when it comes to getting a good deal or service wherever she is.

My eyes are opening and closing. It's 2:00pm here but my body thinks it's 9:00pm and I'm exhausted after a nine-hour flight. I suspect Dee's body doesn't care what time it is, but while she sits on the balcony my thoughts inevitably wander back to the hospital and the events of the past few days, and then forward to our plans to meet up with Stevie next week in Florida. To steal a tired cliché from many a reality television talent show, we've been on quite a journey. And to shamelessly continue the theme, we've also worked so hard to achieve our dreams and learned a lot about ourselves. But it really has been an emotional ride and we've achieved a meaningful success. Stevie once said to me that to have successes we need to develop stamina to overcome failure, and by God we've done that. We also need to seize opportunities and work well with people who can help us. I think we did just that as well, and throughout Stevie helped me to develop clarity of thought.

He also convinced me of the concept that there's an inherent simplicity in reality, and gave me the courage to challenge conflicts.

The people who ultimately made it happen are all good people; from the management team to the doctors and nurses, everyone who was willing to turn an idea into new behaviours. We overcame the entrenched philosophy in the service that we'd already done everything we could to try to improve. But we hadn't, and we soon came to realise that the hospital's performance could be substantially improved, though not without healthy dollops of blood, sweat and tears. But once we were on the right track, the harder we tried, the more we achieved; and we were galvanised by a passion to do it again. For a second I've forgotten that I'm no longer acting CEO, and suddenly I'm a little disappointed.

"Wakey, wakey! Rise and shine… It's lunchtime!"

Dee crashes into my consciousness, poking me in the arm.

"We're not staying in here with all the sun out there, sweetheart."

"OK, OK. Why don't you go and do a reccy, maybe find the best pool? I think I'll take a quick shower."

It turns out Dee has already had a shower while I was dozing so she sets off, not before leaving the strict instruction that I've half an hour to find her.

♦

Sunday morning. And after a wonderfully relaxing evening I feel refreshed and ready to holiday. I ring little Kirk to wish him a happy birthday and I'm in a good mood. We saunter down to a terrace restaurant for breakfast, the one in which we'd enjoyed a sumptuous buffet last night. Now it's all immaculately laid out again, crisp white linen on the tables, every imaginable colour of fruit on a big stand, and then a selection of hams and bacons and some corned beef hash (odd) with pastries on one section, and on the other side a huge refilling pile of waffles and a silver bucket of maple syrup. The Europeans seem to migrate to the ham and pastries and our American cousins enthusiastically head for the waffles. Dee orders Eggs Benjamin and I help myself to a bowl of fruit and yoghurt.

"Do you want a glass of juice?" she asks.

Full of vitality and generosity of spirit I offer to go and fetch it, and head towards the dispensers which are next to the syrup container. I excuse my way past the waffle queue (it's a tight squeeze) and collect two glasses from a tray which is next to three enormous glass tanks, each containing gallons of juice, one orange, one mango and one pineapple. Hydration is taken seriously in these temperatures and there are juice and water dispensers everywhere, as well as an ice-cold beer tap that Dee discovered yesterday afternoon. Dee asks for orange, which I collect first, but I fancy a glass of pineapple from a tank which is full to the brim. Undeterred by the apparent unpopularity of pineapple, I hold my glass in place and turn the tap. But it won't turn. Maybe that's why the tank is full. I'm determined to get my pineapple though so I twist the lever a little further around and success... the juice begins to trickle and then flow. That's the good news. The bad news is that the lever's come off in my hand and I can't stop the juice so when my small glass is full I can do little else but replace it with another glass... then another... then another. I'm intermittently waving at Dee and the waiter, who doesn't seem to see me as I fill the fourteen glasses available. But the tank is still full and still flowing:

"*Dee!*" I do a sort of whispered shout, but Dee has just put her shades on and is pretending not to hear. In my desperation I grab a huge canoe-shaped tray which is half full of ice cubes. The tray is about the size of a child's sledge and I wedge it under the spurting pineapple tap, placing the tray of pineapple juice I've poured on the nearest table, which has been temporarily vacated by a couple who have ventured off to select their pastries. On my side of the restaurant, the waffle queue is now mesmerised by my antics and waiting with bated breath to see what I do next. As a crowd gathers outside the terrace to see what the fuss is about, two men – one with **PLUMBER** emblazoned on his red T-shirt, the other's saying **GARDENER** – stride purposefully into view, and then one half of the restaurant is quickly evacuated.

Three hours later we pass the terrace restaurant, the majority of which is still encircled by red and white tape and now houses only two fruit juice tanks. I put on my sunglasses to conceal my newly attained celebrity.

"Bet you wish you'd had mango now," says Dee unhelpfully.

As we pass I'm recognised by a group of lads, and a polite ripple of applause breaks out.

Chapter Twenty

Strategy and tactics

Thankfully, the remainder of our first week passes relatively uneventfully and we fly to Florida tanned, massaged and entirely chilled. And Dee's clearly up for more of the same when we arrive at the Four Seasons: a fabulously over-the-top resort with lavish facilities and stratospheric service levels. A pair of concierges collect our cases and scuttle inside, not a bead of sweat in sight, as we follow and are hit by a chilling blast of air conditioning and then soothed by the gentle sound of Chopin's *Nocturnes* being piped throughout reception, a bit of a change from the Bob Marley fest we've left behind.

Stevie waves at us as he descends an elaborate staircase, looking the quintessential Englishman, dressed in cream slacks and open-neck shirt and carrying a copy of the FT.

"Morning, ladies. Good flight?"

We hug and exchange greetings before following an immaculate bell boy towards the lift. We briefly return, having realised he wasn't carrying our cases, to be met by the right bell boy. We should have known as ours was pushing a trolley, it being humanly impossible to carry all Dee's luggage which has grown by one holdall over the past week. Stevie says he'll give us a call in an hour and we can meet for a coffee.

This is just brilliant. One week of my holiday to go and I honestly can't think of two people I'd rather be with. The way I feel right now is as far from the tension and worry of my job situation as it can be. I feel like I don't have a care in the world, and I'm so grateful to Dee and Stevie for setting this up. A friend in need is a friend indeed, and I'm lucky to have these two to support me. Mind you, support sometimes comes in funny ways when those two are involved. When they received the news that I'd not got the job they quickly concocted the plot of a holiday. But, as ever, from Stevie's standpoint a holiday isn't an opportunity to unwind, sometimes quite the opposite. He uses holidays to quickly recuperate with a change of scene and then immediately draws on the energy he gains. His two weeks involved meeting with his pharma clients last week and then staying on this week to work on some document. Dee managed to get us the flights to join him and, being Dee, booked the penthouse suite with private pool. The hotel doesn't seem packed out to me, but who's complaining? The bathroom alone is bigger than my house.

Stevie's plan was that we could help him write his document but Dee isn't particularly in agreement; her plan is to lie down by the pool and relax.

"Stevie thinks we're going to help him work, but he's got no chance."

I have no idea who's going to win.

After a relaxing day the three of us are sitting down for pre-dinner drinks on our first evening together. We're on a wonderful veranda with a beautiful panoramic view leading from the golf course across the bay. The sun is setting and the whole situation is perfect, and Dee is confident she'll get her way.

"Don't let us interrupt you this week, Stevie. When you're busy we'll just get out of the way."

"No, don't worry," comes the reply. "I'm sure you can help me."

Work-focused as ever, he doesn't seem even slightly concerned by the prospect of disturbing the ambiance.

"Look, Linda, you have worked your butt off over recent months turning around the hospital and you have just received a mighty kick in the teeth. But staring into space or wallowing is not an option. Don't expect any sympathy from me. My idea was for you to help me with my document and I will help you with yours."

"Who's wallowing?" I say indignantly, subconsciously siding with Dee, and then realising what he's just said.

"And what document? I don't have a document to write. I might not even have a bloody job when I get back."

Dee seizes the moment.

259

"We're here to carry on the sterling work on our tans and make you look good. We can watch you work and then the three of us can spend the evenings having fun out on the town."

"Who says work can't be fun as well?" Stevie is persistent. "If I know you and Linda, I suspect you are both going to be bored in less than one hour just lying in the sun."

"Just try us. And we could always just have another mojito," replies Dee.

I think it's best to try to find out what Stevie has planned for us, so I ask and he replies:

"OK, but firstly I want to see if you agree there is a job to be done. If you look back to when you first described the situation that your hospital was in, it was rather grotesque."

I'm briefly taken aback, but he carries on to say that there wasn't only a life struggle for the patients; the organisation itself was clinging on to its own survival. Quality of care was at risk and the finances were perilously close to meltdown. As Stevie got to understand the situation, he realised how many of the staff had become disenfranchised in the fallout.

"If we are honest, there were more than a few whose frustration had slipped into apathy. There were a small number who had gone as far as spending their time bad-mouthing others, which in itself began sending yet more negative vibes through the hospital and stirring up others to moan about the constant struggles they were claiming were impossible to solve."

I'm listening carefully as he goes on to describe the sense of hopelessness that prevailed. He admits he thought we might be a freak example at first, but when we started to identify the underlying core issues it became obvious that this was probably an example of a more generic problem around the world.

I think to myself that at least we shouldn't feel that special according to Stevie's analysis. He ploughs relentlessly on as Dee tries to attract the waiter's attention.

"We discovered that medical costs were rising faster than revenues in your hospital and that this was only going to intensify over time. But now we also know this problem is not simply isolated to the UK. Did you watch the news before you came down? The American TV is saturated with the same stories. It's naive and plain wrong to assume that the cause of this is the specific approach to healthcare that the UK takes."

Then he tells us Tam is investigating what's been happening in the USA, as it looks like it's such a hot topic here that presidential elections can be won or lost on this issue alone. To some extent it's even dwarfed discussions on the economy, partly as there have been early signs of growth. He shares the data she has uncovered, which is very revealing. Firstly, in the USA the total spend on healthcare as a percentage of Gross Domestic Product (GDP) is one of the highest in the world. Over the last three decades it's continued to accelerate and has gone from nine per cent to seventeen point six per cent. This is by no stretch of the imagination a small percentage of GDP and the speed it's growing at is terrifying for a country. Demographics and mortality rates may continue the momentum of this runaway train.

As Stevie speaks, even Dee is listening agog. This is jaw-dropping stuff. Unless things change, the only way to sustain the position is to ensure GDP grows faster than the growth in healthcare. A challenge even with any encouraging signs on offer. The other less palatable option is for healthcare to be rationed. And the twist in the tale is that while the amount spent on healthcare has been growing, America has one of the slowest rates of reducing preventable deaths, which you certainly wouldn't expect. Dee joins the discussion.

"Are you suggesting the US should adopt a UK healthcare style of approach? The Boston Tea Party people would choke on their Earl Grey."

"Nope, that's not it," says Stevie. "The UK and the US are very different, but the UK does have a cost of healthcare per head of less than half of that in the US."

Two countries separated by an ocean are suffering the same underlying dilemma. Stevie explains it's not a matter of choosing one approach over the other; both have their flaws.

This has just reached Dee's tolerance to gloom threshold.

"Bloody hell, Stevie! I thought we were on holiday, not at a global healthcare conference. Can't we just leave this one to the politicians and order another mojito now?"

She waves to the waiter and Stevie nods.

"We can definitely order another drink but I am not so sure leaving it to the politicians alone is such a sound idea."

Then he returns to my own situation at the hospital, telling me I wasn't the first person to try to find a better way forward. Many people have had a go in the past but for many others inertia was too strong for them. Often, after a brief attempt they decided it was just too difficult to continue to push new ways of working through, and accepted the only way forward was to try to manage the compromise between quality, timeliness and availability of care, and the finances. It's played out in different ways in different countries but the underlying dilemma is the same. Stevie tips his glass towards me.

"The interesting thing about your success is that all you had to guide you was the sextant that we built to answer two simple questions: of all the patients I could work on next which one should I work on next? And, of all the things I could try to improve, which should I improve first?"

Stevie likes to use the analogy of the sextant and explains this very simple instrument can actually help describe where you are at any point in time; and from a better understanding of where you are, it's easier to establish the direction of travel. Vasco de Gama managed to find a new route to India around the southern tip of Africa, opening up a whole new trade route that lasted centuries.

"Good knowledge," smiles Dee.

Together we used our version of the sextant to find a simple way to place the hospital on a rapid process of improvement. More importantly, we found a way of bringing almost everyone with us in an amazingly short timescale.

"You overcame the traditional yearnings for security by achieving unprecedented results in a timescale previously unheard of. And by using a simple explanation of what you were trying to achieve," he adds, "you made the new way forward seem just common sense even if not common practice."

Also we were very careful not to shout too loudly about our impressive results despite the temptation. We held our nerve and opened up the potential of becoming a leading research hospital which achieves levels of profitability that even a high-tech company would be in awe of. But these ideas were not followed by exhortations for others to blindly follow.

Then Stevie gathers momentum.

"In this journey we have all learned a little bit about ourselves as well. Perhaps we've seen what has been limiting our own and others' achievements. It wasn't just about changing our understanding. You helped them close the chasm between a lack of understanding and a change in behaviour. You helped people to see that there was a way of thriving when it seemed that all around them was nothing but pain. You helped staff shed entrenched assumptions and achieve a seemingly insurmountable goal."

Dee is looking at me to gauge my reaction. The sunbed seems a distance away now but this doesn't feel like work. And I realise that, despite my recent disappointment, it means the world to me. Stevie continues.

"It may feel like not getting the job is just bad luck because they chose someone else over you. But for me there is another way bad luck can strike. What happens if leaders in a dozen or even thirty hospitals also succeed like you have succeeded?"

"Bad luck!" I'm stunned. "How can you claim it would be bad luck if thirty or so hospitals managed to achieve the sort of results we've had?"

"It would be bad luck because nobody would have made the necessary effort to properly learn and articulate exactly how to achieve this level of breakthrough. It will just leave more lost souls swimming around in the fish bowl year after year without addressing the same old fears of changing."

I see what he means. Without reviewing and uprooting any of the assumptions that are holding them back, those who will have succeeded will just come forward with more shouts of '*look what I have done*'. Just a few case studies claiming results will continue for a while, and the global health system will have to wait for another coincidence to start its journey towards finding a truly sustainable solution. Stevie looks at us both.

"What I'm saying is we have an opportunity to articulate exactly what we believe are the strategy and tactics required to achieve a breakthrough in a hospital, and a breakthrough in healthcare for a nation. And if someone finds a flaw in our argument they can use it to form the basis of the next leap forward. Are you with me? Are you happy to spend this week learning how to do just this?"

Dee and I look at each other before Stevie implores again:

"We could all have a great time, get tanned in the day and eat and drink too much in the evening, then check out and go home. But I really believe we would be leaving this important need behind. And that's not in any of us, is it? Is it?"

Dee sighs.

"Looks like we're in on one condition. If you think we're going to be seen outside of this hotel with you wearing those shorts, you've got another thing coming. So you go shopping tomorrow and it's a deal."

Stevie's delighted.

"Let's see if we can't create two great documents, one for healthcare and one for my pharma clients."

"Do you know exactly how we can articulate what Linda has done in a way that can be understood across the world?" asks Dee.

"Not exactly," admits Stevie. "This is why I am here in Florida. This is exactly what I have to do for my client so they can spread the results we have had through their two hundred plants around the world."

I tap Stevie on the hand.

"So just to be clear, we're going to spend a good proportion of the next week of our holiday articulating how to achieve a breakthrough in healthcare that can be applied across the globe."

"And the pharma version as well."

"Using a process that you have only ever used once or twice before?"

Stevie nods.

"Sounds like a blast," says Dee. "That's why you wanted us here. You don't have the time to do it all on your own. So when do we start?"

"How about eight in the morning after breakfast? And don't worry... the juice dispensers are easy to use."

Dee splutters into her mojito.

♦

I'm sitting with Stevie in an air-conditioned meeting room, projector at one end, huge whiteboard, flip charts, water dispenser and a box of branded pencils. We could be in any meeting room in the world, were it not for the sliding doors leading out on to a balcony which overlooks the bay. Dee breezes in, beach bag over her shoulder and sunglasses perched on her head.

"Morning, campers. Are you done?"

"We were waiting for you," smiles Stevie.

"OK, but before we start, what's my specific role in this?" She looks at me. "You're the health professional, and you're the expert, but what am I?"

"You're Dee," says Stevie.

Dee nods and sits down. Stevie gets to his feet and walks over to the whiteboard.

"Let's see how we get on. If we are going to explain any major change in a massive organisation, the first question we need to ask is '*why?*': why is the change necessary?"

He writes on the whiteboard: 1) **The Necessary Assumptions**

"So in our case, that covers the detail behind the state we were in a few months ago," I say.

Stevie agrees.

"Yep. We saw simultaneous pressure on the quality of care, the timeliness and availability of care, and the hospital's financial mire. Added to that, too many people were bitching and moaning."

He then writes on the whiteboard: 2) **The Strategy**

Dee speaks up.

"To make a step change in providing exceptional quality and timely care, while rectifying the finances."

"Pretty much," says Stevie. "The ambition was a flourishing hospital providing exceptional quality and timely care, and crucially a rewarding working environment for staff. We also wanted sufficient financial success to reinvest in research and staff development to ultimately become an ever-flourishing hospital."

Then he writes: 3) **Why is it possible/what are the risks and obstacles?**

Stevie's third question was why on earth had this not already been achieved and why does it appear so difficult. Through my own experience it appears to be eminently possible and what's more, repeatable on a grand scale. But we need to understand why people claim change is difficult. Only by understanding and challenging the assumptions that were in place did we find the breakthrough required, and in our case there was a combination of assumptions.

Firstly, it was assumed that medical costs were rising faster than revenues on a runaway train that was impossible to catch and change direction. Secondly, the complexity appeared bewildering and where to start improving things was difficult to find. But once we uncovered the inherent simplicity – that there are relatively few constraints in any goal-oriented system – we were on our way. Thirdly, it was assumed that effort demanded by change would either exhaust staff or involve extremely high risks that would endanger the organisation's existence.

Stevie writes: **4) Steps/Tactics**

"So if you claim it is possible to make this gargantuan change then what are the steps or tactics I need to take to achieve what you claim is possible?"

"We know it's possible because we've done it," I say. "The hospital is now providing higher-quality and more timely care and the finances are improving month on month. And our staff have fully embraced the approach and are more engaged than ever before."

I feel a tinge of pride as I speak and I can't help but smile. Dee smiles back at me. Stevie says:

"For sure, showing you have succeeded is a good start but just stating this alone is insufficient for everyone to know what to actually do."

He goes on to say we need to explain to any readers that without a thorough explanation of what should be stopped and what should be started people will flounder. He reminds us of the paramount importance of stopping local efficiency measures, and points out that without testing and irrefutable results in their own environment a broader acceptance of success is unlikely. Also, if the detail of the explanation is insufficient we need to explain why it's insufficient, and then explain what else is necessary to achieve sufficient proof of the effectiveness of our proposed approach.

As we pause Stevie looks at his phone. He needs to make a call so Dee and I step out on the balcony.

"Where do you think all this is going?" she asks.

I look out towards the bay.

"I don't know, but what I do know is that Stevie has put a hell of a lot of time into this. And it certainly helped us at the hospital. Maybe he plans to scale it up pretty quickly."

"But why ask us to help him with it?"

"I guess because he's doing it already in the pharma game and he thought we could do two at once. Maybe he just thinks I should occupy my mind at this moment. And it was my hospital that went first."

Dee plops a cup of water on the balcony in front of me and continues:

"You know what. I think this could lead to something for you."

"In what way?"

"Well… you're going to be in demand fairly soon I should think. Anyone who knows about your work at the hospital will be fairly keen to speak to you. Maybe you could join Stevie."

"No, that's not for me. I'm healthcare through and through," I quickly reply. Dee raises her eyebrows and nods gently. I sometimes think she believes she knows me better than I know myself. Maybe she does. She probes a little more.

"Are you happy?"

"Are you?" I expertly deflect.

"Talented, attractive, unattached and at Palm Beach… of course I'm bloody happy."

I think for a moment, and then I realise that I'm extremely happy. Over the past few months I've travelled from a daily nightmare fighting fires to working in a hospital where I enjoy going in, love my colleagues, and have pride. I'm very happy. Jobless maybe… but very happy. Dee gives me a nudge.

"Come on. Let's see if he's ready for us."

As we wander back into the room Stevie is pouring three coffees, which he hands out while getting himself immediately back on track. Gesturing towards the whiteboard, he says:

"We need to drill down and keep going through our questions at increasing levels of detail until it becomes blindingly obvious. Let's have a go and see when we have gone too far."

So we do. At the highest level we claimed it was possible to simultaneously improve quality and timeliness of care and grow revenues without exhausting staff. But just having one example was insufficient and therefore, answering question one, we must explain what was necessary to achieve such a multifaceted breakthrough. The answer was clearly that the approach was built on satisfying the patient's significant need, in essence driving everything from a patient-centred perspective. What became increasingly obvious is that as we uncovered the three things that patients really want, it was clear these were the three things we and other hospitals were failing to deliver. All that is required in any hospital is to provide high-quality care accessed in a timely manner to suit the patient, and carried out without unnecessary disruption or delay. Ultimately we were able to prove that it was actually possible to do this within the current resources and without exhausting staff. Moreover, the approach we developed creates so much free capacity that we were able to treat more patients with higher-quality care within the same or fewer resources. This showed that rather than being impossible, what we were actually sitting on was an enormous opportunity. In Stevie's terms: a pot of gold.

The tactic we used was also vitally important because, rather than asking everyone to trust us in the hope it would turn out all right, we used a combination of logic and a highly focused approach that yielded very fast results. This provided irrefutable evidence which enabled us to get and keep everyone on board in record time. This ensured we closed the traditional chasm between a change of understanding and change in behaviour.

But early results were insufficient in isolation. We had to build the capabilities to capitalise on the capacity we exposed and learn how to use it to eliminate backlogs and treat more patients with higher quality and more timely care. This meant that the very first step was to reduce the bad multitasking and mis-synchronisation we knew about. They were negatively impacting the quality and timeliness of care, and creating a grim working environment for staff who were constantly fighting the latest fire that took hold. This is what had caused the gulf between clinicians and managers for so many years, and once we'd resolved this it made the lives of all clinicians, and particularly the doctors, much better and allowed them to do what they love: spending more time on delivering patient care. The bad multitasking and mis-synchronisation were also sucking up our capacity and damaging the opportunity to both grow revenues and reduce unnecessary operating expenses.

While we talk about this, Stevie reminds us how we used the dice game to demonstrate that it was the bad multitasking and mis-synchronisation that were the primary causes of increasingly overstretched resources. People were already aware that the quality and timeliness of care rapidly deteriorates when staff are overstretched. And attempts to offload these overstretched resources increases operating expenses. On the day of the dice game, we also proved that the tactic to achieve such a change was not just improved practice and process but a fundamental shift in culture as well. A shift that was best led by the clinicians themselves rather than exhortations by management.

Diving down to the next level, we were able to show that it was necessary to deal with local optimisation and the resulting conflicting priorities. The strategy that tackled this was to create one simple robust and trustworthy patient-centred priority system for everyone in the hospital to follow. Stevie says:

"This is a crucial point. It is the core of the approach that we need to be able to explain, because previously there were many false assumptions about why this was seen to be impractical."

And of course he's right. We were faced with a list of reasons why it wouldn't work. Firstly, that priorities are constantly disrupted as new tasks emerge throughout a patient journey. No two patients are the same so the expected clinical recovery time can vary significantly from patient to patient even when they are suffering from the same illness. And lack of timely treatment can extend the treatment period for some patients. There were also many claims that the pressure of local measures meant that staff would not always follow the overarching list.

But what we showed as our first example was that the simple tactic of creating a clinically derived planned discharge date (PDD) at the beginning of the patient journey that was based solely on the clinical recovery time formed the basis of an extremely robust and patient-centred priority list. And when it was updated every day, it remained valid and trustworthy.

Stevie gets to his feet again.

"When we realised that setting a PDD and updating the PDD when the rate of recovery changed was insufficient, we needed to augment the process."

He walks over to his flip chart and writes down the five steps:

1) Take account of the latest understanding of disruptions and delays in the tasks required to complete the patient's journey, and update the priority list accordingly.
2) Ensure that when prioritisation alone is insufficient, or a large, unexpected disruption or delay occurs, there is an effective escalation process in place.
3) Ensure each resource manager is able to allocate the correct level of resources to meet the fluctuating demands.
4) Ensure each unit manager is able to follow the overall priority within their own unit.
5) Ensure that when, despite all these efforts, a few patients are delayed there is an effective process to ensure these delays are overcome and further delay is diminished.

As he furiously scribbles I think back to how this played out back at the hospital, and how a welcome by-product emerged in how engaged many of our staff became. I tell Stevie and Dee about Mo's navigator.

"This was a really good person who was about to quit the service to retrain. But Mo's implementation of the process re-ignited her passion. She embraced the system and took personal responsibility for flow and escalations. Mo was delighted. Not only has she stayed on; she's loved by patients and colleague alike, and has found ambition. Mo has recommended her for upgrade and she is taking a management course at night school."

"That's brilliant," says Dee.

Stevie continues:

"The people side was crucial. And once that was achieved, perhaps the most important change we introduced was the way we used the time buffer management system. That helped to identify which task and which resource was most often causing the most disruption and delay to the most patients."

That certainly enabled us to focus our improvement efforts to achieve results in an unprecedented time period, and that was what actually proved to everyone that it was possible. Without the speed of results we would never have had the chance to make it sustainable for the long run.

"And let's not overlook how we managed to increase profitability," says Stevie. "We initially eliminated backlogs to give the best service

270

levels around, and carefully planned growth of those services that had a high throughput per bed day and where we had used the reductions in length of stay to treat more patients."

So that is how we did it. But the question we now have to answer is whether or not this level of explanation is enough to guide people to lead their own breakthrough. What else do we need?

"I'm reasonably happy that we can now articulate how to apply the approach to one hospital, or even possibly one health system," says Stevie as he gets to his feet. "You two take the day off tomorrow and see if you can't get bored by the pool. I can get on with the pharma document. And dinner's on me tonight."

"We're full board," says Dee.

Chapter Twenty-One

Brotherhood

"You know… I could get used to it here," sighs Dee as she twiddles a straw in her cocktail glass. The sun is setting while we sit on the veranda waiting for Stevie. As he offered to pay for dinner we've decided to forgo the hotel restaurant and have booked a taxi to take us to Dyche's Oyster Bar. Dee recounts the last time she had oysters in New York.

"I ordered twelve Hudson Bay oysters at Smith and Wollensky's on the corner of 42nd Street. I had to ask for a knife and fork. They were so big they looked like pork chops!"

Anthony Bourdain eat your heart out.

Stevie arrives, looking a little perturbed.

"Sorry I'm late." He accepts the glass that Dee thrusts in his hand. "My bloody brother."

"Ah yes, I forgot you had a brother. What's he up to these days?" I ask.

"Doing his best to avoid bringing down the family business."

Dee's ears prick up. Stevie explains that the business started up in the early nineteenth century as a fishing and seafood supply company, a small local operation in Kent. Over the next hundred and fifty years it grew organically and now supplies top-end regional supermarkets and independents, at the last count employing over two hundred people and turning over £115 million.

"Vokes Smoke Houses – is that you?" asks Dee.

"Part of the group of companies we own."

On leaving university at twenty-one, Stevie joined the business but soon had furious rows with his dad and brother. He left them to it within two years and went to do some travelling. Family businesses are fraught with danger and often logic flies out of the window. Making a cold, commercial decision isn't always so easy when it's a family discussion, particularly when there are stark clashes of personality. Sparks can fly and apparently they did. Stevie admits though that the business has been a nice source of steady income for him from the age of eighteen. It's given him the freedom to explore the world and his own personality, and has allowed him to set up his own business and, when I think about it, help me at the hospital as well.

But Stevie believes that over the past couple of years the business has been losing direction.

"My brother is buckling under pressure from Dad who is insisting things stay as they are. We're haemorrhaging cash but Dad thinks if we do what we've always done then things will come good. My brother's been shouting down the phone at me. He wants me to go and help."

"So are you going to?" I ask.

"It would drive me mad. I couldn't work with them fifteen years ago and I see no reason why I could work with them now. I've moved on. They have a strong enough management team. They should be able to work it out. And the bank's still supporting."

Dee turns on Stevie.

"You selfish toad! I can't believe you just said that. You've been happy to take an income from it all your life. Don't you think it's time to give something back? How on earth can we be serious about changing the health of a nation if you can't even be bothered to mend the relationships within your family and the family business? Give me strength!"

I know how much Dee loves her own brother. She'd swim back to England if he needed her. She's pretty angry. And I agree with her.

"You can't just let this drift, Stevie. It's not in your nature. I don't care how much your family gets on your nerves; they are still your family. And you know damn well you can help them."

Stevie remains silent, but Dee doesn't.

"You know what? I really don't get you sometimes, Stevie. You're just a bloody fool to continue to fight with your brother. Sort yourself out."

The taxi driver agrees to wait while we have another drink.

♦

The following evening we're sitting on the balcony of Stevie's suite having a late afternoon tea. Dee and I have done the square root of nothing all day, apart from working on our suntans and falling off lilos. We agreed to get together before dinner to continue our discussion on how we can communicate a health turnaround strategy on a wide scale. It didn't seem right last night. We had a lovely meal out and managed to get Stevie smiling again by the main course. He was still smarting from Dee's rebuke while worrying about his family's business for the first hour. So a light and relaxed evening was the order and that's exactly what we had. Dee and I continued in that vein through today at Stevie's invitation, while he worked on his pharma document.

Dee helps herself to a cucumber sandwich as she opens the debate.

"So, colleagues, how are you going to go about communicating to an entire nation?"

It's obvious to us all this is a mammoth and unprecedented challenge. The head of a national health system has huge responsibilities: to continually improve the system and also to ensure there is absolutely no risk of deterioration in the provision of healthcare during any change. Stevie replies:

"As a starting point I think it would be fair to assume that most leaders, politicians and stakeholders would believe it is either impossible or far too risky to attempt to transform the health system of a country rapidly and painlessly."

Too right. He continues:

"And so we need a logical and evidence-based approach that offers the leaders the opportunity to examine how we believe such a vision could be realistic. Then we need a process to firstly evaluate, then verify and finally agree whether or not it can be achieved. Without these ingredients there is not even a snowflake's chance in hell of it being taken up."

The way I see it, even if we had such a vision and the plan to make it realistic, we would still be a long way from getting agreement. The diversity of stakeholders is immense, and any one of them has the power to either stop or ensure its death by snail-like progress in the discussion of whether it should go ahead or not. They are not called politicians for nothing. Yes, they want to contribute to the improvement of the country's healthcare system, but only as long as it doesn't entail taking imprudent risks.

Stevie suggests that our first step must be to do exactly what we have just done at our hospital. For any hospital we must construct the necessary strategies and tactics that lay out the actions required to achieve the desired outcome. Each step must, just as in our one hospital example, be based on the logic and evidence that an experienced person already has, combined with intuition. He says:

"We have to be able to present something that gives the stakeholders a real chance to believe in a vision that they can transform the healthcare system of their nation."

Dee argues.

"Yes, but it's not enough to just convince people through logic that the plan will yield the results you claim are possible. They will want to do all the necessary checks to verify that it will work in their particular country, and show that they've done the checks."

Stevie agrees.

"The best way we can do this is through a controlled set of experiments based on piloting the approach in small and large acute and in community-based care settings in their country."

I add:

"With the rise in mental health issues we will also have to prove the principles are valid in that area as well."

Dee has personal experience with her brother Carl and nods her agreement. Stevie continues.

"The pilots must systematically verify all the key elements of the vision, but they must present no risk to the healthcare system as a whole and be relatively inexpensive."

Any such experiments will need careful guidance to ensure they are successfully executed and that the results do indeed verify the main elements of the vision.

"The results must make continuing a no-brainer," says Stevie.

I ask how we can measure the results and he outlines two primary methods. Firstly, we can measure whether the size of the results are as predicted from the initial analysis. As we know from our own experiment at the hospital, the results that were larger than expected should be treated with as much caution as results that are smaller than hoped. Both are indications that there's something wrong in the underlying logic. The second way is to ask if the results are assumed to be representative, and were successfully implemented across the nation, would they show without a doubt that the health of the nation is improving, and that the spend on health as a percentage of GDP is stabilising or reducing?

"There are two unknowns that are as yet unproven, of course," says Stevie. "Does a healthier nation lead to a more productive nation?" Intuitively one would think so, but the magnitude of this effect is more difficult to work out. "Secondly, does having an effective health system give a nation a decisive competitive edge?"

"Well, when you think about the growing market for health tourism then that could make a real contribution to GDP," says Dee. "Don't forget the opportunity for greater inward investment from the pharma companies. If they see a nation leading the way, they would be mad not to be involved."

Just think, if both of these two effects were real and significant, which country could be the first to have an affordable health system?

"To be successful a pilot will need a CEO who is committed to leading it," I say. "Getting the attention of the CEO of a big organisation won't be easy."

"It needs a CEO like you." Dee winks.

"We'd also need a CEO who knows they are leading the implementation on behalf of the country as a whole."

When someone realises what they are being asked to lead has ramifications beyond their immediate area of responsibility, they will want to ensure they understand the logic of the plan implicitly. Hopefully, they will ensure the process is properly followed and do whatever it takes to ensure there is a decisive outcome. My concern is that with the plan we implemented I couldn't have done it without Stevie's help and guidance.

"We can't just give people a manual and expect them to get on with it," I say.

And there's only so much Stevie to spread around. Particularly as he tells us that he wants to test his approach in areas other than healthcare as well, not to mention trying to help out with his family business, partially motivated by the haranguing he received last night.

"And I wouldn't mind having a closer look at the education sector," he says. "Particularly the universities."

"Does that mean you'll be coming to give me all the attention you've been lavishing on Linda?" asks Dee.

"Be careful what you wish for!"

"Let's try to sort out health first." I bring us back on track.

Stevie suggests the first step would be to build a small group of people from within the country's health system who can support the initiative.

"These individuals must already be respected for their achievements. No rookies, I'm afraid," he says.

"Like me you mean?" I can't resist it. Stevie ignores me and carries on.

"Our role will be to give them the confidence of the most senior CEOs in the industry and to do this they will have to have a deep understanding of the vision and how to make it realistic. They will have to be personally involved in leading the early pilots and be on a constant journey of upgrade and development."

He tells us we would need a few months preparing the group to take their health system through the changes required. And we would need to guide this group of people and ensure the pilots are well designed.

"What do you think?"

"I think you should ask the Prime Minister and President what they think," I offer.

"Me or we?"

Stevie's phone rings; he sees it's his brother and so picks it up. While his brother puts his dad on the phone, Dee and I wander back inside the suite.

"This is getting pretty colossal," says Dee. "Where do you think it will end?"

"I really don't know. But it's kind of exciting, isn't it? What we achieved in the hospital changed the whole character and mood of the place. It's great to work there now. Why shouldn't we be ambitious? Why shouldn't everyone else have at least the right to look at the opportunity even if they turn it down?"

"But what type of person is going to make the first leap of faith?"

I think for a moment back to my predicament when Stevie first came to the hospital.

"Well, I asked Stevie for the help personally, I guess."

"So anyone Stevie knows will search for a better way? That's not it. Why else did you do it?"

"Because I was desperate."

"And you also had to be pretty courageous. But the ideal people to take on this challenge will be people who care, and are blessed with logic and intuition."

That's a little haughtier but it suits, I suppose. As Stevie paces up and down on the balcony I think again about my role at the hospital and, quite frankly, for the first time in a while I can see a clearer path forward, pretty much unknown but different. And I am genuinely excited.

"So which are you then, an intuitive visionary or a desperate hero?" Dee asks.

I smile as I pick up my own phone which is now ringing.

It's Kieran.

Chapter Twenty-Two

Butterfly

On landing, I get a text from Kieran asking me to meet him in his office at 9:00am tomorrow. We had a slightly odd conversation while I was in the US. He just told me he had something to run past me and seemed a little awkward. Maybe he felt bad about calling me on my holiday, particularly after the last conversation we had shortly after I'd been turned down for the CEO job. Either way, I didn't get much of a clue what he wanted to speak about. So now I have the text summoning me in first thing tomorrow. I suppose it'll be better than being at the hospital to welcome Ashcroft into his new role.

Mum has spent the last half hour – while I watched Dee get her luggage off the carousel and the taxi driver cram it into his boot – on the phone telling me how worried she is about me. I don't think she'll ever realise that telling me she's worried about me just gives me something else to worry about.

◆

Bang on 9:00am I walk into Kieran's office, and he offers me a coffee and asks me how my holiday was before moving towards the point.

"I know you're disappointed you didn't get the job, but you gave it your best shot. You've achieved more in a few months than most struggling hospitals could hope to do in years. But, let's be honest, you didn't stand much of a chance. You just didn't have the track record."

Thanks a heap. He could have told me that three weeks ago and saved putting me through the whole painful process. He knows it was a big blow to me but he doesn't know that in my current state of mind I'm seriously considering my future within the health service. I did want the job so we could continue the work we've been doing, and there's no small part of me that feels I've let my colleagues down in some way. It's only fair to put him in the picture, even if he hadn't done likewise when he had the chance.

"So what now? I'll be honest with you, Kieran, I'm wondering what to do. I'm not sure if I can go back to my old job and I really don't know if I can work with Ashcroft. They've appointed a CEO, but right now, the way I feel, they've lost a COO."

"I know you and Ashcroft have never really seen eye to eye," he says, "but I really do think you may have misjudged him to a degree."

"Really?"

"Like I told you, he's been successful as a CEO before, which is why he got the job in regional office. And working here is not particularly conducive to making friends."

"But he doesn't even try."

"Maybe not. But now he's a gamekeeper turned poacher (or is it the other way round?) he may be able to show what he's actually made of." He pauses for a second, and then: "But I didn't ask you to come in to talk about Ashcroft."

I wait to see whether Kieran is ready to tell me what this is all actually about.

"Linda, believe me, there will be a job for you as CEO in the future, I'm sure of it. But not now and not with this hospital. You need to pick yourself up and look for other opportunities. It is the world we live in. It is as simple as that."

Good God. Is he telling me I haven't got the COO job either?

"Has anything like this ever happened to you, Kieran?"

"Not exactly like this. I was once offered a job which was later retracted. But that's in the distant past and neither here nor there."

Well I never! He continues.

"All of us have moments in our careers when things don't go as planned. I have spent the vast majority of my career in the health service, and at one time I had ambitions to make it all the way to the top but it was not to be. I am grateful, though, that I have had a fantastic career and I'm very proud of what I have done."

He then tells me of an old school friend of his who joined the service a couple of years after him. Soon they were in the same group, and then his friend William started to accelerate and has now made it to the very top.

"They chose the right man," he says.

"William Thackeray? You know William Thackeray?"

"Of course I do. Our children have grown up together."

"Wow. But Kieran, I'm not saying I want to run the health service. I just wanted the chance to turn around our hospital."

Then he gives me a look of intent.

"Linda, I asked you to come here today because I want to talk to you about something else." Aha, here comes the point. "Something which I hope will be of interest to you. I want you to take on Ashcroft's old job."

I manage to resist doing a comedy coffee splutter. And then I have the briefest of moments imagining myself bollocking Ashcroft at a regional meeting.

"Me? Ashcroft? Me become a bureaucrat? You have to be kidding!"

"I knew you'd be pleased. Anyway, before you carry on slating Ashcroft please remember I was his boss for three years. It kind of reflects on me."

"Sorry, Kieran. I didn't mean it like that, but I don't think this is my style."

"Just hear me out," he says. "The day I came to visit you before the interviews I saw something different; something I haven't seen in my whole career. Don't get me wrong. I have seen many hospitals struggling and I have seen hospitals turned around, but never so quickly or with such cohesion. I saw a process in place and I started to wonder whether that could be repeated."

It appears that Kieran's line of thinking is not a million miles away from what Stevie, Dee and I were talking about last week. He tells me he was impressed by the way we weren't interested in simply cutting costs quickly to try to make ends meet.

"Your approach was ambitious enough to create conditions in which the hospital could flourish now and into the future. I know you haven't had the chance to play this one out, but there are many other acute hospitals just like that one. There is a big job to do to help others."

"But I don't want to help other acute hospitals just like that one. I wanted the chance to do that one," I say, immediately realising I sound like a nine-year-old. Kieran looks like a disapproving parent.

"I know, Linda. We've already been over that. But the acute hospitals are only one link in a much bigger chain of health and social care. We should talk about seeing whether what you have done can work in different links of the chain, and then if we could use it to manage the whole chain."

As he's talking, a butterfly flies through the window and flaps its wings, helping to push my career in a new direction. It's so funny; a minute ago I was testing my resolve to consider scoffing an industrial container full of humble pie to go and work for Ashcroft. Now it appears I'm being presented with the possibility of testing the ideas that Stevie and I have developed in other parts of the health system. And to get the chance to try it across the whole health and social care system is even more inspiring. Kieran can see he's engaged me.

"Roles like this are few and far between these days. They can be thankless, but from this position we have the opportunity to influence a much wider circle."

Under Kieran's stewardship there are many acute hospitals, community hospitals and mental health services, and tens of thousands of patients being looked after out in the community. Both he and I are wondering whether we can achieve a similar breakthrough in performance in other environments. He tells me that if we can, he will be on the phone to William insisting that he listen to what we have discovered.

"I may well have appeared to you as just another bureaucrat, but I have spent a lot of my time seeking out what works and what doesn't", he says. "When I first heard what you were doing I thought it was pretentious. It sounded too simple. It sounded just like common sense. Dare I say it, I wondered if you were taking us for a ride. But when I came in on that visit and I could see into the eyes of the people myself, it didn't take me long to decide that it works."

Equally, Kieran understands that without examples of breakthroughs across the rest of the links in the chain, even his friendship with the top man won't get us an audience.

"So this is my plan. You are seconded with me for the next twelve months and we work together to bring about these changes in the other links. This is a fantastic opportunity for you."

Someone, probably my dad, once said to me '*gambling only pays when you're winning*', but this is a gamble I can't dismiss. And in any case, I've been winning. When will I get another opportunity like this? I know I've loved the last few months and I know I've learned a lot. So what better chance to test these ideas out but in the environments that I don't have the same level of experience and intuition about?

"OK, Kieran, you're on. When do I start?"

"About five minutes ago. Linda, you do understand this is a different game, don't you? This is about achieving changes through influencing others rather than leading others."

"Yes, I get it. Think Ashcroft with a happy gene."

Kieran sighs then smiles.

"Take the rest of the day off and meet me back here tomorrow. I'll sort out the paperwork and let everyone know what is happening."

♦

Sitting in the car I give Mum a ring first, if only to stop her worrying and me worrying about her worrying. Then I phone Stevie and Dee with the snazzy multi-call facility on my phone.

"Hi, Linda." It's Stevie.

"Hi, it's Dee."

"Oh Dee, I thought it was Linda calling."

"It is, you idiot. She's called us both."

I consider staying quiet to see how this one plays out.

"So where's Linda then?"

"I'm here. Are you both sitting down? I've got a new job."

"Oh my god – that's fantastic!" yelps Dee.

"Hey… well congratulations," says Stevie. "So what have you got us all into now?"

"I've got Ashcroft's job!"

After a moment of incredulous silence Dee pipes up.

"You're joking, aren't you?"

"No… listen to me…"

Then I take them through the whole story of my conversation

with Kieran, amid sporadic whoops from Dee and nothing from Stevie. So at the end I say:

"So, Stevie, what do you think?"

"I think it's perfect. Next time I'm in town we'll all go out and celebrate."

Then I come over a tad emotional.

"Listen to me, both of you. Without you two there is no way I could have done that job over the recent months, and I'm not letting you off the hook now!"

"You'll need some new clothes," says Dee. "We'll go shopping at the weekend. Well done – got to go. Bye."

Stevie stays on the phone.

"Are you still there, Stevie?"

"Yes, I'm still here."

"You know I've never really thanked you for all you've done this year. Without the approach you taught us I would never have been able to achieve the results. But more than that, you stood by me throughout all the good and bad times and you've given me your unconditional support. I've learned a lot from you but most of all I've learned what it is to have a true friend. And the funny thing is it's a friend I knew I always had."

A moment of quiet follows so I say:

"Stevie, are you awake?"

"Yes I'm awake." I'm sure I can hear a slight wobble in his voice. "No problem, mate, anytime and anywhere. You'd best get on. You've got the nation's health to improve."

Typical! Even when he's weakening he can raise the bar.

Chapter Twenty-Three

Yes, but…

Barely four weeks into my new role and I'm already missing the old place, and even more so the old team. So I'm pleased to see an envelope on my desk in handwriting that I recognise to be Cath's. It's clearly a greeting card of some sort, but it's not my birthday (although Cath is less likely to get that one wrong than I am). I bet it's a *'good luck in your new job'* card, and hopefully it'll have an update of how things are at the hospital. I've seen the last month's figures, which are very good, but that's not quite the same as hearing how things really are from someone on the inside.

I eagerly open the envelope to find a brightly coloured card with a picture of a champagne glass on the front. It's an invitation… to Cath's retirement party! My goodness, that was quick. Cath made it clear to me on my last day that she wasn't looking forward to working with Ashcroft, and maybe she's taken just about as much as she can. I pick up the phone.

"Cath… it's me, Linda."

"Oh hello, Linda. It's lovely to hear from you. How are you doing?"

"I'm not sure," I reply. "It's early days. I'm enjoying it but I'm not exactly sure if it's working. But I'll be OK. Anyhow, what about you? I've just opened your card."

"Oh yes. It's wonderful news, isn't it?"

"Is it?"

"Yes, Linda. It's the right time to go for me, while I still have the energy to take up something else… and maybe see more of the world."

"But what really made you decide now?"

285

I suspect, and maybe a tiny part of me hopes, that Cath has had enough of her new boss.

"I'm not getting any younger. Everything's fine here and the team, with Mr Ashcroft's help, are carrying on just as you left off. You'd be proud to see it."

Oh. I take a moment to gather my thoughts. That wasn't exactly what I'd expected to hear. Cath speaks again.

"Well actually, most things are going smoothly but Charlie had a blazing row with Mr Ashcroft last week. I didn't hear about it until the following day but Jo says it was explosive to say the least."

That's more like it.

"So what happened?"

"I don't know, Linda, but they seem to be getting on with it. Maybe they've settled their differences."

I begin to picture Charlie bellowing while Ashcroft removes his paper knife from view, and then Cath brings me back on track.

"So can you make my leaving do?"

"Wild horses couldn't keep me away."

♦

"Yes, but, Linda – you have to understand that we're different."

If I hear those words one more time I might just scream. Since I took up the role with Kieran, I've visited five organisations this month and have taken them all through the story of our success, step by step, in the hope they can visualise the impact it could have on their own set-up. But from the majority, this is the stock response I've had: '*We're different, you don't understand.*' And it's human nature, I guess. If you've tried so hard for so long to find ways of improving your operation, it can take courage to listen to someone from the outside. There's almost a sense of embarrassment.

The only person I have seen actively taking things forward is a woman called Jessica whom I met previously at the dice game session. She runs many of the local community hospitals and has been in constant contact with Jo over the last few months. Together they've taken the ideas and she's been following the same approach in her hospital, while Jo has provided information around planned discharge dates and the buffer status of patients where we're planning to complete their rehabilitation in the community. Jessica has done a tremendous job of minimising the delay in transferring patients from the acute setting to her hospital. When we started, her hospital was the largest external cause of delay and now it does not even appear in the top ten.

To be fair, she had a head start as she made contact with Jo straight after the dice game and started to plan her changes back then. But I must confess I felt the merest tinge of envy when Jo told me the hospital had reduced its length of stay by fifty per cent in a few months. I'm intrigued to find out why her results have been so spectacular. My hunch is that it has really helped to share the information across these two links in the chain.

Frustratingly though, most other people I have spoken to have their own '*yes, but*' response. The mental health service pointed out that so many things are different there, which of course I agree with, but the basic flow is still the biggest issue. Some have said it's purely down to weak leadership (impugning), some entirely down to old IT systems (deluded) and one just said their situation is not as bad as the position our hospital was in (cheeky).

It seems the more I talk through the successes I've had, the more reservations are expressed and the more obstacles raised. The shortest and least successful meetings were when they held the view that there was no problem facing the organisation and no need to change. My nomination for the Linda Seed Head in the Sand Award was for the chap who sat in his office and defiantly explained how his operation was stable, while raising his voice slightly so I could hear above the noise of a worker in the adjacent room screaming at a colleague.

But all too often there was simply disagreement on whether there was a problem at all. When there was such determination there was no need to change, without an answer to the '*why change?*' question, they were never going to take the first step forward. However, one thing I did notice was that now and then, even when there was agreement on the risks of not changing (crocodile) and the potential benefits of changing (pot of gold), it was clearly a combination of the mermaid and the crutches that was the source of resistance.

The phone rings, and I recognise the number from my old office. Strange.

"Hello?"

"Hello, Linda. It's Kevin."

"Kevin?" I'm flummoxed.

"Kevin Ashcroft."

"Oh… hello, Ashcroft – er, Kevin."

Kevin. Who'd have thought it? I always wondered whether Ashcroft had a Christian name.

"To what do I owe this pleasure?" I add, immediately regretting the corny question.

"I wondered if you were free for a catch-up this week. I'd like to pick your brains on something."

Pick my brains? My God, he's moved on to cannibalism now! Stop it, Linda.

"Sure; how about tomorrow?"

"Eleven's good for me."

"Perfect. I'll see you then… Kevin."

Blimey… I've made a date!

We agree to meet at my office. I wouldn't feel comfortable going to my old patch and seeing my old friends in an official capacity. We can do all the catching up we need to at Cath's do.

◆

It's 11:00am on the dot and Ashcroft (Kevin) arrives. We sit down at my desk and I pour the coffee while he fiddles with his phone, amid a brief but odd silence befitting the start of a poker game. I break the ice.

"So are you enjoying your new role?"

"Enjoying?" comes the perfectly reasonable reply. "I wouldn't say I was enjoying it exactly. It's invigorating, rewarding, bloody hard work." (Ashcroft's human!) "But enjoyable? Not yet."

"Yes, wrong word, I suppose. But it sounds like you're doing a good job?"

"Does it?"

Ashcroft immediately suspects me of recruiting a duplicitous mole from within his ranks. I put his mind at ease.

"Cath told me it's going well – I spoke to her when she invited me to her leaving do."

Oops. I instantaneously hope that Ashcroft has been invited.

"Oh yes, Cath. We must make that a memorable occasion for her. She's been a superb employee."

Phew.

"So you want to pick my brains," I offer.

"Yes, thanks Linda." He pauses for a moment, and then: "It has been quite a revelation for me taking the reins at the hospital after the work you have done there; a real eye-opener. I must admit, when I visited you when we were on opposite sides of the desk, I thought you'd lost your marbles. But I have walked into a hospital the likes of which I haven't seen for a long time."

"What do you mean?"

He pauses again.

"Yes, there are the same moments of madness as in any hospital, but not as many. Things go wrong but they get put right more quickly. Do you know what I mean?"

I do. And it gives me a warm feeling. Ashcroft goes on to say that while of course he wants to put his own mark on the hospital, he is worried that he is working on a strategy in an environment unlike anything he has experienced. He talks knowingly of the planned discharge dates and patient-centred lists at the business end of my and Stevie's implementations, and equally sensitively about the people spearheading the strategy. He's concerned that he doesn't have the trust of the senior management team, and that is what he wants to talk to me about. I'm already wondering if I've underestimated him all this time. Maybe he wants me to put in a good word for him.

"Charlie's quite a character, isn't he?" he says.

"He is that. How are you getting on with him?" I ask mischievously.

"Well… we had a little run-in last week."

"Oh?" I continue my façade.

"Hmm. He was annoyed that I'd spoken to a member of his team without asking him first. I was only asking for an update and Charlie wasn't available."

I can see that raising Charlie's heckles. Ashcroft continues.

"One small thing that probably didn't help was that the previous week I had asked the department heads to complete a synopsis –

an executive summary, if you like – to give a clear picture of their area of responsibility. In essence I was after an analysis of strengths, weaknesses, opportunities and threats."

"So you asked Charlie to complete a SWOT analysis and then the following week you spoke to one of his team asking for figures? I think I may understand the problem. What did he say?"

Ashcroft adopts a pained expression.

"It wasn't pretty, Linda. And it isn't repeatable. As for where he threatened to shove my SWOT analysis…"

I can't contain my laughter. Then on recovering:

"I'm sorry, Kevin. I'm not laughing at you," I lie.

He goes on to tell me the person he's most worried about is Mo, who is still an outstanding doctor and leader but maybe has itchy feet. He's begun a part-time MBA and has accepted mentoring support from a successful CEO on the south coast. I'm pleased to hear this as I know Mo harbours ambitions to lead a hospital of his own in the not too distant future. I try to reassure Ashcroft.

"Mo is as diligent, committed and loyal as the day is long. But you can't hold anyone back if they're following an ambition. He won't let you down; he is brim-full of integrity. But he won't be there forever."

Ashcroft nods, and I continue.

"From the very little I can gather, you're doing a good job. You'll want to put your mark on it, but I hope you won't change the hospital's direction."

He assures me he won't. He admits he still hasn't fully grasped the principles underpinning the success of the hospital, but he is experienced enough to know that success continues only if you constantly change to improve, but only the things that need changing. If Ashcroft's as good as Kieran says he is then he'll be OK, and it may simply be the team's loyalty to me that is holding them back from embracing him fully.

"Have you spoken to them about this or how you rate them?"

"I think it's a little early."

But he needs to communicate clearly and do it soon.

"Look, Kevin, when the team sees us chatting at Cath's do, that may convince them you don't plan to ignore what has gone before. They probably already know that but you should keep them in the loop, and it may help them to see that we're on the same page. I'll speak to whoever you want if you think it will help, but I honestly don't think you need me to."

He thanks me and then asks how I am progressing in my newly designed role. So it's my turn to bend an ear. I tell him how I recently spent a day with some front-line care workers in the community, and that it was a little disturbing. In Stevie's parlance, it was very obvious that the crocodiles were out to play and were ravenous. The hard-working people were constantly fighting with the dilemma of doing what was best for the patient immediately in front of them, against rushing through this visit in an attempt to attend to all the other patients on their list. Moreover, it seemed like the patient who arrived closest to their next formal review seemed to be given the greatest priority. This constant yo-yoing between patients was clearly unacceptable to the care workers and their frustration was there for all to see.

"So how can you help?" asks Ashcroft.

After a moment's thought I reply.

"The first step is to engage others to consider a new way forward and go all the way back to identifying the core problem of running any organisation. Then we can look at the problem of changing an organisation and leading that change."

"And I suspect you've discovered it's not as easy as it looks."

"Correct."

"The thing is, Linda, none of these organisations is particularly small. Did you know that if the UK health service was a business, it would be vying with Apple in terms of revenue?"

I didn't know that but it doesn't surprise me. And just like almost every business, controlling such a large span of activities has resulted in the use of a pyramid structure. But the larger these organisations have become, the greater the risk of distorted messages travelling through them; it's like the Chinese whispers game but turbo-charged.

In the community environment the resources are further stretched by geographical spread.

"Treating patients in their own homes means workers can spend as much time travelling as treating," I say. "Also, the treatment is often carried out by a number of different organisations. At least in the acute hospital everyone was working for the same organisation. In the community it's not just the synchronisation within the organisation that's the issue; it's more the synchronisation across organisations."

"I can sympathise with that," says Ashcroft. "Leading your own team is an entirely different ball game to trying to influence others. I often think it would be easier if we could just run these organisations as if they were the World War I army: do as you're told and you might get shot; don't do as you're told and you will."

I don't think he means it.

Another aspect of the dilemma is the monumental number of controls and measures that a CEO is put under. You might wonder why, in today's hostile media environment, anyone would want the job in the first place. And Stevie always said that in these 'for-purpose' organisations, attempts to over-formalise quantifiable measures have failed miserably. If measures were the primary way to run an organisation, how come there are more and more measures in place and an increasing number of organisations struggling? Organisations hide behind measures.

"When they don't know what to do they resort to measuring things," I say. "This is why people rearranged and counted the deckchairs on the *Titanic*. The string quartet had it right."

"But the sad fact of the matter is that in some cases, if you don't measure it, it doesn't happen," says Ashcroft.

"Is that an acceptable way to approach our business?"

"It's not perfect, I'll give you that," he concedes.

"But as you say, I need to influence these leaders, and even if I wanted to measure them I can't. They don't line into me. Unless I can find a way through this conflict between individuals' desire to improve things and their understandable resistance, I'm not going to get anywhere. One of them told me it wouldn't make any difference if they changed. The others needed to change too, and good luck with that!"

"And how did staff react if they could see that part of the proposed change might put their own job at risk?"

Clearly Ashcroft has experience in change management. And I have seen this too.

"Disagreeing on the existence of the problem can be a way of protecting yourself from the negative outcomes of addressing a problem. They're not stupid. How do you ask someone to participate in a process where if it's successful they think they will lose their job?"

When I was at the hospital I just had my own organisation to change. In the broader system we're often asking leaders to work together to achieve change across the whole system. The paradox is that many of them have become leaders precisely because they were willing to stand apart from everyone else. Now we're asking them to be a part of something and their own identity becomes diluted. But the time-honoured idea of leading from the very front, claiming *'follow me, I have a vision, I promise everything will be alright'*, is also unlikely to be welcomed. It just doesn't cut any ice among a group of professionals these days. Instructing people to change can also raise the most subtle but powerful forms of resistance; people just go underground. Trying to negotiate also misses the point, and negotiating across all organisations is more difficult than herding cats.

Ashcroft nods, and then surprises me a little with his insight.

"If the leader you are talking to realises you appreciate they are caught in an impossible situation and are not blaming them for the problem, they will listen to you; for a short while at least. Then they may be willing to acknowledge its full magnitude without fear of personal implications."

I try to recall any previous situation with Ashcroft when I've not felt that all the world's ills were my fault. But then he's beginning to reveal some considerable depth. Maybe his pantomime villain persona while at head office was all part of his brief. Or maybe he has a dark side that he's straining to suppress now that he's out at the coal face. I'm probably being uncharitable.

But there are two other issues I face if I am to win the attention of the leaders and staff. Firstly, how can any success of a solution be judged? And secondly, how can I engage in discussion around valid differences in their environment?

"I know you need to get over the *'it won't work here'* mentality," says Ashcroft, "but only when you properly understand their environment will you have the credibility to move things on.

I appreciate this, but in every case where I've seen a highly complex environment, the core of the breakthrough Stevie developed is also valid. Being able to simplify the perceived complexity and focus on those few critical areas that are causing the most disturbance, then using them to rapidly improve the performance of the whole system, was at the heart of the solution every time. And I can see how this could work in every environment I have seen so far. It's just a case of winning the hearts and minds. Ashcroft begins to chew his thumbnail.

"Have you convinced anyone yet?"

I think for a moment and then:

"There's one young chap who really impressed me. He's called Nick and he's a manager in the children's mental health hospital. He was an inspiration. He'd built a fantastic organisation in spite of all the usual difficulties. The quality of care for children was truly exceptional. It really looked like everyone who worked there understood it was a privilege, and he'd developed an approach that was not just focused on the child but on the broader family and the whole environment in which the family operates."

This young man definitely understands the importance of building child-centred and clinically driven processes. He'd also ensured his own organisation was an exemplar of the approach.

But Nick's success was having unintended outcomes. There is a guiding statement which is core to the organisation that no child would ever be forgotten. In essence, once a patient is in the heart of the service and possibly admitted into the acute setting, the patient is seen as safe. Inevitably, the focus of the community-based staff is on trying to keep the vast numbers of patients being treated in the community safe. So the more successful Nick's hospital became, the more pressure it experienced.

"So how is that playing out?" asks Ashcroft.

"The number of children waiting is increasing, and the number of cases started but not finished is growing – and growing fastest in the most critical care areas."

"So the system is becoming flooded?"

"Exactly. Quality of care will suffer and stress among the workers is on the rise, which is a tragedy when you think of Nick's ethos. Some have become disheartened and some key people have chosen to leave for a less stressful life."

I explain that Nick is hindered by dependent events: one thing cannot happen until previous activities have been completed by other resources. In fact, the appropriate requirements around treating children mean that the dependencies appear more complex and require more strict reinforcement, for obvious reasons.

There's also a considerable Murphy factor: things very rarely take the time they are predicted to take. At each and every intervention, you would not know exactly what you were going to find. In a funny way, although these are dependent events, the resources carrying out the activities are surprisingly independent, often many resources working for many different organisations all trying to provide care for the child. They are each in their own way trying to be patient-centred. But as an inevitable consequence of their attempts to be patient-centred from within their own resources, there was the enormous and growing delay in the care that I witnessed on my visit.

"So why don't they just shut the front door for a week or two and work through the backlog?" asks Ashcroft.

"Because that would violate their core belief: that no child should be forgotten."

"Of course."

"Geography is a challenge. Communication is a challenge. But does it really make any difference to the core of the problem and how it can be solved? I really don't think so."

Ashcroft places his coffee cup carefully on the desk and says:

"It seems to me that the whole trick is to ensure you articulate the problem in a manner that is directly relevant to each specific environment, without pointing the finger. Using your own example from your own environment is not going to cut through anything."

He pauses, and then:

"It won't be easy. I can see your work first hand and I still have many questions. I can't pretend to have mastered it yet, but on the face of it, it seems to make sense. And you know I'll never argue with figures. Advising and influencing people on their own patch is never easy though, Linda – God knows I've tried often enough myself. But if anyone can do it... I suspect you may have a fighting chance."

He gets to his feet.

"Thanks for your time, Linda, but I must get back, not least to see if Charlie's torched my office."

That makes me chuckle. Well, this is a turn up for the books. I never thought I'd be able to say this but it's been really helpful talking things through with Ashcroft. I'm not sure if we've solved anything but I certainly feel better.

"You probably don't know this, Kevin, but I didn't really take to you when you were at regional office." Ashcroft feigns hurt surprise. "But you're actually human, aren't you?"

He smiles then turns to the door.

"That's very generous of you, Linda, but I'd be grateful if you could keep it to yourself."

Chapter Twenty-Four

Yes, Minister

"I told you it wouldn't be easy. Leading is invariably less complicated than influencing."

I'm sitting in Kieran's office reporting back on last month's activity in the field as he wanders up and down. As I gaze out of the window and see the smart rows of office blocks and restaurants I sort of miss the hospital for a second.

"I didn't appreciate just how much more difficult it is. You can lead a horse to water but…"

"I know. So now you probably know why Ashcroft favoured using a cattle prod from time to time. When you're trying to influence thought and behaviour, all manner of factors come in to play: ego, neurosis, confidence, trust and politics for a start."

"You're telling me."

"Don't be disheartened though."

"Why not? Are you letting me go back to the hospital?"

"Don't be daft. Not now that we've started something."

Kieran's been reading my weekly updates while doing some of his own digging and, with the benefit of his helicopter view, he's seen a slightly more positive landscape than I have.

"Things are happening," he says, slightly cryptically. "The community hospital that your friend Jo's contact is running is starting to resemble a microcosm of your hospital. And I know you are worried about Nick at the children's mental health hospital, but ninety per cent of what he's doing is right."

In addition, another of the regional hospitals has conducted its first set of controlled experiments and the management team is convinced. Also, Kieran has begun lobbying.

"I've seen enough early yet substantial evidence to take this forward," he says with notable enthusiasm in his voice, something he can usually disguise as a skilled politician. "There are pockets of success around the region, enough to tell me we are on safer ground. So I've spoken to William and he has agreed to meet us on Wednesday at 3:00pm. And we have an audience with the minister."

I jolt upright.

"The minister. Bloody hell, Kieran!"

"Yes, the minister. So you'll have to clean up your potty mouth for the afternoon. And can you get on the phone to your pal Stevie? We'll need him with us."

Kieran had quizzed me about Stevie during his visit to the hospital when his name kept cropping up. I'd explained to him that he was my old MBA pal who had passed on to me the theory that had helped us make the breakthrough at the hospital. At the time he told me that he knew months earlier we'd enlisted external help and just hoped we weren't going out on a limb, or spending thousands on a comfort blanket.

"How did William arrange this for us?" I ask.

"Apparently he meets the minister in his club somewhere in Kensington, the Reform Club I think it is."

"Oh yes, I know it."

Kieran raises his eyebrows.

"I knew you moved in the right circles."

As soon as Kieran has started his morning calls I get on the phone to Stevie.

"Whatever you're doing on Wednesday afternoon, you need to cancel it."

"No I don't."

"Yes you do," I insist.

"I'm trying to finish my book this week, and also why would I want to cancel an expenses-paid trip to the races with Scott?"

"To see the head of the health service."

"Go on."

"And, wait for it, the Minister for Health."

"Have you been at the sherry trifle again, Linda?"

"No, really. It's a bit of a story, but Kieran's pal is William Thackeray, the boss of the service, and he goes to the same club as the minister. Your dad's, in fact."

"Yes, of course. William Thackeray. I don't know him but I know his son, Will. He was at St Edmund's College, still in his late twenties I think. He's a corporate financier, nice chap but a bit quieter since the 2008 crash."

"Is there anyone you don't know?" I ask.

"So that's great. Us and the minister on Wednesday afternoon. Are we at Whitehall?"

"No, at William's office."

Then I ring Dee, who almost self-combusts on the other end of the phone, and insist she meet us at the coffee lounge near William's office after our meeting so that we can let her know how we got on.

"Great. We'll be there by six."

♦

We climb two flights of stairs and arrive at the office occupied by the leader of the whole health service. Just outside his meeting room there's a flat screen television on the wall showing Sky News. There's a reporter standing outside a hospital. A quick glance confirms it's not one of ours. Thank goodness for that!

I'm not sure what I expected, but as we sit down in the smart room it's no more grandiose than Kieran's office. Kieran introduces us to William, an imposing man who must be six foot four, and who welcomes us in before ordering tea. As we sit, I wonder where the Minister is. Kieran, Stevie and I are on one side of the table with William in splendid isolation on the other.

"Thank you for coming. I was hoping the minister would be able to join us. He was expecting to, but has been caught up in a de-briefing session following PM's question time. His PPS has called me to say he hasn't ruled out being able to get here, but has asked that I report back."

That's a blow. I glance at Stevie, who thankfully is smiling. Even if the minister can't get here we're still in front of a man who can certainly make things happen. Kieran starts.

"Thank you for the opportunity to talk to you about our plans,

William. As I mentioned last week, we believe it is possible for our country to have a flourishing health and social care system again."

"Not at all, Kieran. The approach we have talked about, which you have tested in your region, has raised some eyebrows here and at Whitehall. I'm very keen to gain a better understanding of what you've been getting up to out in the sticks."

Out in the sticks!

Kieran sets the scene. As we all know, the nation is finding it increasingly difficult to meet the health needs of a growing population, and the demand for healthcare is increasingly costly to fulfil. Without adding more and more money into our health budget, it's inevitable that in some areas there are life and death issues and critical quality of care issues left unaddressed.

"In your position, William, you know better than most that in this predicament the ability to do more with the current resources answers a significant need."

"Indeed," he replies. "But this, without doubt, is a mammoth and unprecedented challenge."

"But as the head of our nation's health system you take this huge responsibility very seriously. And your task is to improve the health system while at the same time ensuring there is absolutely no risk of further deterioration in the provision of healthcare."

"And that's a crucial point," says William. "Anyone presenting a radical change initiative will have to pull up some deep-rooted trees to convince leaders, politicians and stakeholders that firstly it is possible, and secondly the risks are managed."

"This is why we are so appreciative that you are giving us the chance to explain why we believe that a rapid breakthrough may actually be possible."

Then he turns to Stevie and me.

"You know Linda Seed. We've discussed at length the wonderful work she did in turning around one of our worst-performing hospitals in a matter of months. And this is Stevie Vokes, the person who introduced us to the approach we've taken, adapted it to healthcare and then guided Linda throughout that first experiment."

He then explains that I have been working with him to repeat these tests in the community environment, in mental health and in health-related social care.

"Our objective today is to explain the core of our breakthrough," he says. "We will talk through results we have achieved in the various environments and make a proposal for how we believe this could be taken forward."

Then he asks Stevie to explain the fundamentals of the approach, and he obliges.

"All the work conducted in the health service has been done in what is seen to be a highly complex environment. The core of the breakthrough we have developed is being able to simplify the perceived complexity, and focus in on those few critical areas that are causing the most disruption. We then utilise those areas to rapidly improve the performance of the whole system. This is the heart of the direction of the solution."

William is listening intently and then turns to me.

"So, Linda, how did this work out in your hospital?"

"In the hospital where I took over as temporary CEO, we managed to achieve a simultaneous improvement in the quality of care, the timeliness of care and the financial performance of the hospital."

I go on to explain that within a few months we had reduced length of stay in many wards by twenty-five per cent, consistently hit all emergency access targets and turned a loss of £15 million per year to a small monthly profit. In some specialties we improved access times by over fifty per cent. In the community environment the reduction in length of stay has been much greater, and within several weeks we've been able to reduce length of stay by fifty per cent. In the mental health environment we've achieved a reduction of almost thirty per cent.

Kieran adds:

"What is so impressive about these results is that the improvements have been achieved with the full collaboration, engagement and leadership of the clinical teams."

William leans forward.

"Yes, and this is what I find the most interesting. How did you get them on board?"

At this point there is a knock on the door. William goes to meet a smartly dressed lady and after a brief whispered exchange she introduces the minister, who joins William as he returns to the table. We all stand and shake hands. Bizarrely I get some butterflies in my stomach and imagine what Mum would do in this situation.

"Sorry I'm late, everybody. There was a bit of an unexpected ding-dong happening up in Yorkshire and then the spotlight flashing at us at the weekly mud-chucking. What have I missed?"

William introduces us all to the minister and explains what we have talked about. Then Stevie continues:

"William was asking how we managed to get the clinicians on board with the necessary changes, minister. Well, we have used a combination of sharing our initial analysis of their current reality and sharing the logic of our approach. Without a logic- and evidence-based approach we would never have got such a highly qualified group to accept and lead the proposed changes. To every one of them, what we were proposing seemed like common sense, even if not their common practice."

William asks Stevie to go over the central focus of the approach, and he explains that we've adopted a patient-centred and clinically led approach in every environment.

"We made this patient-centred by basing the expectation of timeliness solely on each individual patient's need, and we made it clinically led by setting the expectation on clinical grounds alone. It was then easy to identify the few critical areas causing the most disturbances by identifying which task or resource was most often causing the most delay to the most patients."

"And that allowed you to rapidly identify which part of the system was least able to meet expectations," says the minister, immediately up to speed.

"Exactly," says Stevie, "and this drove all the subsequent improvement efforts."

"It also uncovered the most damaging local measures, policies and behaviours that were optimising the performance of each individual link in the chain rather than the whole chain," I add, and then Kieran speaks.

"Once I had seen the approach create such dramatic results in one part of the system, I was keen to check everywhere else. And in each experiment, under Stevie's guidance, we have detailed at the finest level the strategies and tactics we believe are necessary to guide further implementations."

He explains to the minister that we've done this to ensure moving forward on a grand scale would not entail taking imprudent risks. He also wanted to check that the successes achieved in the initial work were not simply down to my leadership and Stevie's hands-on involvement. In the subsequent experiments the incumbent management team has led the way under my guidance and Stevie has not been involved. William says:

"Minister, you know as well as I that the diversity of stakeholders involved in taking this type of initiative forward is immense."

"Indeed, and all have some power of veto up their sleeves," replies the minister. "But beneath it all, every one of them wants to contribute to the improvement of the country's healthcare system, or they shouldn't be there. But they will not take imprudent risks."

Kieran, Stevie and I have previously discussed how merely articulating how we achieved a breakthrough is unlikely to succeed on its own. Kieran speaks.

"Absolutely. They will want to check, and show their own stakeholders they have checked, to verify it does work in the wider environment."

"This can only be done through a carefully designed, planned and controlled set of experiments," says Stevie. "The pilot projects must systematically verify all the key elements of the approach."

"There must be minimal risk to the healthcare system as a whole," adds Kieran. "And we need to keep a lid on costs."

William seeks more comfort.

"Experiments like this will need careful guidance to ensure they are successfully executed and results would need to be verified by third parties. Only then would the results of the experiment convince the decision makers to go with it."

The minister then asks how we could measure success and I explain that we can either measure it against predicted outcomes or, if it's assumed the results can scale up across the whole nation, the measures would have to show that the health of the nation is improving. Also the expenditure on health as a percentage of GDP should stabilise or reduce. The minister nods his agreement (I think) and William interjects.

"I am constantly trying to persuade my colleagues in government that a healthier nation should lead to a more productive nation."

"We know that instinctively, William," says the minister. "What we don't know is by how much and precisely how to get there."

Stevie says:

"This work would help us to answer those questions because it would enable us to establish the causal link between the health of the nation and the relative spend on health as a nation. We have already started our own research across nations. Maybe we should take this a step further."

He glances at me, and then at Kieran, who gives him the nod.

"Every country in the world is looking for a breakthrough in its healthcare system. Having a more effective health system should also become a platform for the nation itself. Rather than just being seen as a drain on GDP, if you consider the growing market for health tourism then we don't yet know how much of a contribution to GDP this could grow to."

Well done, Dee! I must tell her Stevie used her thoughts.

William says:

"Are you suggesting we could improve the system enough to attract revenues and investment from outside the country?"

Stevie nods.

"That's exactly what I'm suggesting."

Then after a rather long pause, William says:

"Linda, you were the first. You were strong enough to try something very different when acting as a temporary leader in such a difficult situation. How do you think we could get other CEOs to give this their serious attention?"

I think for a moment before responding.

"Any chief executive who takes continuous improvement seriously has an open mind to begin with, but if they know they are leading an implementation on behalf of the country as a whole it becomes more difficult to resist. Then they will want to ensure they understand the logic and ensure the approach is properly followed. We can help them with that."

The minister asks:

"How much help did Stevie give you at your hospital, Linda?"

"Well, I was lucky to have Stevie's help, and without him developing the core of the approach I would not have stood a chance. But I feel with all the work we've done in testing and carefully articulating the approach it is now different."

Kieran looks at the minister and then William and says:

"I am not suggesting the three of us take this forward on our own. My proposal is we build a group of people from within the health system who can support and lead this type of initiative. These individuals must be a combination of successful senior clinicians and the most capable managers. We can help them to gain a deep understanding of the vision and how to make it work. They will have to be personally involved in leading the early pilots, just like Linda was, and then the best of them join the team to help others."

Stevie adds:

"The very first step should be to select the right people who can then spend the first six months leading their own organisation through the change before guiding others."

William leans over to pour us all another cup of tea and the minister helps himself to a biscuit.

"Kieran, we go back a long way and in all the time I've known you this is the first time you have ever been so forthright about such an initiative."

Then the minister says:

"Kieran, what are you asking us to do?"

Without hesitation he replies:

"Sir, we want your proactive sponsorship from the heart of government."

Acutely aware that the minister won't even dip his toe in the water if there is any uncalculated risk, William eyes Stevie.

"From where you are sitting, can you see any insurmountable obstacle?"

"There will be obstacles but I do not believe any will be insurmountable."

Then the minister turns to me.

"Linda, are you prepared to lead this initiative?"

"Yes, Minister."

♦

It's 7:00pm as we approach Dee. She's sat in the corner of the coffee lounge nursing an Americano and with three helium balloons which say **I ♥ London** tied to her chair.

"Have you two any idea how much coffee and carrot cake I've eaten while you've been in there? I'm starting to feel like a rabbit on speed!"

"The balloons are a nice touch," I smile, "but what made you think we'd have a good afternoon?"

"Well, did you?"

"We got the early stages of some kind of commitment," says Stevie. Dee grins.

"I knew it – Bonnie and Clyde with a half decent idea; who could ever say no to an offer like that?"

"It's very early days," says Stevie, "but we have sponsorship in the right place now."

Dee thrusts a balloon into each of our hands. We pay her impressive coffee bill and the three of us walk down the road together in search of a taxi. As we round the corner we see William acknowledge us as he passes in his chauffeur-driven car. Then the blacked-out ministerial limousine follows and we collectively hope the minister is looking the other way.

I walk with Dee on my left and Stevie on my right as the sun is setting over the Houses of Parliament. We pass a stack of *London Evening Standard*s and a board reading:

HEALTH SERVICE IN CRISIS

Stevie picks up a copy. Dee looks at me with a glint in her eye and says:

"We'd better get a move on," and then, "I know this is going to be a big thing for you two."

Stevie stops in his tracks, smiles at Dee and says:

"You should never say… '*I know*'."

Coda

"So why did you decide to write this book?"

Stevie takes another gulp of his coffee while Dee and I wait for his answer.

"Do you really want to know?"

We both nod. He takes a deep breath.

"Well… there were three core reasons I guess, and together they created an overpowering force in me to give it a go.

"The first was driven out of a deepening frustration with the health debate. It seems wherever you look in the world healthcare is in the news. And usually the discussion is about who to blame for a crisis. Every time a new undesirable outcome emerges, the immediate focus is on trying to isolate the individual causes: one for the spiralling costs, another for the reducing quality of care, and yet another for the backlogs.

"But these discussions are utterly futile. Everything I have been taught in this area is about trying to seek and validate a common cause; one which explains why good people with honest intent find it so difficult to achieve necessary change. And you know, when you look in from the outside you see it is because those people directly involved feel stuck between a rock and a hard place where there appears to be no way out."

That strikes a chord with me. I recall, as if it was yesterday, the moment when I realised I couldn't simply add more front-line staff to address the deteriorating quality of care in my hospital, or reduce headcount to address the financial overrun. Stevie continues.

"All too often the solutions being proposed are just more examples of intolerable compromise: decentralise with more autonomy, centralise with more controls and, if necessary, more 'special measures'. This is a sign of the level of desperation we have reached."

Dee speaks.

"I must say our brightest students at the university are in no rush to start a career in healthcare management. And where's the surprise in that when the ultimate sanction for not achieving targets is just more pressure applied?"

Taking a less travelled path takes some nerve. And at our hospital, we could only really contemplate a new way forward once Stevie had helped me to see the situation differently. He knew I was in between that rock and hard place, and I suspect, allied to his frustration with the healthcare debate, that prompted him to help us find a solution.

"But do you know what the real eye-opener was?" I ask. "It was when you told us that the more complex the system appeared, the greater the improvement we should expect."

"Exactly," he replies. "Our task was to understand and challenge the false assumptions that led us to this complex view of the world. As long as medical costs are rising faster than budgets, we can explain the multitude and seemingly diverse nature of the effects we see today. The growing intensity of these undesirable effects also becomes visible. So we can easily see how the disparate and increasingly desperate actions to tackle individual effects are futile. Attempts to resolve one part of the system simply exaggerate the negatives of another part.

"My book describes our search for a working hypothesis which enabled us to seek out a common underlying cause for these effects and a common-sense solution to overcome them all."

I'm wondering about Stevie's chosen format in his book.

"But why write it as a novel? Surely this type of work would normally sit in a text book. Writing a novel is a very different process and the outcome equally different."

Stevie ponders for a second, and then:

"There are too many good text books that quickly become shelfware. Even if they have been read, very few have actually made the world a better place, which is sad. But I thought many more people love and enjoy reading novel after novel.

"My conclusion was that although a good textbook may enhance people's understanding of a topic, as human beings we are inherently inclined to avoid examining our own behaviour according to our changing understanding. This places an incredibly strong brake on our rate of progress when dealing with such an important topic. By embedding the evolution in a novel I hope it helps the reader to notice this tendency in the characters of the book, as well as in themselves. I truly hope this story will help them to see and overcome this tendency.

"It isn't easy to get a new idea across to thousands of people consistently. So I wrote this book in a manner that I hope is accessible to all parties and stakeholders including the patient and the wider society."

"Maybe it will also help to reduce the number of instances where a new insight with acute common sense takes so long to become practice," adds Dee. "But why did you write the novel through Linda's eyes?"

"Because," he replies, "Linda was the one at the centre of the story. She felt every triumph and disaster more acutely than anyone else. She knows."

"Did you alter our characters or change our names? Dee is keen to check."

"Foibles and eccentricities, no… Names, yes."

"So I think that's two reasons for the book," I say. "What's the third?"

"I promised the man who taught me these principles that I would," he replies.

I'm still troubled by the challenge we face.

"I understand that a core of these principles is we should promote growth of the more successful hospitals rather than cutting our way out of the financial difficulties. But this is counter-intuitive when the overall budget is finite and already seen as unaffordable. How do you think this works on a grander scale?"

"If we try to cut our way to increasing productivity we will end up with hospitals running on the edge of the thin line between a non-chaotic and a chaotic system. This transition is non-linear, and the most likely outcome is we will have a nation with many hospitals experiencing wandering bottlenecks and an increasingly stressed health system. In an environment of wandering bottlenecks, management attention will be splintered into addressing the latest crisis; we see it time and time again. Another ramification of cost reduction is that almost all initiatives to foster a process of ongoing improvement quickly reach the point of diminishing returns and as a result many deteriorate to lip service. The approach I have suggested is built on the idea of progressive equilibrium, which I was lucky enough to be introduced to by my mentor. This is where an organisation can safely grow without disturbing the underlying core processes.

"When you apply this across a whole network of hospitals, you can achieve the aggregation of variation that we used so effectively in the theatre scheduling on a grand scale. We'll end up with a safer system that can cope with both fluctuations and a growing demand."

"While you have been working with us, I've learned a lot about becoming a leader," I say. "They were right not to give me the CEO job, and that may come in the future. But in the meantime, I can support the next generation of potential CEOs to gain the necessary development and experience to lead the changes required."

Stevie turns to Dee.

"And what about you?"

"I guess," she begins, "as a society we have to decide what level of responsibility we have as individuals to help tackle the issues we face. It's about time my university started to address this properly."

Dee turns to me.

"So have you read this book?"

I nod. Then she asks:

"Does it make me look good?"

"Don't worry, Dee, I'm sure you'll be pleased."

"So what about you, Linda? Are you pleased?"

I pause briefly, and then:

"Well, I suppose it's reminded me of how this journey has brought new meaning to my life. And the tireless efforts of my colleagues to help us find a new way forward in the face of a seemingly hopeless situation has been truly amazing.

"So I suppose it has made me proud of everyone… and yes, I'm happy and excited about the next jump we can now make."

Index

About the author

Alex has worked around the world with many great leaders in health, social care, for-profit and not-for-profit organisations. His consulting, lecturing and coaching work has shown him the joys and struggles people face in their endeavours to improve their services and businesses. He is recognised as one of the world's leading authorities in the Theory of Constraints.

Alex lives in England. In his spare time he plays guitar in a band known as One2Many.